A MAN WHO "FLIES" LIKE A BAT   DECEMBER 12, 1937

MANOS MORGAN OF SIOUX FALLS, S.D., PHOTO-
GRAPHED IN THE AIR ABOVE OAKLAND, CALIF., AS
HE STARTED HIS JUMP FROM A PLANE FLYING AT
10,000 FEET. FOR 90 SECONDS HE GLIDED UNTIL HE
HAD DESCENDED TO 1,400 FEET, WHEN HE PULLED
THE RIP CORD OF HIS PARACHUTE AND LANDED
SAFELY. HIS WINGS ARE THREE AND A HALF FEET
ACROSS AND ARE MADE OF STEEL TUBING WITH
AIRPLANE FABRIC ATTACHED TO THE ARMS.
                (INTERNATIONAL)

NEWSPAPER ARTICLE: (GLEN SOHN)

"IN HIS FLYING GARB OF "BAT WINGS", CONSISTING
OF TREATED CANVAS OVER METAL RODS STRAPPED
TO HIS ARMS, WAIST AND LEGS, AND WITH
ANOTHER PIECE OF CANVAS FIXED BETWEEN HIS
LEGS, SOHN TRIED FOR THE LAST TIME THE STUNT
THAT HAD THRILLED CROWDS ALL OVER THE
UNITED STATES. HE JUMPED FROM A PLANE AT A
LITTLE LESS THAN 10,000 FEET. WHEN HE WAS
WITHIN 700 FEET OF THE GROUND HE TRIED TO
OPEN THE FIRST OF HIS TWO PARACHUTES. IT
OPENED LIKE A TORCH INSTEAD OF BILLOWING
OUT AND SLOWING HIS DESCENT. THEN HE TRIED
TO OPEN THE SECOND ONE AT 270 FEET, BUT
HIS ARMS WERE ENTANGLED IN THE FIRST PARA-
CHUTE AND HE DROPPED LIKE A PLUMMET."

DECEMBER 1935
GLEN SOHN, WHO AGAIN DEMONSTRATED HIS WINGS
AT THE MIAMI AIR-MEET.

SUNDAY NEWS

GOING DOWN! LEAPING FROM A PLANE ONLY 3,000
FEET UP OVER PORTSMOUTH AIRPORT, HANTS,
ENGLAND, GLEN SOHN SWOOPED LIKE A BIRD FOR
A MILE, THEN PARACHUTED INTO A TREE. HERE
YOU SEE HIM FALLING THROUGH THE AIR WITH
NEITHER WINGS NOR PARACHUTE OPEN.
                (WIDE WORLD)

THE NEAREST THING TO A MAN BIRD THIS EARTH HAS
YET SEEN
GLEN SOHN, AS HE APPEARED SOARING IN THE AIR
AFTER HE LEAPED FROM A PLANE AT 10,000 FT.
DURING THE EIGHTH ANNUAL ALL-AMERICAN AIR
MANEUVERS IN MIAMI.   (WIDE WORLD)

SOHN ALSO HAD AN ARRANGEMENT ON HIS FIN TO
LEAVE A SMOKE TRAIL AS HE FELL. YOU CAN SEE
THE SMALL CYLINDER BETWEEN HIS ANKLES.
SOHN WAS EVENTUALLY KILLED IN VICENNES,
FRANCE ON APRIL 25, 1937. THE PILOT PARACHUTE
OF THE MAIN PARACHUTE - HE USED A SEAT PACK-
FOULED HIS WINGS. WHEN HE USED HIS RESERVE
PARACHUTE THIS WRAPPED IN THE UNOPENED
MAIN PARACHUTE.

OMMY BOYD - WINGS FOLDED. NOTE SEAT AND
BACK PARACHUTES; CLOTHES PINS ON POWDER
POUCH.

TOMMY BOYD - CONSIDERED ONE OF THE BEST
BATMEN, READY TO JUMP WITH FLEXIBLE WINGS.
BROOMSTICK HANDLES, HELD BY HANDS, WERE
ONLY RIGID MEMBERS.
USED TRIANGLE PARACHUTE AS MAIN CHUTE AND
SEAT PACK AS RESERVE CHUTE.
WINGS WERE SEWED DIRECTLY TO JUMP SUIT.
APPEARED TO GLIDE AT 30°-40° ANGLE
OPENED PARACHUTE 400 TO 500 FEET ABOVE
GROUND.

TOMMY BOYD - IN BATMAN GEAR BUT WITHOUT
PARACHUTES. NOTE CLOTHES PINS IN BOTTOM
CENTER OF LEG FIN. CLOTHES PINS CLOSED POUCH
IN FIN CONTAINING RED POWDER. AT BAILOUT,
STATIC LINE PULLED CLOTHES PINS, LETTING RED
POWDER TRAIL BEHIND FALLING JUMPER.

BIRDMEN, BATMEN, and SKYFLYERS

BIRDMEN, BATMEN, AND SKYFLYERS

Wingsuits
and the
Pioneers
Who Flew
in Them,
Fell in
Them, and
Perfected
Them

Michael Abrams

HARMONY
BOOKS
NEW YORK

Published in the United States by Harmony Books, an imprint of the Crown Publishing Group, a division of Random House, Inc., New York.
www.crownpublishing.com

Harmony Books is a registered trademark and the Harmony Books colophon is a trademark of Random House, Inc.

Library of Congress Cataloging-in-Publication Data
Abrams, Michael, 1971–
    Birdmen, batmen, and skyflyers : wingsuits and the pioneers who flew in them, fell in them, and perfected them / Michael Abrams.
    Includes bibliographical references and index.
    1. Aeronautics—Biography. 2. Skydivers—Anecdotes. 3. Skydiving—History. 4. Flying-machines—History. 5. Gliders (Aeronautics)—History.
6. Personal propulsion units—History. I. Title.
TL539.A27 2006
629.1'4—dc22   2005032409

ISBN-13: 978-1-4000-5491-6
ISBN-10: 1-4000-5491-5

Printed in the United States of America

The collage of birdmen on the endpapers courtesy Archives of Tom Sitton.
Photograph on page ii: The batman with the longest career, Tommy Boyd.
Courtesy of the Smithsonian.

DESIGN BY BARBARA STURMAN

10 9 8 7 6 5 4 3 2 1

First Edition

For Shenglan

The spirit's wings will not change our shape:

Our body grows no wings and cannot fly.

Yet it is innate in our race

That our feelings surge in us and long

When over us, lost in the azure space

The lark trills out her glorious song;

When over crags where fir trees quake

In icy winds, the eagle soars,

And over plains and over lakes

The crane returns to homeward shores.

—Goethe, *Faust*

BIRDMEN, BATMEN, AND SKYFLYERS

DeLand of the Free:
Wingsuits for Whuffos

I'm in a plane climbing through the sky above DeLand. The giant Belgian I'm strapped to, Vladi Pesa, goes over the plan one more time—we will jump out of the plane together (actually, I'll lift my legs, and he'll do the jumping) and hurtle toward earth at 120 miles per hour. After thirty seconds or so, our parachute will open and then we will look directly up to see Jari Kuosma flying in our direction. The flyby is made possible by Kuosma's wingsuit: a white jumper with red webbing between the legs and triangular wings connecting the arms and the torso. "If I hit you on the way down," Kuosma cheerfully adds by way of ending the briefing, "you die."

At 13,000 feet the door opens, and the earth rushes past us, a blur in the square doorframe. I manage to make it to the edge and put myself in position: head up, arms back, thumbs behind my harness. Pesa tightens the straps that bind us together, grabs my legs with his. The fact that Kuosma has been stuck outside the country and hasn't used

1

his wingsuit for the past three months worries me for an instant. But it's a bit late to voice any concerns. Pesa is counting down in my ear.

✦

How, exactly, did I find myself in such a situation? In the early autumn of 2002, a friend of mine took me for a drive to Gardiner, New York, where a drop zone known as The Ranch was holding a "pond swooping" contest. This was the first time I'd seen any skydiving of any kind, and this particular variation of the sport—unlike others that take place thousands of feet above the ground—was well suited for viewing. After their invisible free fall, these sportsman would open their tiny, high-performance parachutes, glide down to fifty or so yards from the ground, and do a kind of hard turn that would flip them and their canopies facedown, parallel to the earth. The parachute, in other words, would stop slowing them. But before they hit the ground they would straighten out again, hurtle horizontally over the earth—with their legs bent so their feet wouldn't touch the ground, though their knees might brush the taller weeds—toward a pond in the center of which a spongy square raft floated serenely. Skimming across the pond, and dipping an occasional toe into its murky water, they would do their best to land on the buoyant target to earn ten points.

I was entranced by the sight of human bodies falling and fluttering out of the heavens. But I was also attracted to this subculture made up of people highly skilled at a potentially lethal activity, which, though stunning, no one had heard of outside the sport. But swooping, it turned out, was not the most obscure of skydiving's potentially lethal subsets. Talking to some of the veteran divers, I learned that there was a "birdman" who jumped with a set of wings of his own devising who was supposed to have been at the competition. He didn't show, though, thanks to visa troubles that kept him out of the country.

I decided to track down this birdman, Jari Kuosma, and subsequently discovered that he was not alone in his pursuit. Not only were skydivers in the thousands beginning to use the wings he was selling, but there was a long history of men trying—and failing—to do what had only become possible in the last few years. A little research revealed that from Icarus to airplanes, human history was filled with a certain kind of inventor and dreamer who, with homemade wings, had tried to fly from whatever precipice he could find—risking, and often losing, his life in the attempt. Peasants, kings, and scholars had leapt from rooftops, towers, and cliffs wearing an endless variety of frames and feathers and breaking a similar variety of bones. And the plane, to this type of daredevil, was just another precipice from which to try his more organic form of flight: as soon as parachutes and propellers appeared, a bat-wing phenomenon swept— and swooped—the country, with proto-skydivers doing their best to glide through the air on wings of stretched canvas for crowds often in the tens of thousands. They were, however, little better than their predecessors at keeping their bones whole. But now modern technology had finally caught up with the imagination. And Kuosma, it turned out, had competitors. Not only were there several wingsuits on the market, but hi-tech rigid wings were being built that could send people shooting across the sky as fast as 180 miles per hour. After some three thousand years of failure, we were living in a veritable renaissance of personal flight.

One particular statistic intrigued me: seventy-two of the seventy-five batmen who jumped from planes for air shows from the 1930s to the 1960s were killed in their wings. Months earlier I hadn't even heard of such "birdmen," and now there were seventy-five of them, most of whom had died some kind of presumably spectacular death.* Who were they? Why did they keep at it? Why didn't the rest of the world know about them?

Though the subject appeared somewhat comic at first—a seemingly endless litany of the injuries and deaths of daredevils unwilling to learn from the endless injuries and deaths of those before them— the fact was that their efforts had somehow led to flocks of skydivers now flying about the clouds, more or less safely, and others now pushing the limits of what could be done with a set of wings.

Theirs was the true history of flight, it seemed to me—one that the airplane had usurped. Both before and after the appearance of mechanized flight, men have yearned and struggled to fly *like birds.* As one skydiver told me, if piloting a plane is flying, then rowing a canoe is swimming. The airplane is merely a product of this initial drive, a minor offshoot in the long tale of human flight.

The Wright brothers succeeded thanks to engines with ever-greater power-to-weight ratios that were able to overcome the limitations of the human body that had stymied so many of the birdmen before them (and, of course, their patient, scientific approach had something to do with it). We may think of them as the legends who made the first airplane, but in their minds their inventions were meant

---

*After the article about Kuosma came out, it quickly became apparent that the statistic was not quite accurate. Several birdmen (most of them calling themselves batmen now as well as in their winged heyday) contacted me, usually claiming to be one of the first to use a bat-wing. Adding them to the bat-wing jumpers I already knew had survived proved the estimate way off the mark. Further research revealed that the numbers came from a quote by Red Grant, himself a bat-wing survivor, who was merely taking a wild guess at how many of his compatriots had died trying to fly.

to achieve the dream of human flight, the realization of the ancient myth of Icarus and Daedalus. They were part of a rush of inventors competing to be the first to fly, to succeed with new materials and understanding at what was to them the end of a long, absurd, and repetitive history of attempts to flit birdlike about the air. The Wright brothers' success, though, did not allow us to flit. Instead, now that their wings have evolved from glider to biplane to jumbo jet, we sit crammed into a pressurized cabin with two carry-ons and no leg room. Today, airplanes dominate the sky and the story of man in the air. But the development of the airplane is only one part of man's grand quest to fly. While many dedicated their lives to perfecting the machinery that we soar in today, others persisted in the dream of a more personal flying experience.

Kuosma's wings mark the culmination of that dream and the beginning of a new era of flight. Of course, the invention of a wingsuit that would allow anyone to play among the clouds with palatable odds of survival came in bits and pieces during the twentieth century. But Kuosma is the first to mass-produce such suits. And as president and founder of BirdMan, Inc., he's had more mileage in wings and has developed more skill with them than any known human. If you buy a wingsuit from him, he'll be glad to give you personal instruction. "It's as if a basketball fan could take a few lessons from Michael Jordan," one skyflyer told me.

I located the man some months after the pond-swooping contest I had witnessed, and he suggested the possibility of flying by me while I made a tandem jump of my own. Whuffo that I was (that's skydivese for a virgin of the air), I waffled, but after watching a video-tape of Kuosma steering around the edge of a cloud, I couldn't resist the idea of seeing it with my own eyes. Unfortunately, Kuosma, whose business was in DeLand, was still stuck in Finland, and it would be months before we could try any such demonstration. That meant months for my imagination, fueled by parachute disaster stories I'd been reading, to establish a rather strong and ever-building thrum of fear. It also meant months of stagnation on the ground for Kuosma (you're only as good as your last jump, they say), and he had to take up ski-jumping to satisfy his adrenaline addiction. Finally, in January of 2003, I met Kuosma in DeLand, just days after he had arrived there himself.

Kuosma looks like the European expat extreme sportsman that he is. Put a surfboard under his arm instead of a wing, and he'd fit right in on some Southern California beach. His two-toned sandy blond hair has a Tintin flip in the front that points straight toward the heavens. Around his neck he wears an Incan figurine on a black band, and on his right shoulder there's a tattoo of Leonardo da Vinci's Vitruvian Man—but instead of a second pair of arms, it has a set of wings. "When the perfect man creates, he can fly," he told me, explaining the drawing in what he refers to as his "Finglish."

Mom and Pop Kuosma were a bit less daring than their child. His mother was a secretary and his father ran a shop that sold old U.S. army surplus. He was also an amateur pilot, and as a child Kuosma remembers being in awe of the skydivers he saw at the airport with his father. As a teenager, Kuosma took up martial arts and started jumping off roofs with his pals. His mother's friends thought the boy might "need some help," but their advice went unheeded.

When his father died in 1990, Kuosma was all set to take over the family business, but a few lawyers managed to make off with the inventory. "They ended up stealing everything we had: all those nice army clothes, boots, and everything. But I don't think I would be here right now if that didn't happen. So thank you to those lawyers." With nothing to do, he headed to the old airport and took up skydiving. In the lives of the birdmen, the loss of a parent turns out to be one of the few common threads.

Soon he was something of a big bird in a little birdbath. In 1994 he was one of fifty-seven people who broke the Finnish record for the largest free-falling formation. Later he took a trip to Estonia, where he learned a Russian technique for jumping at frighteningly low altitudes. Kuosma was the first to try the stunt in Finland—he jumped out of a plane flying at 250 mph, a mere 300 feet above the ground. At that speed the wind should open a parachute instantaneously. "In my case it did," says Kuosma, "And I was pretty glad."

Kuosma was flying the smallest parachute in Finland at the time—135 square feet, compared with the usual 300 or so. The size went some way to placating his need for speed (currently he uses a canopy of 75 square feet) by allowing him to perform what is now a standard maneuver called a hook-turn—the same trick the pond-swoopers used to zip across the earth at 60 miles per hour. A slight miscalculation can cause a jumper to snap his legs against the ground instead of skimming over it (skydivers call it "femuring"), and the whole business made the Finnish skydiving association skittish. They passed rules banning certain kinds of landings just to get Kuosma to quit his hijinks.*

By then, Kuosma had earned a bachelor's in business and administration, had followed that up with a degree in international business, and had taken a job at Sonera, Finland's largest telecommunications company. "I thought, okay, now the good job at the big corporation, and the career, and that will be my thing to do. So I went for that and I got the very nice job at the big corporation. I had a suit on and all that good stuff. It took me two weeks to realize that it was not for me."

---

*Hook-turns are the primary cause of death and injury in skydiving.

Within a few months, Kuosma had quit his job and drawn up a business plan to manufacture and distribute a new parachute that was well made and super-fast, but still unknown to the skydiving community. But the plan would end up being used to produce something else entirely.

Not long after Kuosma left his job, he and his friend Robert Pecnik traveled to a 3,700-foot cliff in Arco, Italy, that they planned to jump from. At an Internet café there, they came across a photo of a skydiver named Patrick de Gayardon in a wingsuit. Gayardon was the world's most famous skydiver, and he had built the first truly successful "ram-air" wings. Unlike the single-layered wings that had failed his predecessors, Gayardon's wings were made of cells that filled with air—like modern square parachutes—and gave his wing enough shape and rigidity to truly fly. At the sight of Gayardon streaking across the sky, the two friends instantly knew what they had to do— build a set of wings like that for themselves.

Pecnik already had some experience making jumpsuits for skydivers, and Kuosma had already devised a business plan to manufacture speedy parachutes. "We thought, 'Hey, it's easy,' " says Kuosma. "We have wings and we can make suits, so why not put them together?" By the end of the year Pecnik had made three wingsuits. They headed to DeLand to try them out.

Gayardon had invented the wingsuit and wowed the skydiving world with spectacular stunts, but after 500 flights he went the way of the batmen of the thirties and forties—a malfunction sent him to his death in a Hawaiian banana field just months after Pecnik and Kuosma had seen his photo. Undeterred, the pair based their wingsuits on what they had seen of Gayardon's getup, but neither Pecnik nor Kuosma was an engineer of any kind, and when they went to test their wings for the first time, they gave themselves a 50-percent chance of surviving. "It was just such a big jump into the unknown," says Kuosma. "We were doing something that we knew some people had done before . . . but they were all dead."

Kuosma and his partner did not die. In fact, everything went as planned, except for one thing. "I could never have expected it to be so mind-blowing, so beautiful, so absolutely addicting. I came down and I was absolutely high."

Armed with a business plan and a little money, they set up shop in Slovenia, where Pecnik had his jumpsuit business, and made the first eighty wingsuits. In June of 1999 they packed the suits into a car and headed to Austria. They were down to their last Finnish mark and had to smuggle the wingsuits across the border to avoid paying customs. From there they set out to visit every drop zone they could find. Many of the airfields wouldn't allow Kuosma even to demonstrate his suit; the head of England's largest drop zone told them they would have to leave if they so much as said the word "wingsuit." Where he could, Kuosma gave a seminar, flew his suit, and then offered to pay for the flight of anyone daring enough to try it. Volunteers returned to earth slack-jawed, and word began to spread.

The experience, they said, was wholly different from an ordinary skydive. The wings of the BirdMan suit fill with air as soon a skyflyer spreads his limbs (not something he should do right away, or he risks hitting the tail of the plane), and within seconds the noise of the wind dies off and the body begins moving forward. The suit is made of ripstop nylon, a fabric with "zero porosity," so the wings remain rigid in flight. The shape of the wing is made by the arms and shoulders of the person in the suit, and it takes a few flights to find the ideal position. Cutaway cables enable the flyer's arms to be freed in an instant, which reduces the danger of being caught in the kind of inescapable flat spin that killed many of the bat-wing jumpers.

Anyone who's logged 200 skydiving jumps and has at least $799 to spare can buy a BirdMan suit and slow the downward speed of his free fall from 120 mph to 45 mph and cruise horizontally through the clouds. This almost doubles his time in the air before opening his parachute. By 2003, more than 2,000 people—including many women, a first in the history of birdmen—had experienced wingsuit flight. Four had died. (A small number, perhaps, but not exactly comforting when you're sitting in the hull of a rising twin-prop.)

Watching Kuosma fly is breathtaking. At first he drops straight down like any free-faller. But in a matter of seconds the wings catch the air and the fall curves forward in a graceful cycloid. If there's a plump cumulus in sight, Kuosma banks toward it and glissades around its edge, or plunges right through. He can fly on his back, make figure-eights, or soar along a highway—outrunning the cars below. "There are no speeding tickets up there," says Kuosma. And that's more than just a clever way of putting it, coming from a man who's been jailed for exceeding the speed limit while driving through Georgia.

Three of the four deaths attributed to the BirdMan suit occurred on jumps from stationary heights like cliffs or bridges. It's hard to know to what degree the wingsuit can be implicated. The chief thrill in BASE jumping—an acronym for jumps from buildings, antennas, spans (i.e., bridges), and earth—after all, is the threat of death. "Officially, we don't even recommend BASE jumping," says Kuosma. "We can't really recommend Russian roulette to anybody. Although it's fun." The other death occurred when an inexperienced skydiver tried to jump with a friend's wingsuit. No one knows exactly what happened, but he was sent into a spiral and hit the ground wrapped in his parachute.

The deaths give Kuosma pause—but a short one. "Accidents do happen a lot," he acknowledges. "It's always really hard, but you just start getting used to it. It's something you accept as the price for what you are doing."

✦

"That yawning door, opening into space, is like the very jaws of hell," wrote the French birdman of the 1950s, Leo Valentin, of his thoughts in the plane before a jump. "We're not birds, look at us, we're only men! So quick—let's get back to earth. To earth—at once!"

My thoughts exactly. Then the Belgian launches us into space. We flip out the back of the plane and suddenly the fear is gone. I am out there. A pinprick of consciousness punching through the atmosphere. The sun watches from the edge of a 360-degree horizon. The wind blasts against my eardrums and they pop and pop and pop. I eat clouds. Scream with pure joy. The planet spreads out below me, indifferent . . . and then a simple *foomp.*

The world changes from sensory overload to total peace, absolute silence. We're hovering, seemingly motionless. The Belgian taps me on the shoulder and points up to the left. I look up in time to see Kuosma pop out of a bank of puffy clouds, his canopy already open. He spirals around us, grinning. It's like meeting a long-lost friend in a dream. Before long, the drop zone rises to our feet and we've landed.

"I'm in love again," says Kuosma. His eyes are wide and his face is flushed. He's overjoyed, despite the fact that he had to abandon our little plan. "I was like a kid again. My heart was pounding in the plane." He had followed us till we went through the cloud. Rather than risk a collision, Kuosma changed course and found us after he'd opened his canopy. But it hardly matters. I'm just glad I'm no longer a whuffo.*

Soon the beer appears. War stories and life philosophies start spilling out as the sun goes down. "You feel smaller up there," says Kuosma, "but much bigger. Because you know how small you feel and the knowledge makes you feel bigger." A Yorkshireman named Steve Ashman is at the table with us. He, too, has had his first wing-suit flight in months, and he's positively glowing. "I went through my first cloud today," he says with a grand, goofy grin. Steve learned to skydive just to fly the wingsuit. And once he'd flown, he tells us, he never looked at a bird or the sky the same way again. He pauses before quoting Leonardo. "Once you have tasted flight, you will walk the earth with your eyes turned skyward, for there you have been and there you long to return."

---

*Months later we tried the flyby again. Once under an open parachute, I looked up over my right shoulder and saw a speck emerge out of pure blue. The speck soon grew to human size and Kuosma whipped through the air in front of me, just feet away, throwing me a grin and a thumbs-up sign.

Part One

THE FALL OF MAN FROM TOWERS, CLIFFS, AND HILLS

The Legacy of Icarus

The last tower jumper or the first BASE jumper?
Franz Reichlt stands atop the second tier of the Eiffel Tower moments
before leaping to his death on Feburary 12, 1912.

SOURCE: BRITISH PATHÉ

chapter 1

One Small Step for Man =
One Giant Step for Man

For those of us who fly in our dreams, rarely is there any flapping of the arms, nor are there hidden jets or superhero capes. No air, really. The means of propulsion, even for daytime nihilists, is some kind of faith—just a matter of knowing it can be done—that keeps the body suspended and moving. And as that faith wanes, maybe from some creeping knowledge that it must be a dream, instead of plummeting to the ground there's just a slow, soft descent. Sometimes there's only enough faith to hover a few inches or feet above the ground. But those inches are miles when compared to how high we expect to fly after our morning cup of coffee. In the waking world we are utterly certain that any step off a mountain, roof, or table will have the same result: blind obedience to the draconian laws of physics.

We can fantasize that if we could just muster up enough faith, we could launch ourselves off some precipice and hover there like Wile E.

Coyote before he notices the earth's no longer beneath him. But to go any further with the fantasy is to feel gravity's tug. No one will ever persuade us to jump—without a parachute—from anything much higher than the kitchen counter. Fasting, lashing the flesh, walking on coals: these are the limits of what the faithful are asked to do. What religion or cult has ever suggested to its followers that with enough faith they could fly?

And yet every century has had its birdmen, people with enough faith in the possibility of humans taking flight—and enough faith in whatever accoutrements they had devised—to take the literal plunge. Had they heard of a leading edge? No. Was *angle of attack* a part of their vocabulary? Less than unlikely. Lift and drag? Forget about it.

The tower jumpers of centuries past had a kind of faith that separates those who dream of flight from those who try it.

✦

It's hard to talk about humans trying to reach birdy heights without first touching on the Greek myth of Daedalus and his young egg, Icarus. But the tale has more bearing on our story than it might first seem. Daedalus, a metalsmith and inventor of great talent, and Icarus were incarcerated by King Minos, on the island of Crete. To escape, Daedalus assembled wings of feathers, wax, and whatnot and learned to fly. He made another set for Icarus and, before they took off, advised his son not to fly too near the sun, lest the wax melt. "No fancy steering by star or constellation, follow my lead!" as the poet Ovid puts it in the Rolfe Humphries translation. And so they flew, dazzling farmers and boatmen below, who thought them gods. Needless to say, Icarus was having such a heady time that he couldn't resist flying sunward—the wax melted and he plunged to a watery death.

Despite the unhappy ending, the tale seems to inspire flight-minded people of all kinds. Ballooning, aviation, and bungee-jumping companies have named themselves after the wax-winged hero, and Icarus Canopies is perhaps the best-known parachute manufacturer in the world.

The fact that these companies are unafraid to use the name of a figure whose fearless adventurism led directly to his death can only be explained by the fact that those attracted to flight tend to be (or want to be) fearless adventurers. Leo Valentin, whose jumps (and death) in the 1950s inspired a slew of imitators in the second half of the century, did not read the tale of Icarus as a cautionary one. Instead he saw it as "amplified and glorified to strike the imagination, to satisfy the taste for the marvelous." The same stores that sell Icarus skydiving gear also sell bumper stickers that say NO FEAR, NO LIMIT. You might think a skydiving company could just as easily name itself after Daedalus, who did, after all, manage to fly and *live,* but it seems that for those who take to the air, the name Icarus resonates more with the drive to greater extremes than that of his more confidence-inspiring father. Perhaps the school-marminess of Daedalus's warning displeases them. (The Daedalus drop zone in Germany is the exception. Its owner, Christoph Aarns, who flies the rigid Skyray, is safety-obsessed and extends the bumper sticker by two words: NO FEAR, NO LIMIT: NO BRAINS.)

The Greeks certainly didn't have a monopoly on such tales. Myths of human flight abound in almost every ancient culture. The Aztecs had their eagle-knight; the Incas spoke of Ayar Utso, who flew to the sun; and the Hindus have the birdman god Garuda, as well as the story of Jatayu, whose flight closely parallels the story of Icarus. The tomb of Ramses II shows him wearing wings—to what end we'll never know—and the Norse had another flying tinkerer in Wayland, a blacksmith who slapped together some wings, again for the purpose of escaping, only to wind up in a Wagner opera. But the story of Daedalus, in its more complete form, does more for our history of flight than just express the human dream of soaring and warn against trying to make that dream a reality. One subplot of the story more precisely demonstrates what would happen to the first men who tried to fly.

How was it that Daedalus came to be imprisoned in the first place? Well, he was taking care of his nephew Talos, who one day noticed the usefulness of a jawbone for sawing things in two. Talos forged one in iron, thus inventing the saw. Daedalus, who claimed to have invented the tool himself, was either worried that Talos would become future competition or just plain jealous. He led Talos to the Acropolis, ostensibly to show him the view, and there shoved him off the roof of Athena's temple. There was no flying for Talos, just a deadly drop—though some say he turned into a partridge after his death.

What better leaping-off point, as it were, for this history than that of a mortal fall from some high, stationary place? For most of human history, those who tried to fly experienced something similar.

✦

Sorting out what in our written history is pure myth, what is myth based on fact, and what is plain old fact is a notoriously difficult task, and so it's impossible to say who was the first person to make an attempt at flight. But the first possibly plausible account comes from those most ancient of the ancients, the Chinese, and may also tell us of the first use of a parachute. According to the *Bamboo Annals,* the Emperor Shun, as a boy, was imprisoned by the enemies of his father. Somehow he managed to cobble together a bird suit and either leapt out of a tower and flew to freedom or flapped his way over a prison wall. His interest in air travel apparently extended into adulthood, when he stepped off another tower and, with the help of two large, conical hats, made it to the ground without injury.

As with the printed word, explosives, and pasta, the Chinese were centuries ahead of the rest of the world at putting men in the air. Sometime in the sixth century A.D., the emperor Kao Yang began experimenting with the power of large kites to lift the human body. With the typical wisdom of a monarch, he did not use himself as a subject, as Emperor Shun had, but used his subjects as subjects—his imprisoned enemies, to be exact. The emperor forced these kite-accessoried captives to jump from a high tower on the outskirts of the city of Yeh. The kites proved unhelpful, except for one made in the shape of an owl, which placed its payload, the prisoner Yuan Huang-t'ou, on the ground unscathed. For his pains he was locked up again.

The pairing of wind and royalty remains intact across centuries and continents. "Blow, winds, and crack your cheeks! rage! blow!" rails King Lear against the storm, according to Shakespeare. Perhaps, though, Lear was echoing words shouted with more sincerity, and urgency, by his father, the historical King Bladud, in the early years of the ninth century B.C. (The king was also known as Lud Hubibras, which has nothing to do with the etymology of the word *hubris,* but it would make sense if it did.) Bladud was educated in Athens, built the city of Bath, England, and supposedly dabbled in black magic. His own parents banished him when they discovered he was a leper, and he roamed the countryside till the day he chased a mad pig into a pond of muck. The muck cured the prince (as well as the pig), and he was soon accepted at home, where he eventually ruled for twenty years. He built the baths of Bath so that others might enjoy healing similar to his. Whether it was with the assistance of necromancy or science that the king hoped to fly from the Apollo tower in what is now known as London, we will never know. And so we will never know what it was that failed him when he made this jump with wings never described by his contemporaries: the wind did not crack its cheeks quite enough to keep the sovereign aloft—'twas his neck that cracked instead.

English historians tended to use Bladud's tale as an admonishment and a warning to those who strive to outdo God. Some centuries later, Percy Enderbie, the author of *Cambria Triumphans, or Brittain in its Perfect Lustre,* a history of England, felt free to describe Bladud's wings as made with wax and blamed the lord's downfall on his nearness to the sun—"a just reward for his temerity."

In ancient Greece and Rome, flights to the death were not always made by choice. In the first decade or two of the first century A.D., Strabo described in his *Geography* an annual ritual that took place on the island of Leucas. To honor Apollo, the Leucadians would take a criminal to a precipice some 2,000 feet above the sea for the purposes of sacrifice/setting him free. (Sappho, the poet, supposedly leapt from this same cliff, as did many others, to cure her love.) Should the offering survive the fall, fishermen would pick him up and take him to other lands. Having learned from repetition, one guesses, that merely attaching wings or feathers would lead prisoners to certain death— little sport in that—the islanders also tried tying live birds to the unfortunates before giving them a push. The rate of survival is not recorded.

The historian Marcus Antonius Sabellicus, who published a history of the world in 1504, tells us that during Caesar's reign, men imitated birds and managed to leave the ground. At least the notion that such things were possible stuck around till Nero's day, A.D. 54–68. The Sophist and Nero contemporary Dio Chrysostom wrote that Nero would, on occasion, order a man to fly, and as no one would dare disobey such a command, courtiers would keep the man around for some time and pretend he had the ability. Dio Chrysostom does not explain how the chosen birdman escaped demonstrating his supposed skills. Suetonius, who also lived during Nero's reign, tells us that during the "Great Festival," an actor attempting his first flight as Icarus in the *Daedalus and Icarus* ballet "fell beside Nero's couch and spattered him with blood." Sadly, Suetonius does not tell us whether this was a real flight or just an act, if the blood was real blood or just tomato sauce, or whether the bespattering delighted or angered the emperor.

The tyrants of yesteryear managed to contribute to the history of attempted flight even when abusing power in ways other than ordering people to flap or fly. The Persian king Shapur I, who lived in the third century A.D., once had a lovely tower built for himself and feared that others might be moved to requisition one themselves. So, anticipating by 1,300 years the style of Ivan the Terrible—who blinded the architect who built Saint Basil's Cathedral—Shapur ordered his architect to build the tower in such a way that when it was finished he would remain stuck on top. The architect, in no position to reject the offer, requested only that he have enough wood to build a shack to protect himself from vultures. Once the tower was complete, the architect hewed himself a pair of wings with the wood and, with a little help from a strong wind, flew to his escape. (And as for Ivan the Terrible— he treated winged men as brutally as he treated his architects. He executed a man who had the poor luck to survive a jump from a tower wearing wings made of wood and cloth. The event caused the tsar to declare all attempts at flight unnatural.)

In the middle of the ninth century A.D., several Islamic scholar/ adventurers continued the quest for human flight, albeit in a more voluntary fashion. Cordova, at the heart of Moorish Spain, was experiencing something of a renaissance, and as it came to be known as

Europe's intellectual center, it was the perfect place to exhibit the latest aviation technology. To Armen Firman (pronounced "Air-man Firm-man," let's just say) this was a huge canvas cloak, which he donned and leapt with from one of the city's towers. Witnesses tell us that the cloak managed to break Firman's fall enough for him to survive, though not without some scuffing of the flesh.

You'd think these witnesses would share a few more details, but they do not. One of them, though, was a young scholar named Abbas Ibn Firnas. Firnas had come to Cordova to teach music, went on to become a chemist, a physicist, and an astronomer, managed to turn sand into glass, and invented a timekeeping device. Eventually he, too, turned his keen mind to the challenges of aviation. Twenty-three years after Firman made his short drop, Firnas built wings made of feathers mounted on a wooden framework. According to spectators gathered on a nearby mountain, Firnas threw himself off a high point and managed to glide for some distance before stalling and sinking straight to the ground. Firnas injured his back and blamed the less-than-complete success on his having forgotten to use a tail—since that's what birds land on. Firnas died more than a decade later, reportedly from complications with his back. But between his flight and his death, the inventor built a mechanical planetarium, complete with moving planets. Perhaps he was after the view Icarus had as he approached the sun. If he's looking down on us now, he'll be pleased to see the statue of himself on the road to Baghdad's airport.

As we move forward through history, and myth solidifies into reportage, the results of these experiments take a decided turn toward the negative. In the first years of the second millennium another scholar, the brilliant lexicographer Al-Djawhari of Turkistan, had made his way to Nisabur in Arabia. It was there that he announced from the top of a mosque that he was about to make history. He did. Wearing two giant wooden wings, he leapt into the air and fell immediately to his death.

Back in the Christian world, at almost the same time, "the Flying Monk" was practically reliving the life of Ibn Firnas. Eilmer of Malmesbury, as we are told by the chronicler William of Malmesbury, was a scholar and an astronomer who had carefully observed the activities of jackdaws in the area. In 1010 he climbed to the top of a tower in the monastery—probably some eighty feet high—and tied some wings to both feet and hands. Eilmer "collected the breeze" and took off, flying a distance of nearly two and a half football fields. "But agitated by the violence of the wind and the swirling of the air, as well as by awareness of his rashness, he fell, broke his legs, and was lame ever after." Like Firnas, he blamed his injuries on the lack of a tail. He turned his mind to astronomy thereafter and lived long enough to see Halley's comet twice—a fact that made him more famous at the time than his 240-yard dash.

Halley's had come and gone once more before the next reported attempt at hominid flight. A Turk whose name is unknown decided to jump from the top of a tower in Constantinople during the year 1162, during festivities held shortly after a treaty ended a spate of warfare in the region. The Turk spread the word of his plans far and wide, and quite a crowd showed up to see the spectacle. At the appointed time he stood at the top of the tower, draped in a voluminous, pleated white garment, while the throng below heckled and the emperor pleaded. The Turk ignored both, and the story of his jump became widely known in the western world thanks to Richard Knolles's translation of *The History of the Turks*. "In steed of mounting aloft," he wrote, "this foolish *Icarus* came tumbling downe headlong with such violence, that he brake his necke, his armes and legs, with almost all the bones of his bodie." These words were to set off a spate of copycat drops in the seventeenth century, as we shall see.

In 1232 the Florentine Buoncompagno widely advertised his coming flight, just as his Turkish predecessor had. The marketing had its intended effect, and on the day he hoped to fly, he found the entire population of Bologna waiting at the foot of the hill on which he stood bedecked in wings. But Buoncompagno's subsequent behavior brings to mind only one type of bird—the chicken. He told the crowd that he would not fly and that it was enough for them to have set eyes on his face. The people of Bologna promptly chased him away with stones.

Not every scholar of the air was foolish enough to make announcements, gather crowds, and claim he would soon astound the world with the miracle of man-flight. Take the mathematician Giovanni Battista Danti. His stealth approach, more raptor than rooster, skipped the rhetorical introduction. At the very end of the fifteenth century, Danti built himself wings of feather affixed to iron bars. Ernest Edward Walker, in his *Aviation,* calls them "non-vibrant." He tested his wings, alone, over Lake Trasimeno more than once, and, satisfied that he was bound to have some success, the numbers-minded birdman made the trip to Perugia. On the day he planned his flight, there was a rather large wedding taking place, and farther along, in the great square, a throng had gathered to watch a bit of jousting. Many of these fine people were sent into a sudden panic as Danti, having left some high point in the city, came swooping down upon them. No doubt thrilled by the sight of terror on their faces, Danti struggled to fly higher, and, you will not be surprised to hear, it was this audacity that ended the flight. One of his iron bars broke and Danti, carried forward by inertia, crashed into the roof of Saint

Mary's church. The roof, the iron bar, the flight, and a leg were all that were broken. A wealthy member of the wedding party was so impressed that he took Danti to Venice as his private mathematician, where he became famous.

✦

But the most famous of all the early birdmen was none other than Leonardo da Vinci—if, in fact, he was a birdman. The question of whether or not he flew, or tried to fly, is batted about as often as that of the identity of the subject of his *Mona Lisa.* Judging by the success, however limited, of less brilliant tower jumpers before and after him, it's almost harder to imagine him not trying. And then there's that tantalizing quote: *Once you have tasted flight, you will walk the earth with your eyes turned skyward, for there you have been and there you long to return.* Just what did he mean by "tasted"? Do people really write of having "tasted" things they have only studied? Maybe this taste was a short glide from a hill that to any less methodical experimenter would have been cause for braggadocio, but for Leonardo was a failure not worthy of mention.

There are a number of reasons to believe that Leonardo had at least made an effort to get into the air:

+ He dreamt up many flying machines, including a corkscrew helicopter that never would have worked, and a square parachute that would have.
+ He built many a toy bird or small flying machine.
+ In his *Treatise on the Flight of Birds,* Leonardo writes repeatedly, and accurately, of what humans must do to overcome their unbirdlike qualities to fly.

+ Girolamo Cardano wrote in his *De Subtilitate,* thirty-one years after Leonardo's death, that he had "tried, but in vain," to fly.

+ Stories of his flights have been passed down orally since his death.

+ Pierre Boaistuau, in his *Bref Discours de l'Excellence et Dignité de l'Homme,* of 1558, wrote that Leonardo had "nearly achieved that aim."

+ Cusperus, in his *Treatise on the Excellence of Man,* claims Leonardo flew.

+ Among Leonardo's own extensive notes on how to build wings, we find the following sentence: "Tomorrow morning on the second day of January, I will make the thong and the attempt." Also: "From the mountain which takes its name from the great bird, the famous bird will take its flight, which will fill the world with great renown." Of course, this might just as well be evidence that he didn't fly, as the renown was not so great as to have survived as more than rumor.

+ To test out wings, he recommended suspending oneself from a cathedral roof, much as the "Yorkshire Birdman" would do from a crane many years later.

+ In 2003 the BBC commissioned a reconstruction of Leonardo's glider. It flew, piloted by the world's paragliding champion, for 18 seconds.

Regardless of whether or not Leonardo actually soared at all, he did understand many things about balance, gliding, and aeronautics that eluded those who had tried to fly before him. Unfortunately for those who came after, his manuscripts were not found until 1797, which meant—as the world saw few geniuses of his genius thereafter—278 more years of botched attempts at flight.

2

The Plummet Continues

Just a few years after Leonardo's possible attempt, a schemer in the court of Scotland made pronouncements unmatched by any of his feathered predecessors. John Damian, an Italian, managed to worm his way into King James IV's favor with good cheer and dissembling alone—the king apparently thought him funny. No one else did. And so, to make himself useful and less prone to intrigue, Damian set about becoming an alchemist and impersonating a doctor in the Hackenbush style. The tactic worked to a degree—the king made him Abbot of Tungland—but only increased everyone else's animosity toward him. The interpersonal conflict soon came to a head, and Damian was forced to make good on his claims that he was in fact a true genius. So, when, in late September of 1507, some ambassadors and other members of the upper crust were preparing to leave for France, Damian announced that he would beat them there—by flying. He made some wings of feather and leapt from Stirling Castle.

Beating the air with all his might, he soared through the sky and headed south for many miles before gliding across the channel and . . . no, no, my mistake. It was the ground below that he headed for, rather soon after leaving the castle, and upon impact he broke bones. History does not record which ones. His failure, he explained to the king as he lay on the ground, was due to the species of feather he'd used. They were of hen, and it was the nature of hens to stay grounded. He should have used the feathers of eagles, he said, as they favor the sky.

Another bone was broken—in this case the neck—some half a century later, when an unnamed stuntman in cloth wings heaved himself off the Tour de Nesles, right across from the Louvre. If the poet Augié Gaillard can be trusted, the birdman fell "like a pig" in front of some 500,000 gawkers. This was the less than lustrous beginning to the legacy of many a French *homme-oiseau*.

Perhaps João Torto in Portugal had heard of the tragedy, as his wings were a slight improvement on what had preceded him. In addition to making superior bi-wings, of calico on iron hoops, he wore a helmet—with a beak. Sadly, though, the headgear turned Torto's flight into what may be the earliest known evidence in support of the Helmet Law Defense League. Torto left the tower of a cathedral, hoping to make it to a nearby field, but in midflight the helmet slipped over his eyes. Blinded, the journey ended when he slammed into an unexpected roof. He died of his injuries soon after.

Paolo Guidotti of Lucca, Italy, had more luck slamming into roofs. This Rome-educated artist/architect/aviator—a Leonardo imitator, no doubt—crafted his wings from whalebone, covered them with feathers, and somehow used springs to arch them like a bird's wing. The art historian Filippo Baldinucci informs us that after much preparation Guidotti jumped from some eminence and "carried himself forward for about a quarter of a mile, not, in my view, flying, but falling more slowly than he would have done without wings." The underawed Baldinucci goes on to explain how Guidotti was flapping with all his strength as he fell—but eventually he could flap no more. He crashed into a roof, which broke, then fell through to the first floor and landed on a leg, which also broke. Thereafter Guidotti toyed not with wings and exchanged brushes with death for brushes with paint. His *Saint Zita and the Poor* can still be seen in Lucca's Church of Saint Frediano.

Guidotti was not the last polymath in history to be attracted to the skies. Like Guidotti, the monk Kaspar Mohr of Wurtemberg painted and studied in Rome. In addition to receiving a degree in theology, he mastered mathematics, the organ, sculpting, and clockmaking, among other skills. Once he was back at his monastery, Mohr tied goose feathers together with whipcord and secretly practiced flying with the assemblage. But before he could try leaping from a third story as planned, the wings were taken from him—saving, if not his life, at least a bone or two.

Feathers, in those days, were the natural thing to turn to for serious winged experimenters. The Venetian Giovanni Francesco Sagredo had worked with his friend Galileo Galilei, and the scientist's scientific method must have rubbed off on him somewhat. Taking it into his head that human flight was not impossible, he caught a falcon and plucked off its feathers. These he carefully measured, recording the proportions between them and the wingspan of the denuded bird. With these data, he set about building wings of the same proportion for his own person. The resulting flight was like that of a falcon—a featherless one, that is. Sagredo jumped from a high point and landed just yards away. Though he did not fly, when compared to the tests of his peers, we must consider the episode a success, as he emerged from the trial uninjured.

Success, of course, can be measured in many ways. A good glide ratio is one kind of success, and a jump without injury is another. But so is making a splash, figuratively. Many of the tower jumpers of the seventeenth century, like the BASE jumpers of today, sought out peaks both high and historical for purposes of publicity. And so we must count Adriaen Baartjens a success, as well. He tested his ribbed eagle-feather wings with a tail first off a tower in Rotterdam. Having survived that flight, he journeyed to The Hague, where he attempted two more flights. The first, made with some kind of "safety line," produced no injuries. The second, a free fall without safety line, proved less safe, and Baartjens ended up with a broken arm.

The feathers of the seventeenth-century Russian bird must have been better suited for man-flight than those of their more western neighbors. Or perhaps it was the quality of Russian sheets. When a man by the name of Vliskov leapt from the top of a Moscow building in 1610, he survived with nothing worse than a few cuts and bruises, thanks to his wings of eagle feather and linen.

Twenty years later, a prisoner kept in a fortress somewhere near the Black Sea made wood-and-linen wings and with them was able to fly away to a nearby forest. Though the wings put him down safely, they did nothing to hide his smell. Guard dogs soon found him, and he was brought back to the fortress. His jailers were so bowled over by the prisoner's inventiveness that they made the poor man perform the stunt again. Again the linen wings placed him on the ground un-harmed, but the prisoner's strength was not what it had been on his first flight, and he didn't get as far. In fact, he landed next to the execution pike. This seemed a strange coincidence to the guards, and they took advantage of his position and put him to death.

The Russian reward for a failed attempt at flight was somewhat less harsh than the reward for a successful one. A Polish, or possibly Ukrainian, peasant made his way to Moscow in April of 1680, where he promised the residents of that city that in return for an investment on their part, he would make a flight that would wow them all. On two separate occasions, using wings of mica or possibly feathers and wax, this peasant flapped in an effort to leave the ground and failed completely to do so—unless you count his hopping. You might say he was the first to put the hop in ornithopter. He was beaten for his pains and made to return all funds.

In Turkey the flight-minded were treated more kindly. Hezarfen Ahmet Çelebi was to the Turks what Lindbergh would be to Americans, just 300 years earlier and over a slightly smaller body of water. Çelebi, as the tale has been passed down, read Leonardo da Vinci's works on birds and built his own set of wings. Once he felt fully prepared, he announced that he would fly from the Galata Tower in downtown Istanbul. Sometime in 1638 he climbed the 220-foot tower, which still stands today, took off, flew across the Bosporus, and landed in the middle of a market on the Asian side of the city.

The sultan wanted to reward the experimenter with riches, but superstitious or jealous courtesans persuaded him to banish Çelebi to Algeria instead. There he died, at the age of thirty-one. His name lived on, though, as the tower was known as Hezarfen Tower for centuries. It is once again known as Galata, but Çelebi's name has been elevated elsewhere—one of Istanbul's airports is now the Hezarfen Airfield.

✦

The miracle is not to fly in the air or to walk on the water, but to walk on the earth, says one Chinese proverb. But Salomon Idler, a cobbler in Augsburg, Germany, in the mid-seventeenth century, must have felt that after a life in his trade he'd done enough for the miracle of walking on the earth and was ready to try his hand at flying, whatever the thoughts of the Chinese. He briefly turned away from making pairs of shoes to make a pair of wings of iron and feathers, possibly based on some plans that fell into his hands. Idler wanted to jump with these wings from Augsburg's tallest tower, but the villagers persuaded him to take a safer route. They piled mattresses on a bridge and had Idler jump from a nearby roof. The mattresses were apparently well placed, as they broke Idler's fall. But the fall broke the bridge. And the bridge broke some hens that had made a home below. Idler, guilt-stricken by the gallinicide, chopped his wings to bits.

This, of course, was not the last disaster for a birdman on German soil. A surgeon from Grenoble, Charles Bernouin, built himself saillike wings, and rumor had it that he was a whiz at flying them. How many flights he may have made, we'll never know, but in Regensburg, at seven in the evening, on January 15, 1672, Bernouin leapt from a tower and, with the addition of a rocket, made something of a flight, which resulted in a broken neck.

The breaking of the neck seems to have been a habit for winged Frenchmen living abroad. Around the same time that Bernouin rocketed to his demise, a compatriot of his in London was constructing his own wings of leather over wooden ribs. These were hinged, presumably for the purpose of flapping, and they assisted their maker, on his first jump, from the roof of St. Paul's Cathedral to the ground below without incident. But on a second attempt one of the hinges jammed, killing the Frenchman in the manner described above.

Back at home, in Sablé, France, a locksmith by the name of

Besnier took a more measured approach to getting in the air. His wings were like poles that seesawed on the shoulders. On the end of each pole was a hinged frame holding stretched taffeta. The frame operated like a valve: on their way up the air forced them closed, and on the way down they opened, creating more resistance. Besnier mounted the poles over his shoulder and tied the back end to his feet. That way he could use his legs to pull down on the back of, say, the left pole, while pulling the front of the right pole down with his hand.

But Besnier was not so enamored of his ingenuity that he rushed to dive off the nearest parapet. Instead he jumped first from a chair and, having survived the drop, tried again from a tabletop. Finding himself still alive, he leapt from a windowsill, and as he came to no harm after even this fall, he ramped up the experiments and flew from a second-story window. Emboldened after this greater success, he went to the attic and took to the air, flying over a nearby cottage. If all this is to be believed, he went on to even higher and lengthier flights and eventually sold the wings to some kind of con man who performed with them at fairs. Besnier built a second pair and bragged that, given enough height, he could cross rivers in the air. He also earned the distinction of being the first birdman to appear in a magazine article when the *Journal des Sçavans* described his wings.

With the shoulders as the pivot point of two levers, and poles moving up and down in front and in back, Besnier's wings were more or less the first machine used for flying a human. But it was not Besnier's innovation, if we can call it that, or anyone else's, that led men who wanted to fly to leave the path of bird mimickry for the path that would end in the airplane. This change occurred thanks to the thoughts of mathematician, philosopher, and scientist Giovanni Borelli, a contemporary of Besnier's. Borelli proved that it was not the ratio of a bird's feathers to its wingspan that made it able to fly, but the ratio of its weight to its muscle power. Not even the most muscle-bound of humans could approach this ratio,* and after Borelli published these ideas, the rate of aviation experimentation plummeted like so many dense-boned creatures.

Those who dared enter the air now tended to do so with machines. The first was another locksmith, Johann Gabriel Illing, of Halle, Germany. And though his mechanical eagle (which he was to sit inside, though it never flew) might have seemed the logical next step after Besnier—a complete surrender to Borelli's theory that man could not fly on his own—it was the start of an entirely new branch in the evolution of flight, one that would lead, of course, to the airplane, and therefore holds no interest for us.

Flying in a plane, a mechanical eagle, or a winged chariot does not put wings on man, but puts man inside wings. "What we have invented is a rasping malodorous machine which serves as an elaborate prosthetic device to transport us through air," wrote Roger Shattuck in 2003. "It flies us as much as we fly it. Flying now belongs to our long love affair with machinery, to the Toys-R-Us syndrome, not to a bird-like liberation."

While Illing and his malodorous branch of flight-driven inventors in the eighteenth and nineteenth centuries were trying to flap, propel, wind, gear, and pedal themselves into the air, others, who had either not read Borelli or dismissed his notions as so much folderol, continued in the quest for birdlike liberation.

Sometime around 1712, for instance, the thespian Charles Allard made a leap in Saint-Germain, France, with wings on his arms—the landing was fatal. Three decades later the Marquis de Bac-

---

*With the upper body alone, anyway. Paul B. MacCready would cross the English Channel with the pedal-powered *Gossamer Albatross* in 1979.

queville, sixty-two years of age at the time, drew a crowd when he announced that he would jump from an upper story of his opulent home on the edge of the Seine and fly to the other side of the river. He wore four petal-shaped wings strapped to his arms and legs like shields (as depicted in one possibly inaccurate illustration), and with them he made it, at most, a sixth of the way across the river. He landed on a barge, startling the washerwoman thereon, and broke a leg.

The higher your jump, the farther your glide—if in fact you can glide. Alternatively, the higher your jump, the harder your fall—but never mind that. As greater and greater height became available through various technologies, winged men leapt at the opportunity to leap from it. No sooner had the Montgolfier brothers invented the hot-air balloon—in 1783—than birdmen began trying to fly from their baskets. The first of these belong to the mechanical category: Jean-Pierre Blanchard took his oared ship up in the air attached to a balloon's basket in 1784, and Jacob Degen similarly hooked up his ornithopter in 1812. Aside from stooping to the use of machinery, these two experimenters were further lowered in the eyes of bird-man history as they never actually detached themselves from their balloons. The first to try that was Louis-Charles Letur, with his parachute-like glider that more closely resembled a merry-go-round than a set of wings. He successfully made the trip from balloon to ground several times, but in 1854, at a drop in London, he crashed into some trees and later died of his injuries. Twenty-two years later, a man named De Groof, another shoemaker, pulled a similar stunt with similar results. His parachute-ornithopter combo inverted when he dropped from a balloon over London, and he died when he hit the streets of Chelsea.

Oddball wings and huge gliders proliferated like rock doves in the nineteenth century, as a flight craze took hold of humanity. The gliders of Charles Spencer, Octave Chanute, Percy Pilcher, Otto Lilienthal (these last two died flying), and countless—if less successful—others marched the world toward the Wright brothers as well as laid the foundation for the future of hang-gliding. This branch of flight, with its fuel-free soaring, undoubtedly has more in common with the wing-suit than it does with the airplane, but these gliders did lead straight *to* the airplane and mark a significant departure from the wings of those who wanted, as much as possible, to make the human body something that was flight-worthy.

The breed of birdman who wanted to keep wings to a more personal size was not entirely extinct. What could be more personal than the arms themselves, unadorned? George Faux, the deliveryman for Essex's Chigwell Row, in the mid-nineteenth century, had spouted off to his fellow villagers that he could fly with nothing more than these upper limbs. It was a bird's leading edge, he explained, that allowed the creatures to fly—the rest of the wing had little to do with it. His arms were leading edge enough, he felt, even if they weren't leading anything. In 1862, Faux invited his neighbors to watch him put the concept to the test by jumping from the roof of the public house. He succeeded in jumping, but not in flying, and quickly met with the earth below. But he broke no bones and took this remarkable fact as a sign of encouragement. He went on to jump from other roofs in the hamlet and quit only when, finally, he broke a leg.

The era of parachute-free drops from stationary heights came to an end when an Austrian tailor named Franz Reichelt stepped off the newly completed second tier of the Eiffel Tower in 1912. He was wearing something that looked to be an overcoat made for a rhinoceros, and it slowed his fall about as much as holding a grown rhinoceros would. The impact killed him.

It was in that same year that a U.S. Army captain named Albert Berry made the first jump from an airplane with a parachute. And as planes and parachutes became more reliable, the birdmen of the world would raise their launching point by several thousand feet and begin the era of the bat-wing.

Part Two

BAT-WINGS

FROM

AIRPLANES

The Legacy of

Clem Sohn

Clem Sohn models a later and larger set of wings,
hours before his death.

3

The Sohn Also Falls: Clem Sohn

Aviator, batflyer, batman, bat-wing man, batwinged pioneer, bat-winger, birdman, daredevil, giant bird, hawkman, human bat, human bird, human eagle, human glider, man-bird, Michigan Icarus, parachute jumper, pioneer soul, skydiver, sky pioneer, skywriter, stuntman, vampire, wing-man. These were the many names attached to a young man from Michigan also known as Clem Sohn. And though he was a man of many titles, he had but a single aspiration. News of his spectacular attempts to achieve it inspired a lineage of imitators that continues to this day. For most of the twentieth century, Sohn's progeny would do little to improve upon his design, perform with greater skill, or surpass his international fame.

If you must leave your birthplace, become a star, and return to put the town in your shoe, Fowler, Michigan, may be the place to start. This hamlet of 1,136 people—only a few hundred people larger than it was in the days of the Depression—is where the redheaded young Sohn was born and grew up. Like so many of the bat-wing jumpers who would follow him, he lost a parent as a child. Sohn was eight when his mother died of ulcers on the lung. He moved to East Lansing as a teenager and frequented the newly erected Capital City Airport while working his way through high school. Airports were still enough of a curiosity then that they attracted weekend crowds who came just to see the planes take off and land.

The Capital City Airport had one pilot who could do a bit more to entertain the gawkers below. Art Davis had acquired his piloting chops in the First World War and had returned from that adventure with a hankering for more. By the time Sohn started hanging out at the airport, Davis had several air-racing trophies to his name and was a celebrated stuntman: he broke one important record of that era when he took off, flew a mile high, and landed in three minutes and four seconds. He'd also pushed a Waco Taperwing biplane to 200 miles per hour. But he was most famous for a little trick he'd developed called the Kiss of Death. When passing in front of the audience, Davis would edge up next to another plane with a flag planted on the outer edge of its wing. With the tip of *his* wing, Davis would grab the flag midflight.

Sohn, who said he had always wanted to imitate the hawks native to his state, paired up with Davis after he graduated from high school. But he was less interested in actually piloting a plane than in stepping out of one and into the open air. With Davis at the stick, Sohn began making parachute jumps at the airport.

He soon made his first major public outing as a parachutist at the All-American Air Races in Miami with seven other jumpers. They jumped from a plane as a group, each attached to his own "static line." Free-falling was not well understood at that time, and most jumps were made with a cord attached to the parachute at one end and to the plane at the other. As the jumper fell away, the line pulled the parachute open, so the actual drop lasted only a few seconds—properly pulling a ripcord wasn't a worry. The technique of multiple static lines used by Sohn's group paved the way for the masses of paratroopers who would jump together in World War II.

For several years, Sohn toured the air-show circuit making static line jumps. But at the Cleveland National Air Races in 1932, he saw the great Spud Manning make an extended drop from a plane. Manning held the record for the highest-altitude drop—15,000 feet—and had practically invented the controlled free fall, having taught himself to spread his arms and legs to keep from tumbling. By the time Sohn set eyes on him, Manning could do turns and flips, fly head-down, and even position himself to glide a little. Manning would be dead a year later when his plane crashed into Lake Michigan, but when Sohn saw him he was at his peak. By some accounts it was then that Sohn first envisioned using wings and began the long process of building his bat-wings.

Manning kept his trade secrets to himself, lest the competition learn to duplicate his stunts, and only decades later would those same positions be rediscovered and taught freely at parachuting schools. So if Sohn wanted to learn to maneuver through the air, he was on his own. He began experimenting right away and discovered that he could move as much as 300 lateral feet in the air, making swimming motions. Less than a year after watching Manning in Cleveland, Sohn felt ready to make his own free fall at the American Air Races. With a 24-pound bag of flour emptying behind him to create a white trail in the sky, Sohn fell from 10,000 feet, terrifying the crowd below, who had most likely never seen a body fall through space.

To elevate the terror, Sohn began jumping with one Wayne "Mile High" Wagner. Together they would race to the ground in free fall, and whoever opened last was the loser. The pair were the first to stage this act, which became standard fare at flight exhibitions. But they were far more cautious than future participants in these "low-altitude contests" who would push the limits of how low a free-faller could go before opening. Sohn and Wagner never opened below 1,000 feet, and even that is a bit low compared to the minimum recommended opening altitude of 2,500 feet for today's skydivers. Most open at 6,000 feet.

Not every jumper with whom Sohn performed this test of the nerves had a cutoff altitude at which they always pulled. In June of 1934, Sohn made a parallel jump with the nation's top parachutist, Jerry Wessling, at Brooklyn's Floyd Bennett Field. The two sped straight toward zero altitude, and they continued going lower and lower even as they experienced "ground rush." (During free fall, people feel as if they are floating, and that the earth remains at the same distance below them. But somewhere under 1,000 feet, the earth's surface seems to suddenly come up at them or spread out, and it's considered a sign to pull the ripcord immediately.) Perhaps there was a real sense of competition between the two jumpers that day, or maybe Wessling simply wanted to see just how low he could go. Sohn opened his parachute with room to spare, but Wessling pulled his rip-cord with only enough time for his lines to unravel, but not enough for the canopy to inflate. Wessling fractured his skull and was dead when Sohn's feet touched the ground.

Wessling's death didn't seem to rattle Sohn, at least not enough to keep him from jumping. The next day he made his 212th jump at 15,000 feet, teasing the crowd again with another low opening, his open flour sack trailing a white line behind him all the way down. As he approached the earth, the announcer, clearly more shaken by the previous day's accident than Sohn himself, began shouting. "Open that parachute! Why don't you open it, Clem?" With the wind roaring in his ears, Sohn couldn't have heard those words, but he opened his parachute, again with just enough time.*

With every jump, Sohn learned a bit more about how to move in the air to control his fall, as well as how best to put on a show. He eventually broke the record for the highest jump when he fell from 18,500 feet. But in making jumps of several miles, he discovered that if he left the plane any higher than 10,000 feet, the spectators below would not be able to see him. For most shows he made lower exits, and to be extra-sure his audience could keep their eyes on him, he developed another trick. "As soon as I have cleared the plane, I set off a smoke bomb fixed between my legs," Sohn once explained. "This shows my position to the crowds below." He also learned to punch holes in his bag of flour as he fell to create a more even and continuous trail behind him. To further heighten the excitement of every show, he had the announcers plead with him over the loudspeaker to open his chute, whether or not he was in any real danger.

But as he approached the kind of skill and maneuverability that he'd seen in Spud Manning, Sohn began to yearn for an experience more roc-like than rocklike. He studied the techniques of bats and flying squirrels, and, with Art Davis, bought a sheet of sailcloth (this first version may have been waterproof zephyr cloth). Using Sohn's mother's sewing machine, they fashioned the cloth into something that resembled a bat's wings. This they anchored to some steel tubing and stretched it over riblike spokes that would radiate from Sohn's shoulder. A locking device held the wings parallel to the body and kept the wind from dislocating his arms. The wings weighed eight

---

*He continued to perform the act with others throughout his career. At the Cleveland Air Races in 1935, three years after his eyeful of Spud Manning, Sohn raced to the ground with a woman named Babe Smith without incident.

pounds (his parachute added an additional 75) and cost Sohn and Davis a total of sixty dollars to build.*

At Daytona Beach, in late February of 1935, Sohn unfolded his wings for the world, as well as a slew of reporters, several "air experts," and the Department of Commerce. Sohn took a plane up to 12,000 feet, climbed out, and jumped. He kept his wings folded as he fell for the first 2,000 feet to avoid any collision with the plane (just as today's wingsuiters wait a few hundred feet before stretching out), and when he opened them, he immediately went into a glide that was so smooth and easy that the batman began to experiment. He darted back and forth and then, by bending his legs, made three consecutive loops. Several reports even claim that he went *up*. "If I had something to check my drop," he later boasted, "I believe I could move through the air almost at will."

Somewhere around 2,000 feet he folded his wings back against his body, pulled his ripcord, and descended safely to the ground. He'd been in the air for about 75 seconds. "I am sure that I could have glided a mile or more laterally if I had concentrated my efforts on that—it was cold, and I was in a hurry to get to the ground."

News of the jump hit the front pages of newspapers throughout the world, and Sohn, cruising on the attention, took his wings on tour. He hit airfield after airfield, spilling out of Davis's Waco, and delighting earthbound spectators all across the land with his loops and glides. Sohn soared in St. Louis, New Orleans during Mardi Gras, Des Moines, Kansas City, Omaha, and in farmers' fields all over Michigan, learning how to fly better with every show. And though that first jump with wings had been surprisingly deft, there was plenty of room for improvement.

---

*One source put the total at $600.

What the grounded audience could see was the easy part of Sohn's flight. The challenge was opening the wings. "First I spread my legs wide apart so that the fin between will prevent tumbling. Then I slowly open my right wing. In those early moments before I attain full flight, there is a terrific pull at my body. As soon as the strain lets up a little, the left wing goes out."

Other bat-wing jumpers cropped up almost immediately after Sohn's first winged flight, but as the originator he continued to make a good deal of money. When he returned home to Fowler, it was in a shiny new Ford coupe (despite the fact that Chevrolet had sponsored him). He had a gun holstered to the car's ceiling to ward off any malefactors seeking to relieve him of his new-found riches. He also had two planes, which he parked outside of Fowler, and a motorcycle. He was known to buzz the homes of friends and family, taking the plane so low that he could see in the windows. At Miller's bar (still open, if you find yourself thirsty in Fowler someday), all drinks were on him.

But, despite the money, the newspaper articles, the crowds, and the announcer shouting his name, in his mind he was not a showman but an experimenter and an inventor. And though he was known to be a quiet man in his private life, he didn't shrink from making grand pronouncements about his endeavor. "I am not a stuntman," he said.

> I use the fin between my legs in the same manner as a bird uses its tail. It's the stabilizer. By letting one wing down a little, I can bank and spiral. It gives you a wonderful sense of power to be able to control your movements in the air without mechanical aid. I feel that I am my own master. Every movement of my arms and legs is obeyed and magnified in the swoops and turns of my flight. I feel like birds must feel. And someday I think that everyone will have wings and be able to soar from the housetops. But

there must be a lot more experimenting before that can happen.

Certainly, Sohn was serious about furthering the pursuit of personal aviation, but it's unlikely that he truly believed that within his lifetime anyone would successfully launch himself from a roof and avoid the same results that met his millennia of predecessors. "House-tops are out," he said at another time. "That's where Darius Green was nuts—and he cracked up. I'm going at this thing in a sane way."*

Over time, Sohn increased his wingspan and eventually switched the cloth he was using to airplane cloth and oiled canvas. When the air pushed against his wings, it drove the frame on his chest hard against his ribs, so he added three rubber sponges between his body and the frame. He claimed to be able to fly for five miles in one direction— and then back—before landing. His wings, he said, slowed his fall to 60 miles per hour, not yet slow enough to land without a parachute. But that didn't stop him from dreaming.

The glory of touching down like a bird was only part of the reason Sohn talked of a chuteless landing. "Soon I hope to land without my parachute. It weighs seventy-five pounds, and its weight handicaps me in the air. It is the weight of my parachute that makes my bird flight so tiring. I am so tired after copying the birds in the air that I can hardly stand up." He toyed with the idea of landing on water, surrounded by some kind of pneumatic tube.†

---

*John T. Trowbridge's poem "Darius Green and His Flying Machine" can be found in the appendix.

†Sohn also spoke of a possible military application, using bat-wings to send spies into enemy territory—a good seven decades before the U.S. army bought wingsuits from Kuosma, and the German military began working with Alban Geissler's Skray.

With so many ideas flitting around in their heads, Sohn and Davis applied for a patent for their invention, and the pair become reluctant to show the wings to the inquisitive. But their secretiveness did little to thwart copycats. At least two of his imitators ended up dead in Sohn's lifetime. They were killed when minor asymmetries in their wings put them into a "flat spin." If they didn't pass out from the blood running to their heads while they twirled helplessly, they would likely tangle with their parachute when they tried to open. Sohn took the deaths as a warning to be more cautious.

With experience he learned how to stop his own dizzying spins, figured out that opening one wing first kept him from rolling, and gave up making loops. "Looping is dangerous," he said. "I don't often do it now unless I have to. As I reach the top of the loop I lose speed, and losing speed is nearly fatal. The little airplane that is me decides to spin. Over I go, head downward, spinning round and round like a top. It is very difficult to get out of a spin." He began folding his wings back in at 1,500 feet and waiting another hundred before opening his chute, to avoid catching his parachute lines on his wings.

But Sohn's new cautiousness was not enough for him to avoid injury. A reporter for the *London Daily Express* who had seen Sohn's debut flight persuaded his newspaper to bring the jumper across the Atlantic for a tour of England. Sohn was to be paid a thousand dollars per jump for forty jumps. On one of them, for the dedication of London's Gatwick Airport, he pulled his ripcord at 800 feet and the emerging canopy immediately tangled with his wings. At 200 feet he managed to send up his reserve, which slowed his fall enough to save his life—but not enough to keep him from crashing into a taxi and breaking his arm. His steel ribs mangled his arm and shoulder. "Please excuse the terrible writing," he wrote home, "it is my right arm I broke."

Nor was it the altitude that nearly did Sohn in at an exhibition in Miami in December of 1935. Again, after a graceful glide, Sohn opened at 800 feet and managed to touch down safely. Unfortunately he was not the only aircraft on the runway. An army plane, ready to take off for another stunt, had its propellers spinning. The suction took hold of Sohn's still-open parachute and began dragging him straight for the plane's blades. He was saved by the ground crew, who managed to chase him down and throw themselves on the wayward chute.

By 1937, Sohn had already made two lucrative trips to Europe. The flight-mad French, who had greeted Lindbergh ten years earlier with enamored throngs, had missed him and were eager to have another Michigan son land on their soil. The French government agreed to pay Sohn $3,500 for six winged jumps at the Paris Air Show.

Sohn and Davis took a ship across the Atlantic, but a storm delayed the pair and they didn't arrive in Paris until the day the first jump was scheduled. They hurried to the Vincennes airport, where a crowd of 46,000 was waiting to see the batman make his flight. Once there, Sohn quickly climbed into his suit—a new set of wings with the largest wingspan yet—and noticed a damp smell coming from his pack. A mob of enthusiasts surrounded him ("scores of pretty girls," according to one report). When a journalist asked him if he thought his job was "temporary," Sohn told him that he felt as comfortable in the air "as you would in your grandmother's kitchen."

After he pulled himself away from his fans, a French pilot took him up to 10,000 feet and slowed the plane when he saw Sohn's thumbs-up signal. Sohn jumped into the slipstream, spread his wings, and began to fly. Footage of Sohn shows the batman gliding gracefully directly above the spectators and banking several times to keep himself in view. These slow turns seem playful and easy, like a seagull hovering in the breeze. He seems to have learned every nuance of the wings he had invented.

When he'd flown for a minute or so, Sohn spiraled down to about 1,000 feet and pulled his ripcord. The lines went out above him, but the canopy did not open. Sohn opened his reserve, but it too stayed shut, fluttering above him like a flame. By now the crowd could see Sohn struggling with his lines. He fought all the way down, but in vain—he hit the earth with an explosive sound not far from the crowd.

Spectators rushed past police lines to get to Sohn's body. Many wept, some fainted, some crossed themselves. Others removed their hats and stood in silence. Art Davis's wife collapsed, sobbing.

Later that day Mrs. Davis would suggest that the jostling admirers who had fondled Sohn's gear may have had something to do with the accident. She also insisted that Sohn must have fainted and come to after his parachute fouled, otherwise he would have pulled the ripcord to his reserve much sooner. Most likely the storm on the Atlantic had wet Sohn's gear, and in the hurry to get to the air show and perform, he had never repacked his chutes.

Mrs. Davis and eight giant wreaths offered by French aviators accompanied Sohn's body on the liner *Aurania* back to the States. His last crowd greeted his coffin as it arrived by train at the Lansing station.

From our perch in the 21st century, black-and-white photographs of Sohn with his wings stretched taut make him seem at first glance like the kind of nutty daredevil you might read about in "Ripley's Believe It or Not" (which in fact once featured him). But Sohn was both a dreamer and hero for his times. The French put on a ceremony, in which they printed and distributed cards with a long elegy for the twenty-six-year-old skyflyer.* In Michigan a pilot friend of Sohn's, Bob O'Dell, flew over Lansing, spelling Sohn's name in the sky. At

---

*The beginning of which can be found in the appendix.

the funeral a group of planes passed over, dropping wreaths. Sohn's old high school made a plaque that said, "There are some pioneer souls who blaze paths where highways never ran." In 1941 an unknown pilot passed over the grave and dropped flowers, each with a note asking the finder to "Please place on Clem Sohn's grave." The people of Michigan still honor Sohn periodically with museum exhibits and summaries of his life in the local papers, and for many years his wings could be seen hanging in the Lansing airport. Fifty years after Sohn's death, the town of Fowler had a ceremony at his grave, with hundreds of people, half of whom were related to the batman. A new headstone was placed there, calling him a "Contributor to the Advancement of Aviation."

Mocking Birds Don't Sing:
Floyd Davis and Others

Within months of Clem Sohn's debut flight in Daytona, a handful of parachutists and air-circus regulars, inspired by the flight of the batman, built similar wings for themselves and bailed out of planes to see if they, too, could fly. Though they modeled their wings on what they'd seen of Sohn's, they rarely, if ever, began with his skill as a free-faller. Few were successful.

The first was another lad from Michigan—the twenty-two-year-old Floyd Davis. Hailing from Flint, the young man, who had been jumping for about three years, wanted to "improve" upon Sohn's design. To him that meant two four-foot, teardrop-shaped wings of stretched canvas, each attached to his side, just above the waist. Davis planned to control the wings with handles tied to ropes that connected to the outer edge of each wing. A pair of smaller, similarly shaped wings adorned the outside of his ankles—altogether he distinctly resembled the figure Evinrude, the dragonfly from the Disney film *The Rescuers.*

At noon, on March 31, 1935—exactly one month after Sohn's first flight—pilot Gordon Helm took Davis up to 6,000 feet. Below, a handful of spectators, including his parents, watched as he exited the plane and glided for several seconds. He was quick to let out his parachute, but his parachute was quick to become entangled with one of his wings. Davis went into a spin and most likely lost consciousness. Seconds later he hit the ground. The ripcord on his reserve was untouched.

When Sohn, who knew Davis, heard of his death, he attributed it to Davis's lack of experience with wing-free falling and assumed that the spin he went into was similar to the kind of tailspin that happens to a plane when it stalls. "I'm afraid," he added, "that more casualties will be reported if many people without experience in delayed jumping try to fly with their own wings."

News of Sohn's first flight must have spread fast and far and wide. Two weeks later a man named Donnie Marshall appeared in Augusta, Georgia, and drew a crowd of 10,000 people when he announced that he would become the town's first bat-wing jumper. He jumped from 4,000 feet, opened at 500, and safely plopped down at zero. He loved the experience so much he moved to Augusta.

Less than a month after Davis's death, a parachutist left a plane over Moscow at 4,900 feet. He was wearing aluminum wings, which, thankfully, did not tangle with the parachute when he opened it at 1,900 feet. He touched down in the Soviet capital fully intact.

When it comes to people of the risk-taking variety, disaster can inspire as much as success. Just as *Into Thin Air,* Jon Krakauer's haunting narrative about the death of twelve climbers on Mount Everest, inspired more people to attempt to climb the mountain than ever before, Sohn's death gave more jumpers the bat-wing bug than his first flight did.

Jimmy Caraway, of Indianola, Iowa, for example, had been touring with the Hollywood Daredevils. After Sohn's death he became their batman. In late August of 1938, he made a winged jump in Fargo and for some reason never opened his parachute when he was finished with his flight—he fell straight to the ground. His body landed in a park, and he and his untouched parachute were not found for half an hour.

The opening of the eleventh annual Miami All-American Air Maneuvers, during the first week of 1939, began with a memorial for Amelia Earhart. In addition to the unveiling of a plaque and various aircraft formations streaming across the sky, the dedication featured a "race" between two bat-wing jumpers, Charlie Zmuda—yet another daredevil progeny of East Lansing, Michigan, and the new bat-wing jumper with Art Davis's Air Show—and Elmo Bannister. Apparently the winner would be the world champion, but how this winner was decided (a dash to the ground would hardly be made faster by using wings), as well as who the winner was, remain lost to history.

Bannister, we know, survived his bat-wing jumps as well as the Second World War, though somewhere along the line he lost an eye. In 1945, a Private Bannister, wearing a patch over one eye, made a bat-wing flight for the folks of Monticello, Indiana. His wings complemented the wicked aesthetic Bannister achieved with his eye patch. These long, black, pointy wedges, whose shape brings to mind Madonna's mid-1990s brassiere, were clearly the Stealth Bomber of bat-wings. A gravestone in Comanche, Texas, tells us that Bannister died on June 8, 1977.

By late January of 1939, a stunt flyer named Jimmy Goodwin was making regular winged leaps with the Southern Aces air show. Goodwin, who'd played many small parts in Hollywood, found more adulation as a stunt pilot and jumper, and his wings were calculated to make a sensation. Goodwin draped broad-striped canvas on poles that extended more than an extra arm's length past his fingertips. He also pioneered a look that would catch on with the bat-wing flyers of the 1960s—the mustache. Goodwin's was pencil-thin.

After making a jump on January 21 for the Blythe Country Club, he headed to Palm Springs, where he made a jump as a "Man from Mars." Later that year he joined Happy Jack Miller and his Death Dodgers. (Happy Jack's wife dodged death by sitting on the hood of his car while he crashed it into a burning wall.) For these jumps he was opening as low as 150 feet. A pilot who often took Goodwin up to his jumping height of 10,000 feet claimed that he had once flown a distance of 75 miles.

It was not Goodwin's striped wings that did him in, but larger red ones—with an engine. In the fall of 1941, Goodwin was performing with the All-American Air Show at Curles Neck Farm, near Richmond, Virginia. He had outfitted his racing plane, a Mono Special, with a smoke machine so he could create a "smoke screen" in front of the grandstand. After diving and racing past the 400-odd spectators at nearly eye level, Goodwin took the plane to 500 feet and tried to make a "double snap roll"—slowing the plane down and then yanking back on the stick while turning hard to the left. But instead of completing the roll, he was thrown into a spin. He recovered, took the plane back up, and tried again—with the same result. A Civil Aeronautics Administration inspector turned to the manager of the air show and told him that because of his erratic flying, the pilot shouldn't fly at the next day's show. He didn't. Goodwin went up again to 500 feet to try the roll once more, and this time the plane went into a spin Goodwin could not get out of. He was presumed dead on impact.

In June of 1939, George Cook made a bat-wing jump from

10,000 feet at the Denver Air Show. A crowd of 6,000 watched his parachute tangle with his wings. The half-inflated canopy barely slowed his fall, and he broke his back upon hitting the ground.

A month later the Royal Southern Aces performed in Ottumwa, Iowa. Their bat-wing jumper, a Native American going by the name of Walter "Chief" Thatcher, left a plane at 7,000 feet. Three thousand people watched him fall straight down. His wings never slowed him, and his parachute never opened.

At the World's Fair in September of the same year, Earl Stein of Findlay, Ohio, flew from 15,000 feet with his bat-wings. He was also the first to fly bat-wings from one country to another (from Michigan to Canada), a joke that Red Grant would perform for *ABC's Wide World of Sports* decades later. In October, Stein was the final act of two days of festivities for the dedication for the Reading Municipal Airport. He was billed as "Batwing Parachute—Human Bird." *Time* magazine called him the "number one bat-wing stunt man in the world."

Don R. Bost had done some stunt jumping before World War II, so when he went to enlist he naturally joined the 82nd Airborne. During the allied invasion of Sicily, he was the third paratrooper in the air. In Germany, after the war, he amazed a Russian general by using a bedsheet to fake a trailing, uninflated, malfunctioning canopy, much to the horror of every other spectator. The general immediately decorated him. Back in the states, Bost honored Sohn with a bat-wing jump at the AAF-CAP Michigan Air Show.

A man named Cliff Rose, who led the Cliff Rose Death Angels, also used bat-wings to make great spirals above the crowd. "I was a sort of human corkscrew," he said. He started at age seventeen, after a mere thirty regular jumps, and, according to him, he enjoyed his first flight so much that he nearly forgot to pull his ripcord. It was only the sight of faces in the crowd that alerted him to his low altitude. He opened and touched down seconds later.

The bat-wing phenomenon even made it to Brazil, though it took a few years. The following article was printed in the *Chicago Daily News* in 1946:

For Only $9.89 YOU Can Be a Superman (Maybe)

BY ERNIE HILL

RIO DE JANEIRO, Oct. 24—A Brazilian inventor says he has perfected man-sized bat wings so that people can flap their arms and fly like a bird. He is looking for somebody willing to jump off a radio tower and try them.

Amadeo Catao Lopes, 33, declares that he has eliminated all the bugs from his strange gadget. The day is at hand, he says, when every man can be a superman for $9.89.

You just strap a little one-horsepower motor on your back, start flapping, and jump. For a rudder, you use your big toe. The Brazilian Darius Green says he would try it himself, only he has a sore left arm. So he is looking for an assistant to make the leap.

"The man I select," he proclaims, "stands to become more famous than the Wright brothers, Lindbergh, and Wrong-Way Corrigan put together."

Amadeo's last experiment, four years ago, failed. This time, he says, it is a sure go.

Amadeo's last stooge jumped off a radio tower at Pernambuco, Brazil. He flapped for all he was worth. But he "drifted" to earth like a ton of bricks and broke both legs.

"The trouble was," says Amadeo, "that he went only halfway up the radio tower. If he had gone clear to the top it would have been different."

The stooge, however, claims that it would have been different only in that he also would have broken his neck. He declines to try it again.

Amadeo, after this sad experience, went back to work at his house in Pernambuco. He started all over again, with aluminum wings. His wife left him, he says, because he slept during the day and worked only at night when his imagination functions best. Her nightly slumber was interrupted continually by his jumping off chairs and butting his head and wings against the walls.

"I hated to see her go," he says, "but civilization comes first."

Aside from parachute fanatics and those spectators awestruck with childlike glee, bat-wings received little respect during their own era as well as the one that followed. "They tried the wings back in my day, but they were put aside," says Grace Wiggins, widow of the great parachutist and showman Ralph Wiggins. "They were looked down on as going a little bit too far. Too many people got hurt, and their lives lost. They couldn't perform, never did anything—no one looked up to those people."

Where the tower jumpers received beatings, executions, and mockery in verse, the bat-wing jumpers got bad press. Even Clem Sohn received comments like those found in the *Des Moines Tribune* when they reported that the experts who watched Sohn's first flight "did not see much practical value in his achievement." His wings, they said, made him into a mere glider, and they did not believe he could fly any great distance under his own power. But at least they gave Sohn credit for flying. Here's how Bud Sellick described the bat-wing "gimmick" in his book *Parachutes and Parachuting*, from 1971:

The typical bat-winged jumper would walk around in front of the crowds, swooping his canvas and stick contraption up and down, demonstrating how he would be using it in flight. It made a good show on the ground—and still does for that matter—the crowds loved it. But in the air, that's a horse of another color. With few exceptions, the bat-winged parachutist would plummet like a crated piano, usually trailing a sack of flour to mark his trail as he fell."

Of course, to some degree, most birdmen brought such condescending remarks on themselves with their hyperbolic claims of being able to fly—usually adding that they were the first to do so. Rarely, if ever, did they pronounce something as simple and honest as "I will jump from a plane, spread my arms, slow my fall somewhat, and, with luck, achieve a glide ratio of something greater than 1:1."

For some, the claims were part of the show, for others they were part of the dream.

Garden State Bird:
William Picune

Just two and a half months after Sohn's first flight, a young man named William Picune, from Hasbrouck Heights, New Jersey, nineteen years of age, left a plane at 9,800 feet, hoping to help further his and Clem Sohn's dream that the air would someday be filled with winged people.

Picune, like Sohn, lost his mother at a very early age—she fell out a window. Not long after, his father died as well, and he grew up with his stepmother. To help raise his younger siblings, he dropped out of school and took a job at a camera store in Manhattan. When he wasn't working he would ride his bicycle down to the Teterboro airport to watch the planes.

While working at the camera store, he dreamt up the idea of photographing the "gyrations encountered while making a parachute jump" and decided to learn how to make a parachute jump himself. He told his boss his idea and was told in return that he was nuts. He talked to his friends about the idea and was told he was crazy. Undeterred, Picune located the Joe Crane Parachute Jumping School at Roosevelt Field in Westbury, Long Island, the same airfield that Lindbergh, his hero, had started from in his journey across the Atlantic.

By the time Picune got there, he had memorized a pamphlet from the Irvin parachute company that explained how to fold a parachute. Joe Crane was so impressed by the sixteen-year-old's folding abilities that he allowed him to skip most of the usual instruction, though he still charged the fifty-dollar fee.

Picune, of course, would not be taking a camera with him on his first jump, which was to include a free fall. Instead he contacted Pathé News, and they sent two photographers—one to shoot him from another plane, and a second on the ground to capture him under his open parachute. Though Picune changed his mind "over and over again" the night before his scheduled jump, in the morning he told Crane he felt he was ready. Picune was to leap from a Fairchild monoplane from 12,500 feet, and to be sure that the camera would track his fall, Picune was to try his hand at jumping with a sack of flour.

The ingredient may have helped the cameraman spot Picune in the sky, but it completely blinded the jumper himself. It filled Picune's goggles, and he only saved himself by removing them and cleaning them while in free fall.

Soon afterward he was hired at Roosevelt Field to clean airplanes and sweep the floors. It was a long way from Hasbrouck Heights, so he slept on the second floor of a hangar. The job paid three dollars a week, and Picune made ends meet with a steady diet of peanut butter and jelly sandwiches. He would gladly have lived like this for years, but after two weeks his stepmother arrived to take him back home.

Home was still near an airport, and with his new skills with a parachute Picune made a deal with the folks at Teterboro: he would make jumps to attract crowds, and they would teach him how to fly. So he started jumping every weekend, and the crowds came.

Like Sohn, Picune had to discover how to make a stable fall on his own. He first tumbled haphazardly through the air, and each jump seemed to have its own slapstick element. Once his lines caught his helmet and ripped it off his head. Another time the parachute tore the rubber overshoe off his shoe. On his eighty-seventh jump, from 2,800 feet, he found himself shooting toward the earth headfirst. No matter how hard he flailed, he could not change his position, and when he pulled his ripcord he received an opening shock that would pain him for days. Such openings, as well landings on his rear, received plentiful applause from the audience that gathered to watch him every weekend. He began to work for more of it, sometimes pretending to run as he came in under his canopy. His girlfriend, Adelaide, would pass the hat. "We thought he was all nuts," she says today at age ninety.

When he wasn't delighting the crowd with near disaster while jumping, he was making the papers with near disaster while flying. When a fuel line broke on his Aeronca, he narrowly missed a trolley car and crash-landed on a local baseball field. Two weeks later he totaled the plane when he failed to clear a fence, which some farmers, apparently tired of being scared by the takeoffs, had erected in protest at the end of the airfield.

Two months after this last wreck, Picune made what he would call the second successful jump with bat-wings (in fact he was third, if not farther down the line). Just as Sohn had, Picune made his wings on his mother's sewing machine. He used "duck canvas" and hooked the wings to his jumpsuit with clips. He "tested" them by standing behind a spinning propeller. Here's how Picune describes his first bat-wing jump in the detailed log he kept in composition books:

> I went up to 9,800 feet in the Standard Trainer with Jim
> Pollizzi, picked out a nice spot to bail off and no more
> than cleared the ship [when I] opened my wings. I did two
> loops, one spin, which happened to be a right spin, and
> opened my left arm to get out of it. I did floating in a
> zigzag position and opened my chute 3,000 feet from the
> ground. The wings unraveled at the edges but worked
> swell anyway.

A crowd of 10,000 had gathered to watch this nineteen-year-old make his ninety-second jump. They saw Picune glide peacefully and reported seeing him perform several loops (by closing his wings and opening his legs), rolls, and turns, all in the first 7,000 feet. It was then that his canvas wings became frayed. The *New York Times* reported that he "twisted awkwardly and at times appeared like a bat which had been shot and was fluttering listlessly to earth."

Picune spent the following week strengthening his wings in preparation for a second flight. When he made the next jump the wings performed much better—possibly better than even he expected, as he came down two miles off target. The landing, however, was less than ideal, if perhaps fittingly birdlike: he wound up in a tree. Though he managed to climb down without injury, the tree had to be chopped down to retrieve the parachute.

This was not the jumper's last mishap, or his first landing on something other than the ground. While jumping at the Holmes Airport on Long Island, Picune found himself on the top of a 93-foot blimp hanger; his still-open canopy had dragged him across the roof. Picune grabbed hold of a ledge while his parachute went over the other side. There he dangled for fifteen minutes before the fire department showed up and hauled him back up top with a rope.

In Binghamton, New York, Picune made another bat-wing jump,

this time from 4,000 feet out of a Kitty Hawk biplane. At 2,500 feet he opened his parachute and floated gently toward the airfield. But when he'd descended to 500 feet the wind changed course, pushing him out into the middle of the 100-foot-wide Susquehanna River. He was happy to find himself in only three feet of water when he landed, but the current grabbed his parachute and began pulling him downstream. "I climbed out of the harness and two kids swam after the chute and I swam into shore all wet," he wrote.

A few months later he made a jump in Laconia, New Hampshire, and, once under canopy, saw that the wind was blowing him into Lake Winnisquam. Not wanting another struggle like the one he'd had in the Susquehanna, he climbed out of his harness and hung on by his hands. He was now worried about being sliced up by the speedboats chopping the water below him, but the wind changed course and this time put him on land. He made a standing landing while still hanging from his straps.

Despite his obvious proclivity for screwball calamity, by June of 1935 Picune owned his own plane, ran his own jumping school, and began traveling all over the country with his barnstorming show, performing to crowds often in the tens of thousands.* A few years later he began working for Eastern Airlines, and he went on to become a captain for United Airlines. By then he had given up jumping, but his daughter Patricia still called him Batman.

In 1957 he flew the historic reconstruction of Lindbergh's plane for the film *Spirit of St. Louis.* Picune never met Lindbergh on the set of the

---

*He was also becoming a better all-around parachutist. At the 1935 National Air Races in Cleveland, in front of a crowd of 100,000, he placed sixth in the spot-landing contest. It was his second jump that day. (He had to use his reserve on the first and landed in the parking lot.)

movie, but years later he flew the ill hero on what would be his last flight. He was so excited by the honor that he was like a child again. "Mom, you'll never know what I'm going to do today," he told his wife, that same Adelaide who had passed the hat years earlier. "I'm taking Lindbergh home to Hawaii." (During the flight he asked Lindbergh if he wanted to circle Honolulu for the view. Lindbergh declined, saying he didn't want to inconvenience the rest of the passengers, but Picune did it anyway.) The Teterboro Aviation Hall of Fame inducted Picune in 1979.

Picune died of Alzheimer's in the late 1980s, but when he could no longer recognize his own children, he could still remember in detail the planes and jumps of his youth.

High Planes Drifter:
Roland Kumzak

Before his death, Clem Sohn had descended upon Des Moines, Iowa, twice. His first jump there, in May 1935, had only been his thirteenth with his wings, and the jump had been something of a dud. Since his gray suit had blended in with the overcast sky, no one could see him, and the good people of Des Moines were left wanting. Sohn had also failed to show at a jump scheduled before this one, blaming his absence on the weather, so the anticlimactic bat-wing flight further sullied his reputation there.* For his second rain-check flight, in the late summer of 1935, he was ready to do all he could to drop Iowan jaws by a collective two miles or so.

---

*Perhaps the bad luck had something to do with the fact that it was his thirteenth jump in the wings. This was a detail that the superstitious Sohn refused to tell reporters. When they asked how many jumps he had made, he would only say that it was his fourteenth or fifteenth.

It was August, at Iowa's state fair, and 35,000 people wrenched themselves from the riveting attractions of prize hogs and well-fed Angus to watch Sohn. The negative publicity of the no-show and the invisible jump had helped spread the word of this second appearance. This time he was better prepared to delight the eye: on the triangle of cloth between his legs he had attached a "smoke candle" that would make a trail behind him as he flew. And as luck would have it, the day was a clear one, though windy. Sohn took off facing the rear of the small plane so that he could get out without hitting the wing. "It's going to be a job getting out of here," he told a reporter. It was also going to be a job getting to the ground. The wind took him off course, and when he touched down he found himself on Grand Avenue, in the middle of traffic heading to the fair. The crowd soon found him and followed him around, groupie-like.

One fan, who'd seen Sohn's performance at the Clay County Fair a few months earlier, was more affected than the others—a red-haired young man from Milford named Roland Kumzak. As soon as he saw Sohn in the air, he knew that he, too, wanted to be a batman. Before two months were out, he was.

Milford's Junior Chamber of Commerce was putting on an air show for the Spencer airport, and, having heard of Kumzak's aspirations, they offered him fifty dollars to make a winged jump. This was before Kumzak had made any kind of jump at all, but such were his dreams that he signed the contract anyway.

If that seems reckless to you, you'll be glad to know that you're in agreement with the Milford Business Men's Association of 1935: they wrote to the Junior Chamber of Commerce, telling them to call the thing off. And the Junior Chamber of Commerce was ready to call it off until Kumzak explained that, fifty bucks or no fifty bucks, he was making the jump.

On the day of the air show, Kumzak arrived at the airport in an outfit similar to Sohn's. But where Sohn's wings were scalloped like a bat's, Kumzak's were square. They were bound together across the torso with two straps, and each wing had its own frame. Though Kumzak was clearly prepared to make his jump, the weather was less than ideal for winging it—too many clouds, too much wind. But sometime after noon, conditions let up, and Kumzak approached the plane. He was saddened to find that he could not fit inside, as his wings were too big. But the lad persevered, and eventually a roomier Travel-Aire was found, allowing him to jump, after a full day of nerves, at 5:50.

As soon as he hit the air, he found himself on his back. He managed to right himself and open his wings, but then found himself beginning to roll. He fought to stop it, but was thrown into a head-pounding spin, turning faster as he descended. At around 5,000 feet he was conscious enough to notice that the ground seemed to be rushing up at him—he knew it was time to pull. Apparently Kumzak opened both parachutes at the same time and together they placed him safely, if awkwardly, on the ground a mile and a half from the airport.

Kumzak took this first flight as an educational one. "That's when I learned my big lesson about this bat-man business," Kumzak told a reporter. "I think the whole secret is in the beginning of the downward fall."

The Milford Business Men's Association was apparently persuaded that if you could survive one bat-wing jump, you could survive them all. A month later they asked Kumzak to make a jump at a high school football game. So while Terrill and Milford cooled their rivalries during halftime, Kumzak flew down to them from an altitude of 10,000 feet. No malfunctions were reported.

While Clem Sohn was making his way through Europe, Kumzak was touring the Midwest, trying his best to be known as "the Hawk." But he could never shake being called simply "the Iowa Bat Man." By the time another Iowa State Fair rolled around, Kumzak had made thirty-five jumps with his wings and spoke of loving the batman life, which was filled with "plenty of fresh air." Seasoned and better trained, Kumzak was ready to take the Michigan batman's place at the fair. He made several flights, much to the pleasure of his home-turf crowd, and kept the mishaps to a minimum. On one jump the lines of Kumzak's main chute ripped the goggles off his face. They were later returned by a young boy who was pleased to receive a dollar as a reward. On another, Kumzak landed on a roof—Guidotti-like—smashing a few shingles but leaving himself intact. The neighbors called for an ambulance, but Kumzak was gone before it arrived.

Sohn's luck, of course, had not been so good. When Kumzak heard of his death, he spoke of Sohn as a kind man and a skilled jumper, but said he would go on jumping with wings despite the danger. He made more than 100 jumps as a batman before putting his wings away for good. But it wasn't the last parachute he touched. He took a job repairing them and other survival gear for the navy, and later for the U.S. government, to support his wife and four daughters.

New Falls from Sioux Falls:
Manus "Mickey" Morgan

Some men are leaders and some are followers. And some are followers who want to become leaders. Where Roland Kumzak, entranced by the flight of Clem Sohn in Iowa, simply joined the growing flock of Sohn imitators, others were filled with what a literary critic might call an "anxiety of influence." Manus "Mickey" Morgan was of the latter. A handsome man with a determined air, he set out to make better wings, longer flights, and new bat-wing records.

Sohn, as the first of the air-show batmen, held just about every bat-wing record you could dream up. When he died in 1937, no one else had taken their wings anywhere near the 12,500-foot altitude record he'd set. But within months of Sohn's death, Mickey Morgan had beat that record by 3,000 feet when he made a winged jump in his hometown, Sioux Falls, South Dakota.

Morgan started jumping sometime around 1928, with a 3,000-foot free fall for the U.S. Navy as part of a series of experiments

71

meant to help learn how to better save pilots' lives. By 1930, Morgan was flying planes himself, and it wasn't long before he was wing-walking and making parachute jumps for air shows.

In 1935 he began jumping with his own Sohn-inspired wings. In many ways they were similar to the wings of his predecessor: they were white and had three ribs radiating from the armpits, handles on the poles that ran just under the arms, and webbing between the legs, with straps on the feet. And like Sohn, Morgan wore a tight pilot's cap and goggles. But Morgan tried to improve on Sohn's design by increasing the wingspan to eight and a half feet and using poles and ribs made of steel tubing. The cloth itself was airplane fabric. Where Sohn's wings were attached to his jumpsuit all the way down to the thighs, Morgan's were hinged to the square steel frame on his chest only at the armpits—in flight he looked more like a moth than a bat, with the wings tilting up above his back. Morgan seems to have been wary of water, for the biggest change he made was the addition of a bladder worn on his chest. Should he find himself submerged in a sea or lake, he could inflate the bladder by blowing into a valve. The entire getup had the Department of Commerce Air Bureau's stamp of approval.

Popular Mechanics illustrated the ensemble in a spread for their September 1939 issue titled "The Human Glider." The gear was more important than the man, it seems, as they refrained from mentioning the batman by name. "The human glider, getting close to earth, must open his parachute to avoid injury from a rough landing," they wrote.

Rough landings, it turns out, were a pretty rare occurrence for Morgan, possibly because he gave himself some extra room when it came to opening altitude, unlike many of his contemporaries. Morgan routinely jumped at 10,000 feet and opened at 1,400. (By his own calculations this gave him about 90 seconds of glide time—and the

Los Angeles Times concurred.) His jumps eventually attracted the attention of the California State Guard, and they hired Morgan to train their paratroopers to jump with bat-wings so they could better steer themselves to their destination point. By 1940, Morgan had made 108 jumps in his bat-wings (350 jumps altogether) with only a single injury: a sprained shoulder from dodging cars when touching down in a parking lot at an Oakland air show. At another jump for that same air show, he wound up in a tomato patch, but later claimed he'd been attracted by the juicy crop and headed there on purpose.

But the fruits of his jumps were not enough to keep Morgan in the air, and later that same year he was ready to hang up his wings. "So finally I says to this girl, 'Why not get married and I'll take you to San Francisco, which is a swell place to live,' " Morgan told the *San Francisco Chronicle*. "She said she would do it if I would settle down and that she did not mean start from the stratosphere and settle down gradually in a bat outfit, but to give up the human bat business entirely." As with so many of his flights, Morgan ended up slightly off the mark—in Oakland, not San Francisco. There he became a welder.

Seven months later, Morgan had persuaded his wife to let him make one last jump. "What I want to do is hang up a human bat record so high that nobody will break it in my lifetime and I can go on with my electric welding and die happy." Morgan was using the comeback-from-retirement technique for that extra amount of publicity. In fact, the plan was not new to Morgan—two years earlier he'd already been talking about finding someone to sponsor him to break his own record.

The planes he typically found himself in could not go much higher than 15,000 feet, so Morgan's first hope was to find funding for a bigger plane. Then he planned to take it to 20,000 feet, breathing oxygen for the last few thousand feet of the climb. When he exited the plane, he would keep his wings folded so he could quickly dive down 5,000 feet and avoid having to jump with an oxygen tank. He estimated that after unfurling his wings he'd be able to glide for a full five minutes. Apparently inspired by photos of Clem Sohn with advertisements for Chevrolet painted on his wings, Morgan hoped that money might come from "an oil company or something." But such capital must never have materialized, as the jump before his "one-last-jump" turned out to be his last. Stinginess on the part of the oil companies and others kept him from taking that last risk.

Mamas, If You Don't Want Your Babies to Grow to Be Bird-Boys: Tommy Boyd

In the late teens of the twentieth century, a couple broke up shortly after the birth of their son. The father took off to become a teacher at a leper colony. The mother just took off. Their toddler son, Tommy, grew up shuttling between the homes of his grandparents in Iowa and Minnesota. Like many of the most daring and reckless parachutists of all time, he was an orphan.

Before he had hit his teens, Tommy Boyd was wandering off on his own. He eventually found himself in Kansas City, Kansas, where he worked at odd jobs, one of which was sweeping the floors of hangars at the local airport. Entranced by the airplanes and pilots, the young Boyd traded a few hours of work for a few flight lessons. In a matter of days he had made his first flight on his own. He was twelve years old.

Five hours of flight time later, Boyd was taking paying passengers up for a spin. No one questioned the young pilot's credentials, as he was smart enough to dress the part (one could almost call it a disguise): scarf, helmet, riding boots. The fact that he had to sit on a stack of boxes to see over the lip of the cockpit didn't deter them at all. He and his fellow barnstormers began flying from farm to farm, offering to carry anyone who could pony up "a penny per pound."

To pay his five-dollar rent, Boyd moonlighted as a bellhop, but about a year after his first flight he found a way to give up hauling luggage. Boyd's partner, a pilot named Fred, had brought another man along for a flight. When Boyd asked what he was up to, Fred explained that he was paying the newbie five dollars to make a parachute jump for the people below. "To hell with him," Boyd said, as he explained to one reporter. "I'll do it and keep the five dollars." Fred let him. And paid him.

Boyd took to jumping like a bird to the air. With his barnstorming gang he toured the Americas, North and South, usually making little more per jump than what he was paid for his first one. On rare occasions he earned ten dollars. Somewhere along the line, Boyd found out what Clem Sohn was up to with his wings. "He originated the idea, but I didn't care for his design because it looked like you could get killed in it," Boyd said. "In fact, he *did* get killed in it."

Boyd was easily able to improve on Sohn's wings, because he actually had a chance to try on the dead batman's outfit. Standing a good head taller than Sohn, Boyd had to hunch over to keep the wings at his arms. Without having to stretch, his hands rested on the ends of the leading poles, a half-foot or so of which had extended past Sohn's outstretched reach. Boyd refused to jump with them, because "flying like that is something like being a streamlined brick." The upstart wingsuiter believed that other batmen were killed because they had too many rigid parts in their getup. The wings Boyd devised had none, other than the poles at the arms. These jutted out just past his hands when his arms were fully extended, and the cloth ran in a tight line from the poles' edge to the feet, making a giant triangle on either side of him. The insides of the wings were sewn from ankle to armpit, and between his legs he had another triangle, this one isosceles. Later he would include a pouch there, filled with red powder and held shut by clothespins. A line from the pins to the plane would yank them off as he jumped, letting the powder flow out into Boyd's wake.

Apparently Boyd was so fond of the triangle as a shape that even his parachute was triangular. This unusual type of chute was later developed by NASA as a possible alternative to the round parachutes being used to set space capsules safely on the ocean's surface. They were never actually used by NASA because the openings were too hard—a parachute is supposed to lessen an impact, not cause one. For Boyd, the opening shock was so forceful that it would blind him for about fifteen seconds. Though Boyd routinely opened his chute as low as 300 or even 200 feet (after a jump from 15,000), he never broke his neck hitting the ground. Thanks to his mighty parachute, that happened to him once in the air, or so he said.

Boyd believed that so many other bat-wing jumpers died because they didn't know how to fly their rigs, that it was attempts to flap their wings that sent them to their death (certainly untrue in Sohn's case). "What I would try to do was create a ball of air under me. If this happened, I would ride it as far as I could."*

Boyd eventually started making more than five or ten dollars a jump. Having been ripped off by air-show promoters many times, Boyd learned to drive a hard bargain for his act. At his peak in the late 1940s, he made $43,000 a year, and at the Oakland air show he made three jumps on three different days and was paid $1,500 for each.

---

*Jari Kuosma confirms that this is what it feels like to fly near the stall point.

As Boyd's batman career extended toward the 1950s, he became something of a museum piece. A 1948 *New York Times* article, first stating that the bat-winged Boyd "actually maneuvered himself in the air before pulling his parachute," went on to say that the jump accurately demonstrated what "old-timers used to see when flying circuses were popular after World War I." (A year later, though, the Steel Improvement & Forge Company sponsored him to make a seemingly non-nostalgic "Bat Wing Parachute Jump" at the Cleveland National Air Races.) Boyd himself was finally growing tired of the traveling show life. "The money had never been important to me. There was just the thrill of it, of doing something to perfection. But I knew it was over. The suitcases, the hotel rooms, the travel. It was over," he told a reporter from the *Washington Post.* "It became wearying, looking at the ground coming up at you all the time." Boyd retired from the world of parachutes and air shows in 1951. He'd been jumping and flying with his wingsuit for twenty years.

Boyd was paying attention to more than his own wings for those two decades. By the time he quit, he could practically build a plane from scratch, so at the age of thirty-four, Boyd became an aeronautical engineer. But he watched the ground come up at him one last time in 1963. At Taft, in California, he made his final jump with Lyle Cameron, the editor of *Sky Diver* magazine, who at that time was flying his own wings (see chapter 17) and wanted to jump with the legend. But the experience left Boyd feeling too old for the sport. Eventually he quit airplanes altogether, retiring to a farm in Aldie, Virginia. His only flight-related activity was feeding the birds every day.*

In 1974 he became a museum piece in fact. The Smithsonian Air and Space Museum put on an Exhibition Flight exhibit, with an

---

*Boyd eventually retired from farming, as well, and lived until the early 1980s.

appearance by Boyd and a wingsuit he'd made hanging from the ceiling. Afterward he continued his work with the animals at Oak Hill Farm, keeping his earlier life to himself. He would never fly his wings again, but he had lived long enough to see younger generations gape at what he'd once done.

9

When Erks Turn Loony

In 1925, Aircraftsman Number 347766 of the Royal Air Force was refolding a parachute for the demonstration team of the newly formed "parachute section" when his boss, Flight Lieutenant Soden, asked him if he would be willing to jump with what he was packing. Aircraftsman Number 347766, thinking that the lieutenant was inspecting for signs of sloppiness, answered unhesitatingly in the affirmative. Thus he found himself verbally contracted to leap off the wing of a biplane.

Aircraftsman Number 347766 was Harry Ward, and he was an erk, not a loony. That is to say he was a carpenter-rigger and a packer, not a parachutist. *Erk* is pilots' condescending slang for a mechanic (it's derived from *Air C.,* for Air Craftsman, which in Britain, I guess, comes out as *erk*). *Loony* was what the erks called the parachutists who flew around England giving demonstration jumps (etymology superfluous).

The loonies were out to persuade the Royal Air Force to keep parachutes in its planes. World War I pilots had refused to fly with them—both pilots and officers thought the new contraptions would encourage the cowardly abandonment of damaged aircraft that might otherwise be successfully crash-landed.

The erks were in the habit of scoffing at those few men who risked their lives to advocate the circular cloth, and Ward had no intention of breaking that habit. Just months earlier, the loonies had persuaded a sergeant to try a jump. They taught him how to climb down the ladder on the side of the fuselage of a Fairey Fawn and hang with one hand while the other clutched the ripcord. Then he was simply to let go and pull. All very straightforward on the ground. But in the plane, stricken with fear—as all first-time jumpers are—the sergeant waffled. And he waffled at a particularly bad moment. The instant he let go of the ladder's bottom rung, he changed his mind about the whole endeavor and made a grab at the ladder again—with the hand that should have stayed on the ripcord. He somersaulted through the air, and his fingers never made it back to that ring.

The sergeant's death, and others like it, ran through Ward's mind as he began to internalize the pact he had been trapped into making. But there was no backing out. "When a chap verbally commits himself to a parachute jump, it becomes a battle between fear and pride—or, if you like, between fear of actually doing it and fear of being thought a chicken," wrote Ward in his memoirs. "I wasn't going to be anyone's chicken."

Ward's inexperience and disdain for the loonies were exactly what Lieutenant Soden was looking for. Representatives of the upper tiers of the air force were having a look at the activities in Northtolt, where they were based, and the lieutenant hoped to prove to them that a parachute could save the life of someone who'd never jumped before.

Word spread throughout the airfield that Ward the erk was about to make a jump.

Since the sergeant's fatal drop, parachutists no longer left the plane from the cockpit. Now they jumped off the wing—and jumping off the wing meant taking off *on* the wing. (In theory it was safer than climbing down the ladder. In practice, it was far more terrifying.) After a few words about buckles and ripcords, Ward found himself standing on the wing of a Vickers Vimy bomber—a massive cloth-and-wood affair left over from the First World War—hanging on to a rear strut.

The Rolls-Royce engines started, and the plane bounced and shivered down the airstrip. Ward held on to that pole like—well, like a man whose life depended on it. Soon they were in the air, floating over Northolt at 2,000 feet. The pilot, Corporal Arthur East, started waving his hand for Ward to turn and face the wind. Then the hand came down and Ward pulled the ring.

"Nothing happened. For one long second I thought that the chute wasn't going to work . . . that we'd have to go down . . . that I wouldn't have to jump at all. Next thing I knew I was looking up between my legs at the kite disappearing into the distance, while a huge hand was dragging me through the air by the scruff of my neck." With his parachute open, Ward descended safely to the ground—but no one had mentioned anything about landing. Ward ended up on his back, but unhurt.

He was a loony.

+

Ward, the son of a piano maker, was born in the same year that the Wright brothers made their first flight. Air shows made their way to

Ward's hometown, and as a kid he saw parachutists jump from balloons when the famous Spencer brothers came by. (And the first Spencer airships could turn into a huge, umbrella-like parachute if they lost all their gas.) But at that time the young Ward was more interested in putting paint on canvas than trying to break a fall with the material. At the age of fourteen he entered the Bradford Art School, and it was there—confronted with nude models—that he began his career of ogling pretty ladies. His career as an artist, however, did not last long. With six younger siblings to help feed, he needed a steady income and joined the RAF. When the recruiting sergeant discovered Ward's father's profession, he made Ward a carpenter-rigger, and within a few months the new recruit could take apart and reassemble the frames of every known airplane.

He was also taught—informally—how to fly by the future World War II hero Leslie Hollinghurst. Hollinghurst would take Ward along on his longer flights and let him man the stick and rudder from the rear cockpit while he took a nap.

If you could survive a flight with Hollinghurst, you were destined to live a long life. Hollinghurst "flew by Bradshaw," which meant that he navigated by cruising low enough to read the signs at train stations. Once, while skimming over ocean waters, he nearly collided with a ship. As there were no paved runways in those days, sheep were often let out at night to keep the airfield mown. Returning to Northolt a tad early one morning, Hollinghurst and Ward killed two sheep when they collided with the flock.

✦

After his first jump, Ward continued to spend his days fixing planes, packing chutes, and taking the occasional flight with Hollinghurst—

until the death of Corporal East. East, who had piloted the plane that took Ward on his first jump, had established the parachute section at Northolt and was known as England's greatest jumper. Years before Leo Valentin would teach the "Valentin Position," he'd discovered that skydivers could stabilize their fall by stretching out their limbs. The technique made him confident he was ready for more daring derring-do. In March of 1927 he decided to jump from 5,000 feet into a valley near Biggen Hill. He missed the valley and landed in front of a bus. His parachute hadn't yet opened.

Less than a week later, England's second-greatest jumper, Lou "Brainy" Dobbs, killed himself bouncing across the airfield. His newest whimsy was strapping himself to a half-filled balloon that would lift him just enough so he could make repeated giant hops. His last leap was over the trees that lined the airfield and into some power lines. The two deaths created a job opening, and Ward took it. For the next two years he traveled around the country climbing out of cockpits (he'd had enough of standing on the wing), saving his life with a parachute, and teaching others how to do the same. During downtime he and his crew were busy inventing bungee jumping in the hangars or doing the Charleston at the 43 Club.

But in 1929, England was gearing up for "peace in our time," and the RAF suffered a wave of layoffs. By the end of the year, Ward was driving a bus for the London General Omnibus Company.

The earthbound job wasn't going to keep him on the ground, though. Within a year he had organized the "Busman's Flying Club." Seven hundred bus drivers showed up for the opening-day festivities, which featured free rides in a Redwing and a parachute demonstration by Ward—his first jump as a performer. When the owners of the airfield, the Frogley brothers, witnessed Ward's hurtling body, they saw money. Soon they were trading flight lessons for demonstration jumps, and the already flightworthy Ward quickly received his license.

That year the Frogleys asked Ward to make a jump at their annual Herts & Essex Aero Club's air show. The show featured standard fare for the time: mock dogfights, a dive-bomber whose propeller sliced up streams of toilet paper tossed from another plane, and two parachute jumps. The second landed Ward in the center of the crowd.

To make these jumps, Ward had to beg for a loan from the Russell Lobe factory. They made a parachute called the "Lobe," with a distinctive, inward curling lip—a perfect place for advertising—and that's what they offered him. The company employed a Dutchman named Jon Tranum to tour England's airfields, showing off the Lobe. Tranum had spent some time as a stuntman in Hollywood, had wing-walked and barnstormed, and was famous for lighting his plane on fire before leaping out and parachuting back to earth, so demonstrating the Lobe was a breeze. But that didn't mean the daredevil didn't need a stand-in now and again. With Ward already using the Lobe, he was the obvious candidate for the job. On his first jump subbing for Tranum, he spotted a row of beautiful women in the audience. Yanking and pulling on his lines, he did his best to land in front of them, "but rather spoilt the effect by rolling in a cow-pat. I was wearing my best suit, too." Cow-pat or no, Ward had learned to steer and was delighted by the "admiring glance of those pretty girls."

Those glances, and the easy money, kept Ward jumping as often as he could for Tranum. But he kept his day job until 1933, when he threw it all away and joined the circus—Sir Alan Cobham's Air Circus. Cobham was famous for making the first flights from England to South Africa and Australia. In those days, that made him something of a rock star, and his name on the circus banner drew crowds by the thousands. For five shillings anyone could take a ride in a plane. For a bit more they could see the airborne antics—dogfights, wing-walking, upside-down flying, and mock bombings using sacks of flour—while flying themselves. The parachute jumps were saved till last to keep the disaster-hungry crowd around to the end.

Ward did his work for sixteen pounds a week plus two pounds a jump. He made his exits at 1,000 feet and let himself fall for five seconds before opening. Any higher, and the crowd would have had a difficult time keeping an eye on him. He didn't use a backup chute, either. But Ward played down the danger: "On some of the dodgy grounds we used, I often thought it was far safer jumping out of a kite than landing in it."

Whether or not parachuting was safer than piloting, Ward had his share of accidents. When a pilot took his plane a tad too close to Ward—to give his passengers a better look at the madman under the silk—the rush of air collapsed his canopy. The high-speed landing broke his ankle, dislocated his hip, gave him a concussion, and put him in the hospital for a month. The doctor told him he would never jump again.

By the time Ward had healed, Cobham's secretary had started his own competing air show, named the British Hospitals Air Pageant because some unreported percentage of the profits was supposedly donated to hospitals. With the "Hospitals," Ward toured 180 towns in England and made a jaunt through India. There the heat was so intense that Ward's rate of descent was noticeably slower. After a landing, his servant, Gulab Khan—working for two pounds a month—would pick camel thorns out of the silk while Ward went around chasing female members of what should have been off-limits castes.

Back in England, the British Hospitals Air Pageant, hounded by bureaucrats questioning the troupe's devotion to charity, changed its name to the Jubilee Air Pageant. But tax inspectors weren't the worst problem the company faced. That year Ward's friend and co-jumper, Ivor Price, died when his parachute refused to open. He'd forgotten to remove a handkerchief he'd tied around the lines to make packing easier. Price's replacement was killed shortly afterward, tangled in his canopy after jumping off a plane's wing with a Lobe (Lobes, which didn't have a pilot chute—the smaller parachute that emerges first, fills with air, and helps pull out the main canopy—weren't made for wing jumps). Then a pilot died when a wing of his plane fell off in the middle of a loop. Two more pilots—and two passengers—met their end when their planes smashed into each other during a mock dogfight. "Risk was our business. It was what we sold to the public. They didn't come along to see how *safe* it all was." To that end, Ward thrilled a crowd at Castle Douglas that year when he experienced a "Mae West"—his lines came out over the top of his canopy, turning it into a giant Wonder Bra. This sent him spiraling toward the ground, and he saved himself only by falling on his side. Later that year Ward broke ribs in Harrow and foot bones in Guildford. Neither stopped him from jumping. With tape on his torso and a cast on his foot, he still wanted his two pounds per plummet.

By 1936 the English public was no longer thrilled by the mere sight of an airplane, and the circus—now named Tom Campbell-Black's Air Display after the famous monoplane racer—had to rely more and more on death-defying (or death-inviting) stunts to draw in the crowds. It was in that same year that Clem Sohn toured Europe with his bat-wings. A few pilots from Tom Campbell-Black's Air Display had seen Sohn soar in Portsmouth, and when they told Ward about it, he immediately decided to try his own wings. He wasn't about to be upstaged by an American—and he was particularly enticed when he heard that Sohn made 200 pounds for each jump.

Ward called his friend Cecil Rice, who had built the trailer Ward used when on the road, to help him make the wings. Rice immediately ran off to see one of Sohn's shows. The American would soon be dead, Rice reported, because he had no way of getting out of his wings if things went wrong. Rice got hold of a dead bat to use as a model and built Ward two suits that were both bigger and safer than Sohn's. Sohn's wingspan was six feet, Ward's two wingsuits were nine and eleven feet wide. More important, they could easily be jettisoned by pulling two pins. Ward didn't fancy trying to land with the appendages, either, so a cable was attached so that he could lower them to the ground once his parachute was open. The wings themselves were made of linen and black satin, as was his matching jumpsuit: "If I was going to be a 'bat-man,' I might as well *look* like a bloody bat." Four rods embedded into each wing radiated from the armpit. Ward was to hold the wings open with a steel briefcase handle on the front of each wing. To keep Ward from dislocating his shoulders if the wind proved too forceful, Rice used a locking brace to prevent the wings from going back too far. Metal springs connected the whole getup to a strap on the chest; the wings would collapse if Ward let go of the handles, putting them out of the way of an emerging parachute.

To test the outfit, the pair visited a train station and hauled Ward into the air with a cargo crane. Dangling from the giant iron hook did little to prime Ward for actually falling in the suit, but it was great publicity. Passengers in the trains that went by became fascinated ornithologists, and the story of the hanging winged man spread quickly. Later they had to repeat the performance for a group of reporters. But all the attention meant that Ward was again locked into that "battle between fear and pride." It would be hard to back out with England waiting for its own birdman to become fully fledged.

Before he could fly, Ward had to register with the Air Ministry. They'd heard what he was up to and informed him that if he had wings he was a light airplane. Luckily, Ward still had his "A license," so they couldn't prevent him from piloting himself. He registered his aircraft with the thumb-nosing letters "A-CUNT."

On April 15, 1936, after a nervy morning of clouds and rain, Ward, in full birdman regalia, went up in a De Havilland Dragon. He was using the nine-foot wings and had a reserve parachute on his chest—the first time he'd ever felt he needed one. The plan was to jump out at 10,000 feet to give himself some extra time, but the clouds made a ceiling at 4,000. The plane circled for an hour, waiting for a clearing. But there was a crowd down below, waiting to see Ward fly, and he made the decision to exit beneath the clouds. He stepped out onto the plane's wing and dived into the air.

"The next thing I knew I was on my back, slightly head down, and falling fast. As for the wings, it was like fighting a tent in a hurricane." The wind had pinned the wings against his chest and sent him spinning. Ward knew that if he tried to open his parachute upside down and in a spin, he'd just end up wrapped in it. He pulled hard on one of the wings and managed to open it just enough for the wind to flip him over. When he saw land, he yanked the ripcord—a few hundred feet from the ground.

As usual, the near-death experience didn't spook Ward a bit. The next day he decided to try the larger wings. With his arms at his sides they were too long for Ward to stand, and with his arms outstretched they were too wide to fit through the door of the plane. To get around this problem, Rice and a co-parachutist laid Ward down on a board and put him on the floor of the plane with his head sticking out the door. At 11,000 feet, Ward started the smoke bomb that would show his path back to earth. Then his comrades dumped him into open air.

They had failed to tell Ward that the tip of the right wing had broken as they'd loaded him into the plane. As soon as the wind opened the wings, Ward found himself tossed about like a tissue in a typhoon. He pulled the pins and let the wings find their own way down. The throngs below were cheated of the sight of a flying man, but the announcer's tale of near disaster went some way toward placating them.

Before his third flight, Ward renegotiated his contract with his boss. Now he was to earn ten percent of ticket sales instead of a flat rate. And this time everything went just as planned. The wings opened and slowed his fall. By pulling a bit on one wing he could go into a broad spiral. He felt "some lateral movement," and after opening his canopy, he successfully lowered his wings to the ground. As he prepared to land he was dreaming not of the future of human flight, but of the money he would be making. "Must be a few thousand of them, down there," he thought. "A hundred pounds worth, at least."

Back at the club, Ward's boss gave him eleven pounds. The ten percent, it turned out, was after the expenses for running the show had been deducted.

Later that year, Clem Sohn fulfilled Rice's prophecy with his last jump in France. Ward saw another job opening. He contacted the people who had organized Sohn's European tours and asked if they needed another bat-wing jumper.

But Sohn's organizers didn't want another death on their hands, and Ward was forced to go on jumping with the circus, now named the Aircraft Demonstration Company since Tom Campbell-Black had died. (He was taxiing on the runway when an RAF plane, its pilot blinded by the sun, landed on him.) Ward had learned to control his wings and flew them often without a hitch. But despite the attraction of a gliding man, the days of the air circus in England were numbered. "I didn't have to pretend to look frightened. I *was* frightened. Frightened I wasn't going to get paid." With Sohn's death, the *Hindenburg* disaster in May, and the Royal Air Force finally getting ready for the war on the horizon, flight no longer seemed like an entertainment. In Ireland, Ward made his last jump with his wings. After leaping from 5,000 feet he was able to stay in control and keep himself facedown for the whole flight. Weeks later the Aircraft Demonstration Company went belly-up.

So it was carpenter-rigging again for Ward, until 1939. He spent most of the war years as a parachute instructor and managed to earn the Air Force Cross. (As a trainer, he had little tolerance for fear. Psychologists, he said, "wanted to investigate 'the terrors and phobias' involved in this 'inherently unnatural act' of leaping from aeroplanes. What a load of rubbish!") Before he died in 2000, at ninety-seven, Ward ran several pubs in Greece and England, married twice, and had two sons, one of whom still parachutes occasionally for fun.

They Fell for It:
Robert X. Leeds

"The first time I went up in an airplane, I jumped out of it," says Robert X. Leeds, another Michigan son.

Leeds was a child of the Depression who had started his working life, with his Robert Leeds Ash Carryout Service, some five years before that first flight. This career ended when, in seventh grade, rheumatic fever paralyzed Leeds from the waist down. For a year the boy did nothing but read, and he discovered the stories of Charles Lindbergh, Roscoe Turner, and Eddie Rickenbacker, as well as the books of Jack London and especially Cervantes, among others. The literature and tales of life in the air put adventure in the boy's mind, and when he recovered he went to work on the boats that shipped out of Detroit. First he toiled as a "coal passer," shoveling coal on the *Put-in-Bay*. Soon he graduated to "nickel nurser," which meant changing money for the slot machines in the boat's bar. It was while working at this job that a co-worker told him that a daredevil parachutist named

Dour Walker with the Civil Air Patrol was doing some wild things out at the airport.

The fifteen-year-old Leeds headed there at the next opportunity. He found that the Civil Air Patrol was taking passengers up in their Stinson monoplane for a small fee. And, it turned out, for that same fee, passengers could jump out if they felt so inclined. Leeds waited in line, paid his money, went up, and came down the fast way. "There's nothing to it," he says. "As long as the chute opens, you don't have anything to worry about."

Leeds joined the Civil Air Patrol in 1943, soon after that first jump, and though he took off in many airplanes, it was several years before he experienced what it was to land in one. As soon as he joined, he started jumping at air shows and at bond rallies and recruitment drives for the air force.

But the young adventurer was always on the lookout for a way to make his own buck, and he started to realize that if he could bring in money for the war effort making parachute jumps, he could also bring in money for himself doing the same thing. Leeds persuaded a handful of his fellow jumpers to join him and become a traveling air show.

They called themselves "Death's Angels" and made patches for their jumpsuits featuring two skulls and a parachute. Airport owners were glad to have them come and put on a show and draw a crowd—between stunts the owners would take audience members up in a plane for five dollars apiece.

In addition to the standard barnstorming acts—mile-high jumps, wing-walking, a race to the ground—the gang had a few other stunts. They would lower a chair beneath the plane so one of them could skim across the ground, just above the audience's heads, then open his chute and have it pull him off. Another trick was to "jellyfish" to the ground, deliberately collapsing an open chute and then letting it spring open again, and repeating the process all the way down. They also tried to break the record for the most jumps in a single day, but every time they hit the twenty-to-thirty range they had to stop, not because they'd run out of steam, or daylight, but because they'd run out of money to pay the pilots.*

Somewhere along the way, Leeds read an article about some of the earlier bat-wing jumpers and their short lifespans. "A lot of old-time artists were killed in the act of doing it. They used metal ribs in their suits to get more surface area to soar, but it limited their access to movement, and they ended up getting fouled in their chutes," Leeds explains. "I didn't think it was too dangerous if we eliminated the hazards. What we did was leave the ribbing out. Of course, it limited the glide surface, but we could move around." He and his friend Elmer Kanta built ribless wings using an old army flight suit and some heavy canvas. To let their audience see their trajectory, they used the old trick with the flour bags. With one in each hand, they'd loosen their grip as they fell, and the suction of the air behind them would pull the flour out into a trail of seeming smoke. "Today they have canned smoke, in all kinds of colors. I guess we might have changed the hue by giving them rye, wheat, or whole grain."

With a 24-square-foot wing of a single layer of canvas and no ribbing, the Death's Angels had little chance of moving horizontally much more than they could while in a wing-free free fall. But don't tell that to the gawkers who were there below. "The amazing thing is, I don't think we moved twenty feet in those suits, but when we landed people had us soaring across the sky a mile or so. But you

_____

*The current record for most jumps in a single day is held by Jay Stokes, who, in 2003, managed to leap from a plane 534 times in twenty-four hours.

could never pick out a spot and get there. If you're going anywhere, you're going down."

And down they went, both literally and figuratively. The Death's Angels disbanded after a disastrous jump at a show in Monroe, Michigan:

> I was pulling a one-mile delayed jump and when I opened my chute I found that one of the shroud lines crossed over in packing. The canopy couldn't expand. The minute it happened, I started shaking my lines, but I realized it was hopeless. I'd already fallen 1,000 feet, so I opened the reserve, and the chute came out in front of me all folded up just like it was packed. I threw it out and the silk went up and wrapped right around my main canopy and completely enclosed it—something about the suction from the main canopy—and now I had both parachutes fouled. I used to think that if it didn't open, that was it, but when you're falling you're completely conscious, you could thread a needle coming down. I remember looking up at the chutes, and then down.
>
> The ground was coming up. I had slowed down to maybe sixty miles an hour, and I knew if I wasn't killed I would be an invalid. Did I want to die? I decided I wanted to live, and I started pulling on those shroud lines, pulled the chute all the way in, and it popped at telephone pole height. Sent me into an oscillation: I went straight up, the canopy hit the ground, and then I did.
>
> But I landed in a farmer's field that had just been plowed. I had made a pretty good indentation in the newly mown dirt and I just lay there, afraid to move. I started moving first my fingers, then my hands. In the meantime a crowd had formed around me, watching with

a deathly silence—they thought I was dead. But when they saw me trying to see what part of my body was working, they helped me up. The farmer walked me into his house and gave me a shot of whiskey, first whiskey I'd ever had. Believe it or not, a lot of the audience drove away thinking I was killed, which is not the kind of morbidity you expect from a crowd.

Now, we used to pass the hat to make our money, and I asked the other jumpers what kind of collection they got. They said, "Oh, we forgot." The best jump of my life and I didn't get paid for it. That's what made me go off—I could see there wasn't any money in those free shows.

Leeds went freelance. As his own agent, he was able to travel the country making bat-wing jumps for $200 a pop. In his journeys he met some of the heroes he had read about when he was laid up with rheumatic fever. He even made a jump with Roscoe Turner, the famous air racer and barnstormer. "I had the same booking agent as Ann Coryle, the stripper. I never met her, but that was my one claim to show-biz fame."

As wild as those days may seem, Leed's years as a bat-wing jumper were perhaps the dullest of his youth. In 1944 he tried to enlist in the air force, but they didn't want him—he was too young and he didn't know algebra. So he joined the merchant marines and was shipped off to the Pacific. By the time he was twenty, he had fought in three wars and was the head of his own air battalion. He smuggled diamonds out of Sierra Leone, and guns into Madagascar. He was shot down in Soviet airspace, was a prisoner of war in South Africa, and became a soldier for the Nationalist Chinese army. There he found himself in front of a firing squad, accused of being a Communist spy.

Soon after, in 1948, the Israeli army hired him to train their paratroopers, and he commanded their first airborne brigade.

It was in that same year that Leeds made his last jump. "I married the girl who packed my chute and brought her over here. Of course, once I married her I couldn't let her pack my chute anymore." They've been married for fifty-eight years, and Leeds hasn't left a plane without landing first the whole time.

11

International Playbird:
Roy W. Grant

When the American soldiers got back from World War II and finished marching through ticker tape and kissing nurses in Times Square, some settled down. Others did not. War is hell, no doubt, but a multilevel one, à la Dante, and the soldiers who'd spent time under silk were one rung deeper than the rest. Back at home the paratroopers were a little more lost than the rest of their generation. And just as after the First World War, when the aviation enthusiasts bought up surplus Jennies and started flying them aimlessly around the country, in 1945 there were a lot of extra planes and parachutes floating around as well as roaming ex-soldiers trained to use them.

One of them, a private in the 507th Parachute Infantry, wandered into Denver, after trading in his uniform, to meet his fiancée. This Romeo was hanging out in a bar one day when a soldier started abusing a female patron both verbally and physically. Roy W. "Red" Grant rose to her defense and, in his own words, "clipped that bird twice."

The sight of Grant, in his civvies, taking down a man in uniform brought the other soldiers into the fray, and Grant left the bar running. After covering a few blocks he ran straight into a second group of uniformed men. They grabbed him, but instead of grinding him into the sidewalk, they offered to help him take on the small but angry mob in pursuit. They were members of the 82nd Airborne, men whom Grant knew well.

The next day, when he met his lady friend, he was alarmed to find her disappointed in him. She wanted to see her soldier in his uniform. He'd had enough of uniforms. That was the end of that.

Grant soon found himself with another woman, and this time she was a pilot—one who happened to need a man with a parachute for an air show that the Civil Air Patrol was putting on. At that time Grant's jumps had all been with a static line, but he wasn't about to say no to the first adventure he'd seen since the war ended. On the day of the show, his new girlfriend flew him up to 3,000 feet in a Fairchild PT-23, a two-seat monoplane. That meant that instead of leaping out of a big door like the one he was used to on a "gooney bird"—a C-47—he would be climbing out onto the wing, falling into the wind, and pulling his own ripcord. He managed it without a snag and found himself on the ground one free fall and fifty dollars richer, and a showman to boot.

Grant became a traveling parachutist, doing nothing more than falling from planes, often with flour streaming from bags under his armpits. On a jump in North Dakota, Grant was alarmed to find that after pulling his ripcord, his D-ring handle was in his hand, but the cord itself still in its sheath. He went straight for his reserve, but when it opened he had a triple "line over"—instead of one large silken dome over his head, he had four. He fought with the cords as the earth started making its presence known, but didn't manage it. He hit the ground and went unconscious.

Somehow, Grant managed to survive without breaking so much as a hallux. Rather than scare him off the sport, the event seemed to encourage Grant to take on greater risks. He started wing-walking and more. In one stunt he would jump from a car and, with luck, onto a ladder hanging from a plane flying by. But the job he had his eye on was already filled—the organization already had a bat-wing jumper, and there wasn't room for two.

At a show in Mississippi, Grant watched as his friend, pilot Billy Fisher, lost control of a small biplane and smashed into the ground upside down. To turn the crowd's attention to something else, the announcer asked Grant to take a flight standing on the wings. As Grant's plane took off, he wept as he looked down on the mangled wreck below. And when he landed after his wing-walking, he found that he wasn't the only one on the team to be so moved—the sight of the wreck was too much for the current batman. He quit the circus, and Grant inherited all bat-wing duties.

The wings were essentially giant, stretchy pantaloons made taut by wooden dowels that ran under the arms and connected to the torso just beneath the pits. Webbing filled the area between the legs, as well. With his chute, reserve, altimeter, and the wings worn over his jumpsuit, Grant more than doubled his own weight.

It was the summer of 1949 when he was to make his first flight in the wings. Decked out in full batman splendor, and ready to make the jump, his plane circled above the crowd below. A small woman was holding up the show. With Grant in the air, she had run up to the announcer and begged him to let her go up for a flight. Her persistence and charm, as well as the support of the crowd, persuaded the announcer to let her fly with a pilot in a biplane. The pilot buckled her into the forward seat, but before he climbed into the backseat to take off, the woman pushed on the throttle, skittered across the runway, and wobbled her way off the ground.

The crowd was surely on edge with fear for the woman's safety, but above, Grant and his pilot were not dismayed. Up until that moment everything was going just as planned—the woman in the plane below was a well-trained pilot named Gloria Lynch, and her act was all part of the show. But this was not to be her best flight. Grant saw the plane tossed up by the wind and then dashed back into the ground. The pair sped back to earth and found Lynch alive, but now missing both feet. Grant put off his first bat-wing flight till another day.

When he did finally make that first jump, he survived it with all appendages intact. He made many more bat-wing jumps with the circus, and when he felt he had mastered the wings and flown *across* the earth, rather than just *at* it, he decided to do something that had never been done: fly from one country to another (at least it was something he *thought* hadn't been done—see the story of Earl Stein in chapter 4). As they happen to be rather close, Grant chose the United States of America and its neighbor, Canada. So, when the band of showmen arrived in Houlton, Maine, a mere three miles from the border, they spread the word far and wide that a batman would be making a crossing in the air.

On the day of the transnational flight, Grant warmed up an audience of some 25,000 with a few routines. First he jumped through the smoke of two planes circling about him. Then he did a little wingwalking. The pilot deliberately stalled the plane, throwing it into a twirling plunge that dizzied the batman and then caused one of the cables holding him upright to snap—he whipped backward into the windscreen and remained there till the plane landed and mechanics could pry him out.

Having been extricated from one airplane, Grant boarded another, this time in bat-wings. They flew up to 14,600 feet, and once they'd been cruising for a bit, Grant gave the pilot a whack on the shoulder—the signal that they were at the spot where he planned to deplane. The pilot slowed the plane down, and Grant was soon out in the air on his own—and on his back. This was not an unfamiliar position to the jumper, and he rolled over and started gliding for Canada, "a true winged projectile, hurtling steeply and swiftly through the sky." At 8,000 feet, with his arms weakening, he slipped over into New Brunswick, made a large circle for those below who might have their eyes on him, and headed for a clearing in the forest not far from where the two countries met. After a hard opening followed by a hard landing, Grant lay on the ground, too exhausted to move.

After recovering, the migrant was not immediately free to celebrate his new world record. Customs agents fought over his body at the border—a stunt staged for the newspapers.

Grant supposedly covered four miles on his quasi-historic flight, achieving a glide ratio greater than the one-foot-down-for-every-one foot forward that wingless free-fallers can now achieve.

Not every flight was quite so spectacular. At one show the only plane available to take Grant up to jumping height was a small Cessna whose door was a struggle to get out of, even for the thinnest of wing-free jumpers. Once they had achieved the proper altitude, Grant squeezed awkwardly out the door and jumped. But instead of the freedom of the open air, he found himself strung up beneath the plane—the handle of his wing had caught on a cable beneath the cockpit. And there he stayed, realizing, as time passed, that the

Cessna could not fly forever—before it ran out of gas the pilot was sure to make some kind of landing that, no matter how delicate, would drag Grant's body down the runway.

Meanwhile the weight of Grant and all his gear had snapped the cable against the pilot, pinning him to his seat. Grant, in harmony with the vibrations of the plane, began to swing back and forth, each arc grinding the cable farther into the pilot's chest. A small price to pay, at least for Grant, for the opportunity to grab at the wheels of the plane at the apex of each swing. After rocking back and forth for a while, he snagged a tire. The next step was to climb up the side to unhook himself. The pilot offered Grant his hand, and when Grant took it, he nearly pulled the pilot out there with him. A strap hanging out of the cockpit proved more effective, and Grant was able to yank himself free and fall away from the plane.

Grant eventually ended up in Taft, California, which, in the sixties, was one of the two big drop zones in the country (the other was Elsinore, also in California). There he began to refine his wings, searching for an ever-longer glide, and fell in with the jumpers who made the series *Ripcord*—television's only skydiving show to date. A version of the man, named Gred Rant, began to appear in the comic strip "Smilin' Jack."

By the middle of the 1960s, Grant was no longer nomadic, but he was still up for stunts like the ones he'd done with the flying circus. In fact, his most famous jump was a repeat of the border crossing he'd managed out of Maine. This time the site would be grander, the border would be wider, and, most important, it would be filmed for TV. *ABC's Wide World of Sports* showed Red Grant flying over Niagara Falls—starting from the Canadian side this time. To get enough footage, though, the crew needed Grant to repeat the stunt three times. The border guards were perplexed to see Grant show his pass-port thrice on the same day, but only ever heading in one direction.

Grant put the wings down for a while, but came out of retire-ment in the eighties, when he appeared on the Jerry Lewis telethon. The lure of something like fame must have drawn him to this last performance—he was not known for being particularly generous—and shortly thereafter he disappeared entirely from the skydiving scene. Rumor has it that he owed people money.

12

When a Finn Is a Wing:
Viktor Andro

Jari Kuosma was not the first Finn to enter the ranks of the birdmen. That distinction belongs to Viktor Andro, who made the country's first bat-wing jump a half-century before Kuosma started developing his wingsuits.

Viktor started out in life, on March 3, 1926, as Viktor Androsov, his parents being immigrants from Russia. The decision to shorten his name was probably not a difficult one for Viktor, as he owed his parents little. When he was very young, his mother became sick and he was sent to an orphanage. Once he was old enough to leave, he started working at a glider club and was soon flying the sailplanes himself. This led to harder stuff, and Andro eventually joined the Finnish air force. He did not last long, however, as he was unable to follow the rules.

Free from the military, Andro took to the unregimented life of flight, flying planes and wing-walking for the *Lentosirkus Pilvien*

Huimapäät (Daredevils of the Clouds Air Circus). Andro made his second parachute jump ever at an air show in front of a crowd of 4,000. He left the plane at around 2,300 feet, but, despite the low altitude, his aim—or the pilot's—was off, and he landed in some nearby woods. By his fourth jump, Andro was ready to try something new—new for him as well as for the country—a "double jump." In the late forties it was not yet customary to jump with a reserve, so the audience below was entirely unprepared for what they saw. Andro jumped out at 4,000 feet and opened his chute at around 2,500 feet. After drifting down for a bit he cut the parachute away and was back in free fall, headed, in the eyes of the spectators, to a sure death. He opened his second chute at around 300 feet and saved his life. The stunt became a regular part of the show.

Andro's friend and fellow circus member, Niilo Salo, had been to the United States, performing as a wing-walker and aerial gymnast, and when he returned he was filled with information about how things were done in that far-off land. And so Andro began to build his own bat-wings, keeping his progress hidden from competitors and colleagues alike. Maintaining secrecy would be difficult, though, as before he could jump with them he needed to get official permission.

The inspection committee was not pleased. The canvas wings, they felt, would surely restrict Andro's access to his ripcord. He countered by showing them how he could move the wings away to reach the all-important handle on his chest. The committee requested that Andro make a hole in the wing and bring the ripcord through it to his hand. But Andro refused to change a thing, and somehow, in the end, they acquiesced.

Andro planned his first winged jump for October 12, 1949, and invited a slew of reporters to come cover the event. And they came. Unfortunately, October 12 turned out to be a cloudy day, and after waiting around till evening, they left. But as evening arrived, the sky cleared, and as the sun wouldn't set for a few more hours, Andro had time to make the jump. Ignoring the pilot's recommendation to exit at 10,000 feet to give himself extra time if anything should go wrong, Andro climbed out onto the wing and jumped while the plane was still at 5,000. He immediately began looping backward, unable to completely open his wings. He went through a cloud and came out on the other side still spinning head over heels. Was he unconscious? We'll never know. Andro hit the ground having never touched his ripcord. It was his seventy-seventh jump.

Part Three

THE
BAT-WING
REVIVAL

The Legacy of

Leo Valentin

Leo Valentin, making his first real flight in rigid wings.

CHAPTER

13

L'homme-oiseau:
Leo Valentin

Epinal, France, the 1920s. A youngster strolls about the neighborhood. He's a daydreamer and a birdwatcher. Having moved on from the buzzards and storks that once entranced him in the nearby park, he's making his way to see the bigger birds that come and go at the Dogneville Aerodrome.

On this particular day, one of those bigger birds falls out of the sky and crashes into a field not too far from the child's home. He races over to join the crowd forming around the mess and sees the passengers, blanched, terrified, but alive, emerge from the crumpled plane behind the pilot. But the figure of the pilot, in leather and goggles and as cool as ever, was to the boy nothing less than that of a knight, and the sight instilled in him a permanent longing to be a man of the air.

The boy was Leo Valentin, whose name, for skydivers, is synonymous with "birdman" (which, of course, is synonymous with batman).

No other parachutist had ever come close to reaching the kind of popularity that Valentin was to enjoy. This was because Valentin's dream of flight was pure and unfailing, and he strove to soar with the same determination that brought Roald Amundsen to the South Pole, and Sir Edmund Hillary to the top of Mount Everest. Unlike many of his immediate predecessors and followers, Valentin's flights, though often *at* shows, were never *for* show. Every time he stepped out of a plane he was experimenting, trying to take the dream further. If Sohn was the Charlie Parker of birdmen, Valentin was their Coltrane.

The dream started in earnest when Valentin joined the French air force in 1938 and shipped off to Algeria. Before long the nineteen-year-old was a corporal, but not yet a pilot, and it would take three years of training for him to fly. Impatient to put himself in the air as soon as possible and however possible, Valentin took the rash act—seemingly suicidal to his peers—of volunteering to join the parachutists. His own colonel, disappointed by the decision, offered Valentin a small box as a going-away present. It was meant to hold his remains.

Valentin took his box and headed off to the Maison Blanche Center in Baraki. There he learned how to pack a parachute and little more from instructors with fewer than twenty jumps to their name. Days before his first free fall, Valentin watched a bunkmate make *his* first free fall: the parachute came out but did not open, then the reserve came out and it, too, did not open. Together they fluttered behind the falling body, following it all the way to the ground. It was the first time Valentin had heard the phrase "roman candle" for such a sight, and the phrase surely was echoing in his head when, two days later, he tumbled out of a plane himself. But as soon as Valentin found himself securely under canopy—what they called a "brolly"—he "realized for the first time how delightful it would be to live there in a breathtaking liberty." His taste for the bird life had been whetted.

When the war came, Valentin found himself, and his fellow parachutists, fighting in the mountains, sans silk. When France fell, he snuck his way back to a parachute school in Fez, where, having had some experience, however minimal, he became an instructor and a sergeant. But the details of how a parachute should be handled in the air and cared for on the ground had yet to be perfected. They had not yet discovered, for example, how to prevent the problem that most likely killed Clem Sohn. A parachute needs to be aired and dried between jumps, since moisture can make the cloth stick together. Thanks to this kind of ignorance, the school was losing about one soldier per week.

Valentin and his compatriots who managed to avoid what he called "that slut"—death—were eager to put their new skills, such as they were, to use and serve their country. Several of them caught a boat to England, hoping to join their allies and take part in more-organized warfare. There they found their knowledge and experience completely disregarded. They would have to begin training as if they were beginners. Not so bad, perhaps—a jump is a jump, after all— except that the English did not use reserves.

Valentin survived this retraining, but soon found himself in a more dangerous place: France. With a dozen or so members of a "stick," along with jeeps and other gear, Valentin parachuted into Brittany on June 5, 1939. There the group began a program of sabotage at night. They blew up bridges, ambushed convoys, and eventually found themselves surrounded by Germans. The paratroopers lost half their men before escaping to the Callac forest. Later, in a firefight at Loire, Valentin took a bullet in the arm. By the time he'd healed, the war was over.

The veteran Valentin fell right back into teaching and experimenting in the art of parachuting, though the school was no longer the free-fall free-for-all it had been. Now there were 60-foot parachute towers, and beginners had to go through two weeks of training, including practice hops and falls from two feet, before they got anywhere near a plane. While he was teaching there, army higher-ups decided that all parachute instructors needed to be certified. Valentin, as an uncertified top instructor, found himself in a catch-22: Was he to certify *himself*? His superiors said yes.

At the school, Valentin observed a phenomenon that still plagues the world of skydiving today: the better the equipment, the riskier the daredeviltry. "We realized that now the apparatus had been perfected, men rather than material had to be held responsible for accidents." Seasoned jumpers, with perhaps too much faith in their new parachutes, were testing the limits. They would pull their lines, sometimes till the canopy reached head level, to increase the speed of descent. The technique was called the "death glide," and it couldn't have been more aptly named. "Parachuting is like every other game: prudence does not always increase with skill," wrote Valentin. One instructor was known to cruise in at 100 miles per hour and only let the canopy fully inflate at around 300 feet. It wasn't too long before he was dead. Two other friends of Valentin's, racing in a duel death glide, collided on the way down. Their parachutes collapsed and together they roman-candled into the ground. Valentin saw yet another friend climb out of his harness and hang by his lines to show off to those watching from the ground. Then he tried hanging with one hand. Not able to hold his weight, he let go and fell away from his canopy to his death.

Parachutists who make pride their sin of choice clearly don't fare as well as those who favor sloth. Valentin watched as one of his pupils, under a roman candle, went straight into a farmer's field. He ran over to what he thought would surely be a dead body. Instead, the student stood up and walked over to Valentin to greet him. Tired of carrying a heavy sack on his back during training, the man had replaced the gear with rags, thus saving his life.

The roman candles of the proud, the tired, and the lucky were not, as Valentin pointed out, the result of any malfunction on the part of the parachute, or inattention on the part of student. Despite the experimentation of many jumpers in the 1930s, free-fallers were still hurtling uncontrolled through space, more human cannonball than bird. They had been taught to leave the plane with their arms crossed and their legs bent, which was possibly the worst way to cleave the air imaginable. This fetal-like position was an extension of how sailors were told to leap off the deck of a sinking ship, and its use was reinforced by the pervasive notion that if one reached out with an arm, it would likely be torn off by the force of the air. Even if the arm wasn't ripped from its socket, jumpers assumed it would be impossible to bring it back to the torso to pull the ripcord. As a result, bodies fell from planes turning and twisting, rolling and tumbling—what Valentin called "making a mayonnaise." At best, the jumper came away a little dizzy; at worst, a parachute might wrap around a revolving foot or just twist its way up and never open. But the possibility of such outcomes was considered just part of the assumed risk that comes with stepping out of airplanes, and few considered changing the position.

Valentin was out for a stroll one day, contemplating such issues, when he saw a funnel drop from a second-story window. Who tossed the funnel, and why, history does not record, but for the Frenchman this was a *Eureka!* moment—the cone was falling with its narrow end down, not spinning or tumbling end over end. "If I could give my body a form approaching that of the funnel, perhaps I, too, could fall without twisting, with the same enviable stability." He couldn't wait to get back in the air and begin infundibular experimentation.

In late May of 1947, Valentin left a Junkers at 9,000 feet and gracelessly stretched out his limbs in an effort to imitate a falling funnel. Immediately, though, the sight of his right arm dangling in space away from the rest of his body sent him into a panic. This hand was supposed to be on the ripcord, as he'd been taught—and had taught—ready to yank if things got hairy. Was this appendage still under his command? Would he be able to bring it back? He was too terrified to find out, and reflexively grabbed the ripcord and pulled.

Back on the earth, though, he realized he had had some kind of success—his arm had stretched out and returned, and he was now safely on the ground with all limbs intact. An hour later he was back at 9,000 feet, stretching out again, hands and feet this time. He remained prone, and the stillness of the fall compared to what he'd been used to made him feel as if he were motionless. He couldn't believe that free-fallers had been torturing themselves the way they had—the solution was so simple, it was like discovering that the headache goes away when you stop pounding your temple with a hammer. By the end of the day, Valentin had learned how to roll, turn, and spin and had developed an immense craving for more free-fall time.

The spread-eagle position, the most basic and common pose to take in the air, is still known as the "Valentin position" in much of Europe. (A more relaxed, bent-limbed version is known as the "frog position" in the United States, but this may not refer to the Frenchman.)

Valentin spent that summer refining his technique, and, as he learned to track across the sky and enjoy his first taste of flight, he began to think of ways to extend free-fall time and horizontal motion. "What about wings?" he thought. "I must go easy. I must remember

Clem Sohn; remember the maniacs who went before me along the road of the great temptation."

At that time, several altitude records had been held for more than a decade. The longest free fall had been made by James Williams in 1938, with the assistance of a respirator for oxygen and an ANF Les Mureaux 113 high-wing monoplane—35,450 feet, right where today's jets fly. Another Frenchman, a Colonel Sauvagnac, had managed to survive a fall from 16,200 feet without a respirator, and this was the first record Valentin would try to beat.

In February, Valentin put a Junkers and its pilot through the two-hour schlep to 16,800 feet, the upper limit of the plane's capabilities. With the Pyrenees on one side, the foggy Landes on the other, and the pilot sucking sugar cubes to stay awake, Valentin left the plane. His new-found position kept him stable, and he opened his chute at 1,200 feet, setting a new record for the longest free fall without the assistance of oxygen. For a man like Valentin, of course, such a record could only lead to other attempts at other records, and it wasn't long before he found himself in a pressure tank with a respirator, testing his body's ability to endure another free fall first, this time from 22,000 feet, and this time with official record-keepers watching. A month later, Valentin was in an RAF Halifax bomber—a plane better equipped to reach the heights he was after—in a heated electric suit, breathing oxygen from a mask. The plane's high speed meant that he could not leave through the door. Instead, he dropped from a kind of barrellike chute in the fuselage. He fell till he opened at 1,800 feet, and broke his own record without injury to himself.

But he landed far off course, nearly tackling a farmer working in his field. The farmer was stupefied to see this space-suited being appear from out of nowhere. So to put the man at his ease, Valentin quickly removed his goggles and helmet, pointed toward the sky, and explained that "I've come from up there." This, as well as further explanation, did nothing to bring the farmer to words.

Valentin had now acquired a taste for appearing in the record books as well as the newspapers. After making regular jumps at air shows during the summer, he decided to break yet another free-fall record, for the longest night jump. It would also be a personal record for the parachute artist, who had never made a night jump of any kind before. For this jump he stepped out of a Junkers at 16,000 feet and into pitch blackness. After falling for 70 seconds, according to his calculations, he should have been at his opening altitude of 1,800 feet. Instead, the face of his glowing altimeter said he was at 3,600. If he trusted his stopwatch and the altimeter turned out to be right, he wouldn't have fallen enough to break the current free-fall-at-night-record. But if he trusted his altimeter and the stopwatch turned out to be right, he wouldn't live to find out he'd been wrong. And the invisible ground at that hour was no help. "If I was going to play with fire, why not go the limit? For some inexplicable reason, the more my fear increased, the more I prolonged the adventure."

When the altimeter hit 1,450, he pulled. He'd been falling for 85 seconds. He found out later that air density increases at night, which is why he fell so slowly. Though his parachute opened without a problem, he bounced off a tree and blacked out upon landing. The army officials who had been there to observe had headed home as soon as they heard the chute open, and when Valentin came to, he found himself alone in the woods. Exhausted, in pain, and with only a vague idea of where he was, he had to find his way back on his own. This was not the kind of support he felt he needed, and he decided then that he would take his experiments out of the army. (Not long after this jump, an "international decision" required any jumper leaving a plane above 12,000 feet to wear a respirator. As a result, Valentin's records weren't broken for many years.)

Valentin's first jump as a civilian was into a small football stadium at Nancy. That was the target, anyway. He missed the stadium and landed instead on top of a small hut within a pen of boars. The fire department had to rescue him. After several jumps of similar precision, though free of barnyard animals, Valentin began to realize that what he longed for could not be achieved by simply making drop after drop. "In spite of everything, I felt I was only creeping forward," he wrote. "A great step had to be taken which separated a drop from flying, a step which I had to take to keep faith with myself." As his imagination turned to more birdlike flight, he began to examine the history of men who had tried such things. His studies brought his attention to Abbas Ibn Firnas, Leonardo da Vinci, Giovanni Danti, Otto Lilienthal, all the way up to Clem Sohn.

"The lesson of Clem Sohn was of major importance to me. Had he possessed a sufficiently good free drop and delayed opening technique, Clem Sohn would have been able to save his life." Valentin began to fashion himself a pair of wings fairly similar to the ones Sohn had died in: canvas with several rods to give some rigidity (Valentin's wings differed in that they stretched from wrists to ankles). Valentin's rods, in the tradition of the sixteenth-century birdman Paolo Guidotti, were made of whalebone. Unlike Sohn, Valentin did not have a pole going across the arms, as he felt it was important to be able to reach the ripcord at any moment. Valentin also felt his wingsuit should not be one solid block of cloth—the round parachute Valentin was using had a hole or vent at the top to keep it from oscillating. So, where Sohn had canvas completely covering the triangle between the legs, Valentin filled it only up to the knees. He also left space for air to pass at the armpits.

Once he'd built his wings, Valentin explained to the press that "the American did not have the proper type wings. Now, the nice thing about my wings is that they are both flexible and membranous. This is extremely important, because in that way the air can pass through them." (An article from a Michigan paper of the time explains that the people of Lansing viewed Valentin's remarks with "upraised eyebrows.")

Sohn's death colored Valentin's experiments with wings from the very beginning. In the spring of 1950, the promoter who had put together Sohn's last show at Vincennes asked Valentin if he wanted to be the "Bird Man." Valentin agreed, but tried to argue that he would like to take his wings for a trial flight before the show. The promoter pointed out that if Valentin was going to kill himself, he was sure his spectators would want to watch. Valentin gave in, and soon afterward he started to see posters everywhere touting him as "The New Clem Sohn." The press releases leading up to Valentin's jump claimed that he had been one of the first to reach Sohn's body (though Valentin had been nowhere near Vincennes at the time).

The prefect of police also saw the posters and, not wanting another winged death on his hands, banned any winged jumping. But Valentin decided to make the jump anyway. He would make his surreptitious first flight while the announcer was talking the crowd through some other part of the show.

Valentin went up in a transport plane called a Goéland, and at just under 13,000 feet he brought his hands together and dove out into the air. He had hoped to wait till he was well clear of the plane to spread his arms, but the fierce wind forced the wings open immediately. It also tore from his hands the box of talc he had hoped would show his flight path. Not such a loss, it turned out, as there wasn't much of a flight path to show. Though he kept his arms outstretched in the position that he had discovered was stable in a regular free fall, with his wings the pose gave him no control at all, and he fell head-first for most of the drop. He decided to pull at an early 3,000 feet, but despite the fact that he had nothing rigid along his arm, he found that he couldn't bring his hand in to the ripcord—the pressure of the wind against his wings was too great.

The Valentin position had proved ineffective with wings, but Valentin could still rely on his other moves. He rolled on his back, and the wings instantly collapsed. Turning facedown once more, to avoid an awkward and possibly entangling opening, he pulled the ripcord.

Valentin landed at one end of the airfield and was soon mobbed by a small crowd eager to claim a piece of the man—or his suit—for their own. This group of admirers was made up of the few who had managed to see the birdman fall through the sky. The rest of the crowd, some 250,000 people, remained seated and unimpressed.

News of the failed flight flew across the ocean, and the *Chicago Tribune* reported that the man "who tried to fly like a bird landed like a dodo." The article went on to ridicule Valentin for touching down so far from the spectators and claimed that they booed when he finally returned. But the French press was much worse. With hundreds of thousands of witnesses who had seen nothing, they called Valentin a fraud.

The budding birdman decided to take matters into his own hands. He wrote a letter to the papers offering to repeat his performance.

This time Valentin took two reporters and a lawyer with him in the airplane. And though this may have been a good idea for the purposes of verification and vindication, it encouraged Valentin to make a dangerous jump in questionable weather. The wind was too high at 20 miles per hour, and a bank of clouds had settled at 4,500 feet, but Valentin went up anyway, hoping to find a hole in the clouds and make a short fall from 7,500 feet.

At 6,600 feet, Valentin left the plane and experienced a descent very similar to the one he'd made days earlier. After the jump, he claimed he'd glided somewhat and had slowed his fall by at least 20 miles per hour. The biggest and most important difference, though, was that reporters had seen it happen, and the next day's papers were full of the birdman's flight. The *Chicago Tribune,* however, remained silent.

This last jump really had been just for show. After the first of these two winged jumps, Valentin had realized that canvas was unlikely to let him fly the way he wanted to. His arms needed to be free to get at his ripcord in any position, and the wings themselves would have to have a leading edge with much greater rigidity. The canvas suit was, at best, working as a miniature parachute. And so Valentin began to design wings that were a major break from the bat-wings of those who had flown before him.

Valentin teamed up with pilot and manufacturer Monsieur Collignon. The pair built miniature models of several wing designs and fitted them onto tiny Valentin stand-ins. Scientists at the Institut Mécanique des Fluides let them try these models in their wind tunnel, and after a little tweaking, the pair went on to build the life-size wings. These were very much like the wings of a real plane, made of three-ply wood with internal strutting. The wings would be hinged to a steel cage that would surround Valentin's chest and take some of the pressure of the wind off his arms.

To test out the full-sized wings, Valentin took them to a larger wind tunnel, at Chalais-Meudon. Scientists there were eager to help him, and they ran several tests on the wings alone. But when it came time for Valentin to suit up and climb in the tunnel himself, he was stopped by a frothing director. This man wanted Valentin and his contraption off the premises at once. So appalled was he that Valentin might try his wings in the tunnel that he smashed them to bits in front of the experimenter.

This set the birdman back several months. Around the time the second pair of rigid wings was ready, Valentin received an invitation from two Italian bat-wing jumpers, Salvator Canarrozzo and Soro Rinaldi, to join the "Birdmen of the World" for a jump in Milan. Valentin agreed, but first wanted to test his new wings.

For this initial test jump with wooden wings, he arranged to go up in a helicopter. As the aircraft, a Hiller 360, was rather small, Valentin had to ascend on a structure on the outside, in the open air. With his nine-foot wingspan folded in front of him, and his colorful, concentrically painted wings, he looked like some kind of parasitic moth attached to the side of the helicopter. They had only reached 4,000 feet when the pilot motioned to Valentin that he could go no higher. The height offered practically nothing in the way of a free fall—today's jumpers usually pull at that altitude—but Valentin had faced so much in the way of risk and obstacles that there was no way he was going return to the ground still attached to the helicopter.

Valentin fell face-forward from his platform, and the air pushed his wings open. Then the air pushed him on his back. Then the air pushed the wings closed. And kept them closed. Spinning on his back, he found himself utterly helpless. He could not fly, turn over, or release his wings. With his altimeter shouting 900 feet, Valentin pulled his ripcord on his back. The open chute flipped Valentin into an upright position, and he was able to remove his wings and lower them to the ground on a cord, as planned.

What he needed was a locking system that would keep the wings open no matter where the wind took him. By the time he reached Italy to meet his fellow Birdmen, he had one. There he and Canarrozzo and Rinaldi hit it off, talking of human flight for hours on end. But however well the trio got along together, they were not destined to fly together. Valentin again needed a helicopter to take his large wings to jumping height, and again he had to hang on to a strut on the outside of the aircraft as it took him up. But at just 600 feet the engine overheated, and the pilot had to take them straight back down. There was no spare helicopter, and Valentin had to stay on the ground and watch his compatriots put on their show without him. This turned into a valuable lesson for Valentin, as he could plainly see that Canarrozzo and Rinaldi, jumping from 6,000 feet, did little to no gliding across the sky. He vowed never to touch canvas wings again.

Back home, Valentin began to devise a way of showing the Italians that, despite his canceled jump, he was the better birdman. He organized another gathering of the small flock, and this round was to be on home turf—Dogneville, where he'd watched the planes come in as a child. This event was to be a contest to see which of the three, jumping from 9,000 feet and opening no lower than 1,200 feet, could sustain the longest free fall. Meanwhile, to further his abilities with his own wings, Valentin was finally learning how to fly a plane.

In Dogneville, on July 2, 1951, the first jump of the competition was Valentin's. Having had his fill of attaching himself to the sides of helicopters, he attached himself to the side of an airplane. The Fieseler-Storch that was to take him to 9,000 feet was again too small for his wings, so he went up facing the rear on a jerry-rigged seat fitted to some struts. But as soon as the plane took off, Valentin began slipping off the seat. He grabbed hold of a strut, but with his 28-pound wings and all his gear, his arm soon became numb. They were at 300 feet when his arm began to give out. Altitudes between 40 and 400 feet are considered particularly dangerous for aircraft—should a problem arise at that height, the fall is enough to cause disaster upon impact with the ground, but at the same time it's not enough to make any corrections and begin flying after a stall. Similarly, for the human there's not enough height for a parachute to deploy, but plenty of height for breaking a neck. Luckily the pilot heard Valentin's cries, and they returned to the ground immediately.

That meant the others would take their turns before him. Again they did not seem to travel horizontally, but Canarrozzo fell for 43 seconds, Rinaldi for 55.

Valentin persuaded a visiting pilot with a Junkers to take him up again. It was big enough that he could get out of the plane without smashing his wings on the fuselage, as long as a friend gave him a hefty shove.

At 9,000 feet, Valentin received his shove. Body and wings cleared the plane, but only one wing opened. The asymmetry put him into an immediate and violent spin that tore off his altimeter. Helpless, he spun toward the ground for about 20 seconds before the other wing snapped open. Just as quickly, it snapped closed again, and Valentin was back to spinning toward the ground. He managed to open his parachute before passing out, but continued to spin under his canopy, winding and unwinding and swinging like a watch on a chain.

Upon landing he was informed that he had won the contest. Though his wings had failed him, his free fall had lasted 59 seconds.

While he and Collignon were working out ways to improve the aerodynamics of his wings, Valentin was paying the bills with more-typical show jumps. For these he was advertised as "Valentin, the Most Daring Man in the World." In one routine, called the "Aerial Duet," Valentin and a woman named Monique Laroche would leave the plane holding each other's harnesses and fall together for 30 seconds. On one jump, Laroche, having already stepped out onto the plane's wheel, grew terrified that the prop would slice them as they left the plane. Unable to convince her that there was nothing to fear, Valentin asked her to climb back inside. But in her state of terror, Laroche was unable to do this, either. The plane circled, waiting for her to go one way or another, and eventually, running out of fuel, it began to descend. At 1,200 feet she simply had to jump—anything lower would have meant death. Valentin, though, had no reason to head into the air at that risky altitude, and stayed in the plane till it landed. When the press heard that the woman had jumped but Valentin had not, they ridiculed the birdman once again.

At another show jump, bad weather pushed Valentin off course and he ended up in the Mediterranean. To protect his watch, he put it in his mouth before hitting the water. The result was his bloodiest but most harmless injury. The sailors who rescued him found the parachutist with a mouth of blood and glass.

Many of these jumps were done with Salvator Canarrozzo, and the two birdmen grew very close. Canarrozzo was a lover of the low-altitude opening, routinely pulling his ripcord under 500 feet. "When I see the eyes of the terrified spectators, that's when I open my parachute," he said. Should a malfunction occur at that height, there would be no time to open a reserve, so Canarrozzo didn't bother to wear one. In April of 1953 he was killed when, during a jump in Venice, his main did not open after he pulled his ripcord at 450 feet.

Not long after, a woman Valentin had been working with in an "Aerial Trio" fell to the ground without ever touching her ripcord. Upon jumping, something on the plane had ripped her face from eye to chin.

Proximity to death and disaster had never stopped Valentin from making the next jump, and these recent fatalities did nothing to slow his pursuit of what he called "pure flight." By September, Valentin had a new set of wings. Instead of using his arms and shoulders as a leading edge, these wings had a rounded front, behind which the arms rested. This would give the wings much greater lift and allow the arms to move independently. He kept the tail on his jumpsuit, but no longer had a gap at the crotch—he wanted as much surface area as he could get and didn't want to worry about the possibility of the pilot chute getting caught there. The width and overall area of the wings had increased, and at the end of each wing was a perpendicular plane to give them stability, much like the winglets of today's airplanes. The whole ensemble looked remarkably like the wings Felix Baumgartner would use to cross the English Channel nearly fifty years later.

Valentin had done nothing to repair relations with the director of the wind tunnel at the Institut Mécanique des Fluides, and so he decided to test small models of his wings in actual wind. These flew beautifully, and by late September he was ready to test the full-sized wings on his full-sized self.

The plan was to exit at 11,000 feet, which gave Valentin time to suit up during the flight. But after climbing into his jumpsuit and attaching his wings, he discovered that the new reserve he had brought did not fit his harness. Rather than waste the trip, Valentin decided to jump with just the tail to test it separately. In the air he found that the slightest movement of his legs produced spins as violent as those he'd experienced during his last winged jump. And again he was nearly unconscious by the time he finally opened his parachute.

Several days later Valentin was invited by the air ministry to jump at a benefit, but within twenty-four hours this same ministry banned Valentin from using his wings at all. (Furious, Valentin made a typical jump at the benefit, without wings, but deliberately landed far from the spectators.) He then began to petition the ministry to allow him to try his wings, but they had him in another catch-22: he couldn't get permission to fly the wings because they hadn't been tested, and he couldn't test them because he didn't have permission.

Months later the ministry permitted Valentin to put his wings through a round of experiments at the state wind tunnel at the Bréguet works. The experts there were amazed by the profile and performance of the wings as the breeze passed over them and the dummy they were strapped to. The next day, Valentin himself donned the airfoils and was able to practice in the wind tunnel how best to fly, without the threat of an ever-approaching ground. He found that to keep his center of gravity in the right place, he needed to bring his arms forward, tuck up his legs, and arch his back.

With this invaluable experience and the all-important green light from the air ministry, Valentin was finally ready to try his new wings on May 13. This time, jumping at 9,000 feet, both wings opened without a hitch. He went into a dive, turned onto his front, and then, instead of the deathly spirals he had experienced before, went into several slow turns. He was gliding. At 3,000 feet he opened his parachute, then removed his wings, lowered them to the ground, and touched down without incident. "Yes, I had flown, in fact I was the first man ever to have flown. Bird Man now meant something," he wrote. He had covered three miles.

For the next two years, Valentin continued slowly to refine his wings, and he jumped with them at several air shows. By the time he went to fly in Liverpool in May of 1956, his wings were longer and considerably more aerodynamic. For this jump, on the bank holiday Whitmonday, Valentin was to fly for a crowd of 100,000.

A roomy C-47 Dakota took him and an assistant to 9,000 feet, and with five minutes left till the leaping-off point, the pilot began the countdown. But with one minute to go, Valentin decided he wasn't ready. The plane made another pass, and again the pilot began to count down from five minutes. When they reached the last minute for the second time, Valentin saw that the Mersey River was on his right—he had planned to keep it on his left to navigate this foreign land—and again the jump was put off. On the third pass, Valentin stood at the doorway, his wings folded in front of him, waiting for the final minute. His assistant wished him good luck and patted him on the back. Valentin gave the thumbs-up sign, and then rushing air yanked him out of the plane. The sound of splintering wood filled the hull, and then a thump as something hit the tail. Outside, Valentin, in shattered wings, spun crazily toward the ground. After falling for about a thousand feet, he opened his parachute. The audience below saw the white cloth pop into the air. But instead of opening, it caught on the ruined wings. They watched as Valentin fell another 1,000 feet under the roman candle. Then his reserve emerged. But this, too, wrapped itself around him, and he was fighting to free himself as he went into the ground.

In a tidy wheatfield he lay, his body and wings shrouded in the white of his parachute, as helicopters guided medics to the spot of the disaster.

"It always does something to you to see a man fling himself into space," he had written. "It is a mad action. You want to turn your eyes away, but you are fascinated. You remain there open-mouthed, staring at the man who takes his pleasure taunting death."

It certainly did something to those who saw or heard of Valentin's flight and death. In addition to the many parachutists who would be inspired by his efforts to try something similar on their own, Valentin infected the mind of one four-year-old who was at the show in Liverpool. This was Clive Barker, now the famous fantasy/horror novelist. As Valentin fell, Barker's mother ordered him, "Don't look, don't look." But Barker was looking. He saw Valentin's body fall out of the sky, saw it hit the ground. His father was one of the first to reach the man, and said that Valentin "had made a shape from the flattened grain, and he lay with his wings spread wide, so that it looked as though an enormous bird had fallen to earth." They turned him over and were surprised to see that his face was not bloody. Barker, struck by the sight of a man falling from the heavens to his death—myth made real—incorporated the image, the idea, and even the name Leo Valentin into many of his stories. For Barker as well as for those that would imitate Valentin in fact, his death became "a *private legend,* an image drawn on the rock of my skull."

CHAPTER

14

Mockingbirds Still Don't Sing:
Louis Faure and Others

Valentin was the first of several French flying men who would become shooting stars, wowing their contemporaries, inspiring scores of imitators, and achieving international fame. Forty years after Valentin's death, Patrick de Gayardon took what Valentin started to extremes that the birdman undoubtedly dreamed of but never approached. More recently, Loïc Jean-Albert stunned the sky-diving world with his flights down Mount Verbier. But the country, with its own history of air shows and barnstormers, also had its bat-wing flyers of lesser renown.

The first of these, Louis Faure, was more a descendent of Clem Sohn, who, after all, died on French soil, than of Valentin. Faure, like Valentin, learned to jump from planes at the school for paratroopers at Pau. But in 1946, four years before Valentin would experiment with his fabric wings, Faure built two wooden sleeves and attached cloth to them. With them he made at least one recorded successful flight. The wings now hang at a museum in Pau.

Then there was André Vassard, whose handsome cloth wings were duplicates of Sohn's, but much bigger. The stick that ran along the shoulder and arm extended more than a foot past the hand on either side. These extensions, as well as two long ribs of similar size on either side, would most likely have tangled with Vassard's emerging parachute. But he never had the chance to fight his way out of that predicament: before he ever tried his wings, he was killed when his canopy roman-candled during a regular jump.

Sam Chasac had a pair of wings made by a seamstress in his hometown, Chalon-sur-Saône, that were like two miniature parachutes. Chasac found that he didn't get any more forward movement with his wings than he did without them, though they did slow his fall somewhat. The crowds came to see him at air shows anyway, probably, he felt, because they looked forward to the spectacle of his death. But this treat was denied them—a friend of Chasac's borrowed the wings and never returned them.

Four years after Valentin's death, two brothers with the same dreams, drives, and, perhaps, foolhardiness attempted to continue pursuing Valentin's goal of human flight. Guy and Gerard Masselin first tested a cloth suit they built in June of 1960. They swore to each other that if one of them should perish in the wings, the other would go on with the experiment. In June of 1961, the brothers advertised themselves as the decedents of Sohn and Valentin for a jump at Doncourt. Guy was to make a winged flight for a crowd of 6,000. The weather, though, was wet and miserable, and Guy announced that he would not make the jump. The small crowd responded with jeers. Cowed, Guy put on the suit and took a single-prop biplane to just above the clouds and jumped at about 1,800 feet. He waited to pull till he was at 300 feet, presumably to give the crowd something to see once he emerged from the low clouds. This did not give his canopy enough time to inflate, and Guy slammed into the mud, leaving a four-inch depression. The crowd saw nothing.

A year later, Gerard was ready to fulfill the vow he had made to his brother. At Doncourt again, in front of a crowd of 15,000 this time, Gerard made a successful jump with the wings. *Paris-Match* ran an article celebrating the comeback of the birdman. But weeks later the magazine ran another piece about the remaining Masselin brother, claiming that he would eventually go the way of Guy, Valentin, and so many others. In little more than a year after the article appeared, Masselin made a jump in Germany. His wife and parents and a crowd of 10,000 watched as yet another roman candle took yet another winged man's life.

Right around the same time that Guy Masselin was making his first jump at Doncourt, a Frenchman from Cannes, Roger Malaussena, was taking similar risks in New Caledonia. With a checkered helmet and white wings made of the same doped cotton used to cover planes at the time, Malaussena hopped out of a Stampe biplane, talc trailing him as he descended. Malaussena fell more than flew, according to the press, but after he opened at 1,000 feet, oscillated a bit, and safely touched down, the crowd of 1,200 offered him nothing but applause.

Malaussena went on to make some fifty-odd jumps with his cloth wings. But when he wasn't in a plane or in the air, he was inventing a new kind of wing that was fifty years ahead of its time. Made of tubes with an eight-inch diameter and a bicycle's inner-tube valve, Malaussena's invention was inflatable. When fully pumped, the wingspan reached twenty-six feet. Wings of this kind would not be seen again till Yves Rossy's flights in the twenty-first century (see chapter 30). Malaussena also predated another current wing-man, Tom Sitton (chapter 21), when he tested his wings by putting them in the wind while driving his Peugeot 403 convertible (Sitton uses a set of pulleys to hang his wings out the passenger window of his pickup).

Having tested the wings to his satisfaction, Malaussena chartered a helicopter to take him up for his first flight. But the getup—deflated wings rolled up to his arms and a canister of compressed air to be used in free fall—scared off the pilot, and the jump never took place.

The word "wing," like most words when you really start dissecting them, is difficult to define with hard and fast boundaries. As bat-wing jumper Charlie Laurin put it, "You can fly a barn door if it's moving fast enough." But barn doors aren't wings. On the other end of the spectrum, there are the appendages of penguins, ostriches, and a certain percentage of bat-wing jumpers, which anyone would call wings even though they don't fly. Perhaps it is the intention that defines the object.

And so the aluminum wedges that Gil Delamare attached to his wrists and ankles, though nothing like the wings of any birdman or bird that preceded him, *were* wings, considering his intention to do exactly what those predecessors intended to do with theirs—that is, fly.

Delamare was a stuntman who smashed up cars and made parachute jumps for French movies and television. For one particular shoot meant to demonstrate the effectiveness of seatbelts, the bird-man enlisted a fellow jumper, Marie-France de Gayardon, to sit in the passenger seat. For the cameras, the pair dutifully strapped themselves in and drove the car into a variety of accidents from which they emerged whole. Delamare couldn't have known it, but he was sitting next to the mother of the man who would invent the ram-air wingsuit, allowing thousands of skydivers to fly: Patrick de Gayardon. Delamare also couldn't have know that several years later, Marie-France would be in another accident, and this time her seatbelt would not save her. (Patrick was two years old.)

Delamare's wings made him look more like a can opener than a bird, unless that bird was a fighting cock—the aluminum shards were strapped to his wrists and ankles like the blades on a rooster ready to shiv his opponent. Perhaps he modeled them after illustrations of the Marquis de Bacqueville with his winglets on hands and feet. Unlike Bacqueville, though, he went on to make many jumps with his wings.

Delamare's wings did him little harm, but another stunt would prove fatal, though not to him: In 1965 Delamare threw Rupert out of a plane. Rupert was the name for the dummy paratroopers in World War II used to convince the Germans that there were more soldiers falling from the skies than there really were. At one air show there was a particularly fierce wind, and Delamare decided to use a fully outfitted Rupert to see which way it was blowing—he chucked him out of the door of the plane on a static line. But Rupert's parachute did not open, and Rupert fell straight into the crowd below, giving one spectator a heart attack.

Delamare was known to tinker with his getup endlessly between jumps, and he experimented all the way up to his 117th jump with his wings. But it wasn't that last jump that put an end to his career as birdman. Like Marie-France de Gayardon, Delamare met his end in a car accident. He was racing a convertible for a film in May of 1966, when the car flipped over and killed him.

Shiver of Death:
Rudolf R. Boehlen

"One day, a jump will be the last. The jump of death. But that idea does not hold me back. Aren't we aware, us humans, of all the dangers?"

So wrote Rudolf Richard Boehlen in a pamphlet he called "My First Parachute Jump," making it quite clear that he knew what he was getting into. But it's safe to say that despite his predictive powers, Boehlen was not aware of *all* the dangers.

He certainly came from a safe enough place. Boehlen was born in Basel, Switzerland, two years before the turn of the twentieth century, making him the oldest of all the bat-wing jumpers. In true Swiss fashion, Boehlen became a banker as an adult. And at the age of twenty-eight, he remained a banker. But by then his interests had turned to aviation, and in June of 1926 he took a parachuting course in Berlin. On his first jump, from 2,600 feet, he had his first injury, a cut above the left eye. This small harbinger of things to come did not put

Boehlen off further jumps. In fact, his banking days were over: he immediately became a professional jumper (though he started driving a taxi to help pay the bills). In addition to eighty-six jumps made in the next three years, Boehlen performed much high-altitude daredeviltry. He hung from the strut between a plane's wheels, dangled and swung from a plane on a trapeze, and enacted something called "The Shiver of Death on One Wing."

In 1933 he was enough of a professional to join the ranks of jumpers trying to break records for drops from the highest altitude. With the assistance of bottled oxygen, he entered subzero air at 26,900 feet, setting a new world record.

Perhaps he felt imbalanced as holder of *just* the high-altitude record. Six years later, at Zurich's Aviation Day, Boehlen set a *low*-altitude record when he opened his chute at 115 feet. On his team at the festival were Switzerland's first two female parachutists—a fact that may have emboldened him to test the limits of his machismo.

When, exactly, Boehlen began experimenting with wings is not known, but it was probably around the same time he was breaking records. By the early 1950s he had settled into a suit that was significantly different from his American predecessors. The wings weren't scalloped like those of Sohn. Instead, they began at right angles to the arms and then sloped in toward the feet. Between these appendages he had a rudder (extending away from his front side) the size and shape of a shark's fin. When fully extended the wings locked into a taut, flat surface, giving the birdman a wingspan of ten feet. When collapsed, they were too long for Boehlen to stand, and in order to be photographed, and to demonstrate while on the ground how he opened and closed his wings, he was wheeled out hanging on a metal frame and strapped into his harness.

To get into the plane, Boehlen needed a helper at both sides, holding his half-folded wings above the ground as he waddled on tiptoe across the airfield. Once at the plane, they couldn't then slide him all the way in, since, with his large wings, he wouldn't be able to get out on his own without some dangerous sidling. Instead they put him on his back onto a slide—a kind of plank—that stuck out the door of the plane. The slide, and Boehlen's legs, remained outside the plane as it took off and brought him to altitude. Once there, he slid into the open air.

"During the free fall, the wings and the keel must deploy in order to ensure a circular tail dive that is slow and smooth," he said. "Then, thanks to the movement of the arms and legs, one can propel oneself through the air in the same manner as a butterfly."

The butterfly analogy was not too far off. Once he was out of the plane and had unfolded his wings, he bounced around, tossed and buffeted by the air, seemingly out of control, but undoubtedly getting to where he was going—that is, ground level. Landing with wings still attached and fully extended, Boehlen necessarily fell over.

By 1953, Boehlen had made some 400 jumps with and without wings—a real pro for those days—and he had given up every other goal to continue jumping (today's jumpers would call it "breaking away"). "I'd like very much to live like other men, but in reality, I can never manage to forget my parachute."

In June of that year, Boehlen was to make a winged jump in Germany for Aeronautics Day in Augsburg, but the plane that he was to jump out of was owned by Americans who had apparently seen or heard enough of winged disaster. They refused to allow Boehlen to jump from their aircraft with his wings. So the clipped birdman made a regular parachute jump instead, from 1,600 feet. His parachute opened perfectly and brought him gently toward the earth for his short descent. But just before he touched dirt, a gust of wind gave the parachute, and the jumper, a yank. His head hit the ground before his feet did.

Though reportedly dazed, Boehlen wanted to continue making the jumps he'd been scheduled for. Less than an hour later he made another jump, this time from 4,000 feet. He did not pull his ripcord until 600 feet, and then the wind again set him down hard. But the crowd had loved the sight of the low opening, and Boehlen, feeding on the enthusiasm, declared the day one of the greatest in the history of aeronautics and went up for a third time. The jump, titled the "Living Torch," was a success, but by morning the hard landings had caught up with him. A doctor visited him at his hotel, determined that his brain was hemorrhaging, and took him to the hospital.

Boehlen expressed a last wish there: that he be taken back to Switzerland. But by the time the medical plane arrived for him, Boehlen was dead.

"Another birdman parachutist with a fatal destiny, you might say," wrote wingsuit flyer and historian Francis Heilmann, "Yet this one, without a well-known history, and devoid of a biography and published photos, runs the risk like so many others of fading little by little into the darkness of oblivion."

Michigan Shenanigans:
Charlie Laurin and Art Lussier

When Charlie Laurin saw the short, chipmunk-faced young man struggling down the runway with a small plane that seemed to have been recently crashed, burned, or both, he ran up to offer his assistance. Laurin introduced himself and asked if the plane had in fact been in a fire. It had not, explained the mildly peeved Art Lussier. He had just purchased the Taylorcraft and was about to take it up for a flight. "I'm the captain of this ship," he said. He offered to bring Laurin along, and though they did not yet know it, they had just given birth to the Michigan Parachute Club.

Laurin first arrived in Flint on a bus, a baby in his grandmother's arms. After the three-day ride without food, she handed him off to the couple who adopted him. Lussier's parents were French immigrants, his father a toolmaker. Both Lussier and Laurin were ex-paratroopers who had learned how to fly on the GI Bill, and when they met, they were both working in the automobile factories. Soon

143

they were an inseparable pair, and—when they weren't building cars or eating *Mère* Lussier's beans (all that the Lussiers ever ate, according to some)—they were fixing up the plane or taking it into the air. Lussier would run home at lunch, fly the plane over the factory, and put on an impromptu air show for his colleagues chewing their sandwiches below.

The plane had no electrical system whatsoever, and to fly it legally at night, they needed to have lights on the wings. To remedy the situation, they attached flashlights to the ends of the wings and painted the lenses. Of course, this meant that the lights could only be turned on while the plane was earthbound. And the batteries gave them only an hour or so of night-flying time. In their minds, though, this didn't register as a problem—if the lights were on, then anyone in the control tower could see them and they were fine, and if the lights ran out, well, then no one could see them, so they wouldn't get caught.

While they were working in the hangar one day, a man calling himself Commander Parker, six-foot-four, thick of brow, and humorless of demeanor, appeared in the doorway. He wanted to make a parachute jump, he said. Lussier, eager to mount whatever nutty scheme came riding his way, offered to take Parker up, but as his own airplane was too small to fit the oversized man and his two chutes, they decided to rent a Cessna.

It was 1957, and the idea of a voluntary parachute jump—with a free fall, no less—seemed insane, if not actually illegal, to most who owned a plane, and no one at the little airport would rent them one. So they tried to fit him in the Taylorcraft. To do this, they had to remove the co-pilot's stick, and Parker had to forgo his reserve and keep his legs hanging out of the side of the plane. Before they took off, Lussier turned to Laurin and said, with glee, "We're the only ones jumping in Flint today, Charlie. Just look up—when you see something falling out of the sky, that'll be Parker." Lussier rolled the plane down the field and took off. It struggled with all the weight and just barely made it up to 600 feet. Parker squeezed out the door, fell for a few moments, opened his parachute, and landed without injury in a farmer's field.

Laurin and Lussier didn't have to pass a word to each other; they knew they would be next.

The following day Laurin drove to Flint, rented a Cessna, and flew it back. Parker showed them what little he knew, and up they went. They made their jumps at 2,200 feet, waited four seconds, opened their parachutes, and landed—Lussier in the front yard and Laurin in the backyard of the same house.

The trio started making jumps regularly, and eventually a man with a Cessna at the Saginaw airport invited them to jump from his plane. Before long they were jumping every weekend—no matter what the weather, no matter how hard the frozen ground—and drawing a crowd. Soon the small group had a name, matching jumpsuits, an official patch, and a gaggle of regular fans. Sometimes the gawkers came by the hundreds, lining their cars up outside the airport. They also attracted several other ex-paratroopers from the area who were looking to experience free fall.

One of them was a teenager named Jim McCusker, who found the group after responding to an ad in the paper. After jumping with the crew for a while, he once went up with Laurin and Lussier, and in the plane they explained to McCusker that because they wanted to jump that flight, he'd have to land the plane on his own. McCusker had never had a lesson or flown for a single minute—but he had watched the others at the stick and, all alone in the aircraft, he somehow managed to land it without destroying it or himself.

In an effort to increase their stockpile of gear, Laurin came up with the good idea to run around and see if they could buy old parachutes from veteran paratroopers who weren't looking to use them again. At the first place they stopped a farmer pulled an old canopy out of his barn and sold it to them for ten dollars. Laurin and Lussier roared away from the transaction laughing at the deal they'd managed to get away with.

But Laurin was not laughing when he opened the parachute at 2,500 feet. ("I knew something might go wrong," he says, "so I opened high.") Half the panels blew out. The unexpectedly speedy rate of descent was bound to make for a painful landing, and Laurin grabbed the lines and began pulling as hard as he could, trying to maneuver himself to some soft spot. He found himself on his back, and his compatriots ran over, not to help him, but to marvel at the chute with which he had traversed the air. From the ground they had seen Laurin steer better than any of them had ever managed.

Laurin had inadvertently invented what would come to be known as the "blank gore" parachute, and the whole team began experimenting with removing various panels for better navigation. Skydiving was a small enough subculture, and one with access to planes, that jumpers of any importance knew one another. And the man who would later patent the blank-gore parachute had visited the Saginaw airport and seen the Michigan Parachute Team in action.

While they were stumbling upon techniques that would let people land where they actually wanted to in the future, they were also stumbling onto techniques for stable free fall. They had no idea that others had already worked out the basics—they hadn't heard of Spud Manning, and word of Valentin's discoveries had not yet reached them. They had to learn how to stop hurtling randomly through the air through trial and error.

That's not to say that their method was anything like scientific. They simply tried anything that anyone suggested, no matter how odd or seemingly fatal. Low pulls were the norm, and they considered a perfect opening one where the feet touched the ground the very moment the canopy inflated.* On one jump, team member Walt Peca hit a roof when landing, bounced off, and broke a leg when he hit the ground. The bone was protruding through the skin, and when he presented himself to his pals they offered to take him to the hospital—after they made just one more jump. Peca told them that if they were going up for another jump, he was going with them. Peca thus made history as the only skydiver ever to make a second jump after first breaking a leg.

Laurin, too, made history of a sort when *he* broke a leg. Lussier's younger brother Mike, ten years old at the time, saw Laurin in the air under his canopy, heading for the far side of the airfield. Thinking he would be helpful, Mike jumped into his older brother's Buick and drove across the field to pick up Laurin. His timing was impeccable, and Laurin became the first jumper ever to be hit by an automobile while in the air. He never bothered to have the bone set by a doctor or anyone else. "I just hopped all over. It got to the point where I could hop like a fucking kangaroo."

The broken bones would not make a dent in their conviction that they were invincible. For a period they jumped without the reserves—or containers at all. They would just hold their canopies scrunched up in their hands as they leapt out of the plane's door.

Their seeming inability to get killed did not keep them from other kinds of trouble. In the hunt for cheap planes, the founding pair had

---

*"You're a real asshole," one woman said to Laurin after one such jump that was meant to scare the onlookers. This was his future wife, and those were her first words to him.

discovered an old PT-19 flight trainer in a farmer's field. The propeller was cracked, fabric was hanging off it everywhere, and the wings were full of holes. They poured a few gallons of gas into the fuel tank, just for laughs, and were surprised to find that the plane started up. Laurin taxied it up and down the field a few times, and before long he was flying. He flew the plane back to Saginaw and landed it, but he had no license for it. When the FAA heard of the caper, they sent a man down to find Laurin. He would have been arrested if the local sheriff, a regular spectator on the weekends, hadn't tipped him off. Laurin kept a low profile for a while, and they hid the plane in a hangar where they worked on it. As there were no real laws about who could parachute where and when, the officer who trailed Laurin "like stink on shit" had nothing to pin on him in the end. As long as they didn't catch him actually flying the PT-19, he remained a free man.

Since Laurin and Lussier had gotten away with everything they had ever dreamt up, there was no chance they would turn away from the idea of using bat-wings once it came up. In his memoirs, Laurin describes the moment Lussier first decided they needed to try wings:

> It was the winter of 1958 and Leo Valentin had been dead a year—but Art had just found out that morning. I was sitting on a tall stool changing brakes on a Cessna.
>
> "He's the last of 'em, Charlie. Make us a set of wings before someone else gets the idea."
>
> Valentin was a folk hero to Art—he often talked about him, mostly because they were both French, I think, and probably because Art wanted to be a birdman too.
>
> "I suppose you want me to fetch some wood and wire and springs and stuff and have it done by this afternoon, huh?"

"I know you've got to finish that job you're on, but yeah. Then we'll go to Mom's parlor and eat some beans and figure out how to fly them."

I never ceased to be amazed at my friend's innocence. The bat-wing jumpers were all dead to the last man and Arthur wanted me to build in a couple of hours what they had worked a lifetime trying to perfect—and failed. Sure, they may have glided some, but then what? All of them eventually ended up tangled in their own parachutes, lying under a heap of silk and rubble—dead.

"I never liked the idea," I said. "It's tombstone technology at its finest. It ain't natural."

"So you think you know more than Valentin." It was a statement, not a question.

"I know I ain't dead."

Art looked very disappointed.

"So you're not going to do it?"

"I never said that."

Laurin went on to explain that he thought if they stayed away from rigid wings and stuck to canvas, they stood a chance of surviving.

The pair approached Danny Latchford, from whom they'd previously bought parachutes, and for fifty dollars Latchford sewed up a wingsuit for them. But he couldn't understand why they were risking their lives when no one was paying them. "You're going to kill yourselves for free," he said, and it was not the first time he'd used those same parting words with that pair.

The usual weekend crowd was hanging around the airport to watch the parachutes come down—"oblivious to the fact that history was to be made that day"—when Laurin and Lussier pulled up. Laurin took the wings out and held them up for everyone to see.

Now I am aware that people will tell you that the only reason anyone pays to see a car race or an air show is that they're hoping to see someone get killed in the most spectacular of ways. Maybe that's true for some, but not for our regulars, the ones that came out to see us every weekend. They were older than us, World War II guys mostly, and they'd seen enough death for their lifetime.

They'd heard of Valentin, too, and you'd have thought they'd have said something to us, asked us why we were taking such a risk, but they never said a word. I guess that after seeing us week after week, jumping in every kind of weather, being dragged over the frozen ground, bombing down to within inches of the ground, breaking limbs and teeth, being knocked cold and going back for more, they thought this was just one more thing we would learn to survive.

So we took turns flying that day, first Art, then me, and it seemed to us to be just another time to laugh and be with friends, oblivious to the fact that we had joined a very elite but tiny fraternity—the brotherhood of birdmen.

Lussier's recollection is a little more succinct and budgetary: "I'd read that book about Valentin—and I said 'Hey, we gotta start making some money here, you know. We gotta fly bat-wings.' We didn't want to make *much* money, we just didn't want to have to pay, you know, five or six dollars per jump."

However they came to use the wings, it attracted an even larger audience at the airport. With the crowd and the strange antics in the air, the scene must have looked much like an air show. At least it did to a man named William C. Huddlesworth of the Caro Businessmen's Association, who was among the spectators one day. Huddlesworth, knowing that the parachutes and especially the bat-wings could easily draw a paying crowd at his local airport, called Lussier one day and offered him $300 to bring their "air show" to Caro. To Lussier, this sounded like a lot of money. "He wants to pay us for what we do every weekend for free," he explained to Laurin.

The next week the team headed over to Caro. They had the illegal PT-19, two other planes, and a slew of packing tables so the audience could watch what they were up to. As they set up, some two or three hundred people were milling about. This was the local crowd, thought Lussier, but it turned out this was just the crew that had arrived to set up the show. The audience would be some ten times that size. As more and more people showed up around the time the show was to start, Laurin started getting worried. Thousands of people had paid fifty cents to see the air show, and the Michigan Parachute Club hadn't planned a thing. Little did he know that it was to be one of the most exciting air shows ever to take place.

It started with Laurin taking Peca up in the PT-19 to 4,000 feet, where Peca crawled out onto the wing and fell off. Laurin had to bring the tail up quickly to keep Peca from hitting it, then he took the plane for a roll and came back down. The next act featured the greatest span of age between any two jumpers in recorded history. Jack Clapp, at seventy-five, and Art Lussier's younger brother Michael, age twelve, made a jump together from 4,000 feet. (It was the pre-teen's fourth jump.) Behind them Laurin came tumbling, flour streaming behind him, and he pulled at around 5,000 feet. What he had opened was a reserve parachute that he hadn't even bothered to attach to his harness. He hung from the strap for a bit and then let go, cueing the announcer below to start his worried commentary about how Laurin had fallen out of his parachute. He fell till "that visual explosion where everything below simultaneously erupts in size, and people are now visible, no longer vague images." Ladies fainted. He opened his main and touched earth.

When Laurin returned to the packing tables, he found a young man, under the influence of drink, railing against Lussier, informing him with volume that he wasn't as tough as he thought he was. "He had these babes and he's telling them that he was a jumper and actually he wasn't," explains Lussier. The harangue didn't look as though it was letting up, and it took just a single look between Laurin and Lussier for them to know what was next in the afternoon's events. When the man said, "You think you're hot stuff? If I had a chute, I'd go for a jump, too," they made their move.

Laurin grabbed the man and restrained him, and Lussier began to fit him into a harness while Jim McCusker ran off to tell the announcer that they had a volunteer from the audience who was about to make his first jump. The local, overpowered and assuming this was some kind of joke, began to cool down. But when Laurin and Lussier pulled out a rope and started talking about whether or not it would work as a static line, he began to sweat. Laurin kept a tight grip on his arm. "Now I wish I wouldn't have," Laurin writes with semi-feigned regret in his memoir. "It would have been funnier to see our inebriated volunteer running through the crowd, pressured by two evil villains trying to toss him out of an airplane—but that's not what happened."

First they tossed him *in* the plane. The Cessna took off, and the captive protested all the way up to 1,500 feet. They didn't want to go much higher, Laurin and Lussier said, because they wanted to be sure that he landed at the airport, in sight of the crowd. Laurin tied the rope—really just a clothesline—to the handle of the ripcord on their volunteer, and when they were over the airport, Lussier slowed the

Cessna. "You ain't gonna do this," insisted the man. "You ain't gonna get me out of this airplane."

He was wrong.

"He won't do that again," said Lussier, "shoot his mouth off."

"No, I don't think he will."

They had tossed the volunteer backward out of the door, and the rope did its trick, opening the chute and setting the man down without injury. "He survived the jump," says Lussier, "but he shit his pants."

Laurin admits to having had a twinge of remorse at the time. "I thought, 'Jesus Christ, we almost killed a guy.' *I* was thinking that . . . I don't know about the rest of the guys."

The sight of this man landing and walking away, whatever the state of his trousers, was enough to inspire another, actual volunteer—one less in shape for survival. After Lussier and Laurin performed a handful of jumps, with and without bat-wings, and a faked baton pass (it changed hands in the plane, despite what the announcer told the audience), Caro's doctor, an overweight man in his sixties, stepped up to make a jump. To audience members and performers alike, this seemed like a stunt sure to result in broken bones at best and a dead doctor at worst. But the doctor, as well as Lussier and Peca, insisted. They passed the ambulance on the way to the airplane, and Laurin was sure that the doctor would find himself inside of it in a matter of minutes.

Soon the Cessna was up at 1,500 feet again, while below the crowd was quiet, anxious about their old doc. The plane made a pass over the crowd, and it was low enough that they could see the doctor in the door, ready to go.

"They threw him out!" a woman shrieked. And she was right. The doctor's body was flailing through the air. Behind him, in a more stable position, came Lussier. With a jump from just 1,500 feet, it was mere seconds before Lussier opened. But the doctor never did.

The crowd watched as his body slammed into the ground. Women next to Laurin fainted. Others vomited. The ambulance roared over to the body. "We finally did it," thought Laurin. "We finally went too fucking far."

The ambulance rushed the doctor's body to the first-aid tent, and a worried mob formed around it, waiting to hear the bad news. After a short time the tent flaps opened, and instead of a bearer of bad news, out walked the doctor, swathed in bandages.

" 'Jesus,' I said. Not because I thought he'd been saved by divine providence, but because I knew now that I, too, had been duped—by a plan conjured up by a bunch of drunks," writes Laurin. The doctor, of course, though perfectly willing to try a jump, had never been in the plane with Lussier and Peca at all. When they passed the ambulance, they'd traded the doctor for the dummy that did the diving for him.

The lesson they learned was that a crowd was ready to swallow whatever story they were being told. As their friend, the legendary skydiver Bob Sinclair, once told them, all you need for an air show is someone to sell the tickets and an announcer. The MC can work the emotions of the crowd without a single actual jump ever taking place. Since people on the ground have to squint and strain to make out the activities in the air above them anyway, the jumpers themselves were hardly needed.

This fact was hammered home at the next event the Michigan Parachute Team was roped into.

A promoter named Clarence Fields heard word of the bat-wing jumps and hired Laurin and Lussier to make two jumps, at a hundred dollars apiece, at the Flat Rock Speedway over the July Fourth weekend. The racetrack was just a few miles south of Detroit, and likely to bring in a much bigger crowd than the one that had materialized from the boondocks around Caro. Fields assured them that there was plenty of space to land inside the racetrack, but when the pair showed up to scope things out, they found that the track was topped by hundreds of lights and the electric wires to power them—an unpleasant place for a jumper to become enmeshed. Fields had advertised the show extensively in newspapers and on the radio, and the two jumpers didn't want to back out, so they agreed to land in the parking lot outside the track. The cars that would be there during the race, Lussier reasoned, couldn't be any harder than the frozen tundra they were used to landing on.

On the day of the show, the two batmen showed up in their Cessna, at 5,000 feet in the air, just as the sun was going down—that way the audience could easily stare into the sky. Fields worked the crowd through the PA system, telling them to keep their eyes on the plane as it circled higher and higher and to watch for the silhouette of Lussier streaking through the sky. Lussier appeared, separated from the plane, and fell, wings spread, toward the speedway. He landed in the parking lot as planned. That was the show.

The next morning Lussier and Laurin met Fields for breakfast. Fields commended Lussier on an excellent jump and said that the crowd had loved it. Then he turned to Laurin and explained what he wanted for the jump he was to make that evening. "I want you to free-fall down to about 800 feet and fly around the speedway a couple of times. Then fly over the center of the speedway and flap your wings—hover there like a hummingbird for a few minutes so the customers can take pictures of you. Then you can pull your chute and land right in the center of the speedway."

"We're not real birds," said Laurin, and he tried to explain the limits of what they were capable of.

"I know you can fly," said Fields. "I saw it, and ten thousand of my customers saw it."

Laurin stopped arguing with the man. "People see what they believe," he's fond of saying. That evening they went back up in the Cessna, and Charlie made the same flight that Lussier had made the previous day. Fields never complained. In fact, he wrote the pair a letter of recommendation to help them find other venues for their act. He even had them back for a repeat performance on Labor Day.

✦

Whether Laurin and Lussier are totally invincible has yet to be seen. Both gave up air shows—and automotive assembly—to become professional pilots.

Laurin flew freight for many years, then opened a pizza parlor, raised a family, and now has a small farm, coincidentally, in DeLand. There he became a kind of father figure for the younger wingsuit flyer Jari Kuosma, and he has planned for some time to exchange a remake of his single-layer bat-wing suit for one of Kuosma's Birdman suits. If Kuosma will dare to fly Laurin's wings, Laurin will gladly go for a spin in one of Kuosma's. In fact, more than thirty years after his last jump, Laurin, now in his seventies, has taken up parachuting again. And when he landed after his first jump of the new century, he asked his fellow skydivers to excuse the stiffness of his landing: he'd recently had his hip replaced. Soon after, his wife, after years of watching Laurin's madcap adventures in the sky, made her first jump ever.

Art Lussier went on to become a freelance pilot who would fly just about any job anyone offered. He flew questionable goods to South America, piloted a makeshift bomber in Africa, and lived through adventures too numerous to name here. He eventually gave up flying altogether, raised two children, and now lives alone in a cabin he built in the middle of nowhere, Michigan.

Walt Peca wound up working on oil rigs all over the world, smuggled diamonds out of Sierra Leone, and gave parachute demonstrations in South America.

Commander Parker passed away in 2004.

Jim McCusker, who learned how to fly when his friends bailed out of the plane and left him alone in the cockpit, went on to have a long career as a captain for United Airlines.

Every year the group meets at Lussier's cabin in the woods, known as the "billabog," to fire a few guns, rehash the old days, and wonder out loud how they managed to stay alive.

"There are old pilots and bold pilots, but no old bold pilots," said E. Hamilton Lee, one of the first pilots for the U.S. Air Mail. How Charlie Laurin, Art Lussier, and the rest of the Michigan Parachute Club escaped such a prophecy remains a mystery.

Spy vs. Sky:
Lyle Cameron

Lyle Cameron is the editor of a jump publication.
To the skydivers of the world he tries to give an education.
He sells many copies, that is easily seen,
Of his "Yellow journal Jump magazine."
—From *The Hustler,* by Bev Galloway, with additional
verses by Dan Poynter. Sung to the tune of "Bimini."

By the 1960s, the kind of parachutist drawn to try wings
was, almost by definition, a step beyond what the average person
might call daring or reckless. After the deaths of Clem Sohn, Leo
Valentin, and so many others in between, only those who sought out
the face of death, or suffered from some congenital deficiency of fear,
would don bat-wings.

Such characters were not in short supply. By the time the Beatles
descended on the United States, the pursuit of parachuting had become the sport of skydiving, and, thanks largely to the television series *Ripcord,* the number of skydivers in the country was swelling.

The increased interest led to increased experimentation, and not just to work out the fundamentals of how to maneuver during free fall or steer a parachute. Of course, the jumpers attracted to attempting the new would naturally be the more fearless within the subculture. The result was that birdmen of the sixties would also be the innovators and record-breakers of skydiving in general. Inspired by Valentin's book, driven by reports of his death (in *Life,* no less), or just chasing after more air time, these men created something of a bat-wing revival while skydiving blossomed.

They did not, however, have much to add in the way of technique or technology to the evolution of bat-wings. What changes they made were little more than slight variations on the "rag and bones" that Sohn, Manus Morgan, and Tommy Boyd had already taken above the clouds. Their endeavors with bat-wings became just one of many wild and sometimes peculiar activities attempted in the sky.

These activities gave rise to the inevitable tension between the envelope-pushers and those who wanted to see the sport legitimized in the eyes of the rest of the world. The debate, which continues to this day, focused on how skydivers should exhibit themselves to the media. Many jumpers were tired of the popular view that said "they're all nuts," while others were out to perform stunts that, no matter how well prepared, certainly seemed nutty to any outsider. Some were inspired by those who took the sport to further extremes, while others were angered by the near accidents and dead bodies that gave the sport a bad name.

Take the case of Rod Pack. On New Year's Day of 1965, Pack jumped out of a plane without a parachute. He tracked over to another jumper, Bob Allen, who had jumped out of another plane 1,500 feet away, took a reserve from him, put it on, and made it to the ground alive. *Life* had exclusive rights to the story and published an article calling the jump "a terrifying stunt." Soon after, *Sky Diver* magazine ran an article declaring the jump a "simple baton pass, just more serious" (the ability to pass a baton from one jumper to another in midair was, by 1965, a benchmark for anyone trying to master free-fall maneuverability) and "less dangerous than the old plane changes or wing walking." This drew some remarks from the magazine's readers:

> I am thoroughly disgusted to read that you not only condone the chuteless jump by Rod Pack, but went on to say it was a fine example, to the average citizen, that skydivers have maneuverability. This is in my estimation, a lot of baloney . . . Joe Average Citizen already is of the opinion that anyone who jumps out of airplanes for the fun of it is some kind of nut. I doubt whether this display will do any more for his thoughts, except to prove in his own mind that he was right all along.

Another reader complained that now his friends were telling him, "I told you so, skydiving is for nuts." Yet another groused that had anything gone wrong, "the cause of parachuting would suffer under a very demonstrative press."

The magazine's editor was unapologetic, stating that the "Average Joe Whuffo doesn't even realize we can do relative work let alone know there are different areas of parachuting. You can only attempt to point this out to them when they flapjaw at you."

The editor was Lyle Cameron, a name known to anyone making any kind of jump in those days. In addition to putting together *the* periodical for skydivers, he had started the drop zone at Elsinore, which, with Taft, would make California the skydiving capital of the world in the sixties. Undoubtedly he liked to see his fellow skydivers make it to the ground safely on a regular basis, but he also had a fondness for the kind of stunts that skydivers and outsiders alike would put in the category of kookdom.

Cameron was a tall, chiseled adventurer whose life was one long series of pranks and extravagant risks. But his jumps in bat-wings were an attempt to perfect what he thought were the true goals of skydivers, though they did little to achieve them.

On his first jump ever, from a glider, the joke was on him. He walked out on the wing, was surprised at the silence, turned back, and started walking toward the cockpit. The pilot turned toward Lyle to take a picture and accidentally banked the aircraft, popping Cameron over the leading edge of the wing. For Cameron, the error was just more fuel for laughter.

The fun really began when he and his pal Tony Lemus started jumping at Elsinore. After buying out all the parachute gear at an army surplus store, they started experimenting. By the time Cameron had twenty-five jumps under his belt—an abject beginner by today's standards, never mind that he didn't yet know how to stabilize himself during free fall—he was running a jump school, charging students six dollars a jump.

A man named Bruce Williams once showed up at the school, hoping to learn how to parachute. He asked some jumpers where he could find the instructor, and they pointed up. There was Cameron, about fifty feet above the ground, upside down in his harness. After he'd flopped to the ground, Williams asked Cameron what he should do to make his own jump. Cameron said, "Oh, talk to the jumpers and just go ahead."

Two years later the school had put some 500 people through their first jump, all without a single injury. Along the way, Cameron started learning the rudiments of how to get around in the air. It was like riding a motorcycle—on the road, if you want to move into the left lane, you lean right. In the sky it's the same. If you want to move to the left, reach out to the right; if you want to move backward, reach out in front of you. Cameron left Elsinore to start another school in Piru, just north of Los Angeles, and also began working as a freelance free-fall photographer. He eventually purchased *Sky Diver* magazine and also shot the second season of the *Ripcord* series.

As one of skydiving's leading cameramen, he was hired by NASA to shoot footage for an experiment that would enrich his own understanding of how a body moves through the air. If you've ever tried to win a kewpie doll at a carnival by dropping a quarter into a jug of water and hoping it would land in the shot glass at the bottom, then you'll understand the problem. When the coin plops into the water, it immediately begins to fall in a spiral. The same phenomenon is true in that other fluid—air—and NASA thought it might explain why space capsules weren't landing where they were supposed to. So Cameron and another photographer strapped cameras to their heads and began chasing basketball- and medicine-ball-sized spheres around the sky. The balls trailed smoke so that scientists could later track their movement when watching the film, and as they emptied they became lighter. Cameron discovered that the size and seeming balance of each sphere had little to do with the diameter of the spiral they went in.

In free fall he had to change speed constantly while he chased the elusive balls through the smoky skies. A skydiver's velocity can vary by 60 miles per hour, so a collision up there can be as bad as a head-on collision in a car, just without the seatbelt—or the car—as protection. And even if the two skydivers managed to avoid a smash-up, they still had to worry about whether the ball would hit them after they opened their parachutes.

When he wasn't trying to avoid trouble in the skies, Cameron was trying to cause it. Having survived NASA's game of dodge ball, the aerial Till Eulenspiegel was ready to put his new nimbleness in the air to the purposes of harassing his friends. On one jump, Cameron, Bud Kiesow, and Vern Williams were to jump as a trio. Williams would be attached to a static line, and the other two planned on holding on to him as they left the plane. But when Williams wasn't looking, Cameron unclipped the line and attached it to his own ripcord. Williams apparently noticed, and when Cameron wasn't looking, Williams reattached himself to the static line. When the three of them went out together, rather than falling as a single group, as Cameron and Kiesow then expected, Williams's chute popped open, and the others flew off below him. Kiesow's reaction to the prank was to grab immediately for Cameron's ripcord, and he managed to put Cameron unexpectedly under his own chute.

Cameron loved the joke, and afterward a jump with him meant you might find yourself under your canopy long before you were ready. On a jump with Rod Pack, Cameron challenged him to a contest to see who could pop the most chutes of the other people they were jumping with on that load. Pack managed to get three, but when he saw Cameron, he lodged himself on his back and started reaching for Cameron's ripcord. The two tumbled through the air and soon found themselves with both their canopies open at the same time, in danger of having them collapse against each other.

The screwball comedy wasn't limited to skydiving. Cameron was once piloting a plane with a skydiver next to him who was terrified of flying. This aviophobic endured plane rides only for the purpose of jumping. When he complained about the flight, Cameron offered to take him down immediately—and he landed on a highway they happened to be flying over. This terrorized the skydiver even more, so

Cameron began taking off and landing and taking off and landing, skipping down the highway like a bee over a clover field.

Hopping planes and hopping out of planes led to the inevitable—hopping from plane to plane. For one episode of *Ripcord,* Cameron, standing in for the hero, was to jump from one plane onto the tail of another. But before he went up, he saw his pilot, Cliff Winters, wearing a parachute, and teased him about it, asking if he thought they weren't going to make it back with the plane. The sensitive—or macho—Winters then chucked the chute in the backseat. Up in the air, the second plane pulled carefully alongside the one with Winters and Cameron inside. Cameron stepped out of his plane and made it onto the tail of the second. He was climbing toward the front when the second plane lurched upward and ripped a wing off the plane Winters was flying. In the *Ripcord* episode the planes' wings can be seen crumpling.

Cameron reached the ground safely but wondered what had happened to his friend. It turned out that Winters saw the wing come off, left the cockpit, and scrambled for the reserve in the back, which he found resting against the open door, held in only by the lip on the bottom. He and the other pilot made it to the ground, but both planes were lost.

Cameron, ever unfazed by near disaster, was fond of saying that more people die golfing than skydiving. This is not, strictly speaking, *true.* Regardless, the rate of death among bat-wing jumpers was clearly higher than that of golfers, shuffleboarders, and bocce players combined. But Cameron saw bat-wings as the natural evolution of everything they were trying to do during free fall and ignored whatever risk he may have thought they entailed. "In an attempt to slow our rate of descent, to increase our travel distance and eventual elimination of the parachute, we come to bat wings," he wrote in *Sky Diver.*

Skydiving photographers were already using the cloth extensions that they still use today to slow their descent and stay above their subjects. As these attach to the arms and legs no farther from the body than the elbows and knees, they don't restrict movement and can't become entangled with an emerging parachute. What makes them safe, though, makes them of little use for tracking. Cameron explained that these were just a tool and had little to do with the urge to fly. But he had used them as a photographer, and they probably started him thinking of making bat-wings of his own. What he ended up building was very similar to the wings Tommy Boyd used, but rather than starting just below the shoulders, they rode just above the waist.

Cameron attributed the fatality rate of the batmen of the thirties and forties to the fact that they routinely opened their chutes below 500 feet. "The 'perfect' parachute jump was thought to be one where the opening shock and touchdown were simultaneous," he wrote. That gave little or no time to deal with the many snags that could arise. Cameron, therefore, always pulled his ripcord at 2,000 feet when jumping with his bat-wings, but the extra altitude proved only just enough. His wings created a "burble" behind him that wouldn't let the wind pull the pilot chute away, and his parachute wouldn't open till he was two or three hundred feet above the ground.

Cameron once told his son, Lyle Cameron Jr., what it felt like to hold the bat-wings during a jump. "Put your feet on a chair, and then lay out and have two more chairs where your arms are, extended out, like you're skydiving. Hold on to that for sixty seconds, suspended from three chairs. Hang on to that for sixty seconds—you can do that, you can jump the bat-wings." If you can't, Cameron recommended, try doing push-ups with an ever-widening arm placement. But with the wings Cameron was using, even the most bulging-biceped skydiver would add only fifteen seconds to a sixty-second free fall.

The movements used to navigate a free fall were useless with wings. A dip of an arm with a wing would not result in a turn. Instead, Cameron explained, the batman should simply drop his toes, just as a plane turns primarily with the elevators on the tail's horizontal stabilizers. "Six inches to a foot will give extremely fast turns," he wrote.

Cameron made his bat-wing jumps in 1965. But, like others before him, he saw a future of long and easy flights that didn't require a parachute to land. "The size of gliders has been reduced so eventually there will be a meeting point when skydivers can exit the jump ship and soar for hours. This will require a super-lightweight, semi-rigid wing." (This future has almost arrived with Roberto Stickel's Pyxis; see chapter 29.) Cameron understood that for better aerodynamics the reserve would have to come off the stomach, and he was already working out a way to get the ripcord out to where the hands were, so he wouldn't have to let go of the wings to pull.

But Cameron's experiments with wings never progressed beyond a single layer of cloth. Whatever his pronouncements about the future of flight for skydivers, without new, lighter, materials Cameron could not achieve a glide ratio any better than what Clem Sohn had achieved. Had he been able to make some innovation to better their performance, he undoubtedly would have continued experimenting with them. As it was, by the end of the 1960s he had given up bat-wings altogether, though they never caused him the slightest nick.

In fact, the only jumping injury he ever experienced was in Bolivia. Having forgotten to calculate the extra altitude from taking off in the mountains, hypoxia hit Cameron while he was still in the air. Muddled by the lack of oxygen, he botched the landing, broke a shoulder and an ankle, and was injured enough to keep him laid up in a Balboa hospital for six months.

However wild Cameron's life in the sky, he had another life that was far more risky and in which much more was at stake.

By the late eighties, Cameron was planning to retire to Honduras and sell parachutes. He was flying there when for some reason he needed to land on a dirt road. "Either carburetor ice got him, or he ran out of fuel," says Lyle Cameron Jr. "Nobody seems to know, the story's not clear." The plane touched down, but the nose flew back up again. One passenger was ejected, and when the plane came back down, everyone else on board was killed.

"Quite frankly, my dad was—he was a cloak-and-dagger kind of guy. He did things for our government and knew things that he shouldn't have known." One of those things may have been Jack Ruby. Logs of the calls Ruby made the night before he shot Lee Harvey Oswald show that he called Lyle Cameron.

After Cameron's death, his son received a call from someone telling him that his father was connected to the CIA, had "gone rogue," and had been assassinated. "There's a hundred ways to make a plane quit," he was told.

During his prime, Cameron was a controversial, larger-than-life character whose name was known to every jumper. But a sport that focuses on ever-new horizons quickly forgets its past heroes. Cameron's son put it another way: "You'll get your day in the sun, and then that sun will set faster on your ass than you can count." Despite all the pioneering work Cameron did at the dawn of skydiving as a sport, his research with NASA and his time in bat-wings, his longest-lasting contribution is a single word. On one jump, Cameron wound up landing in a farmer's field. The farmer happened to be out farming and came over to see if Cameron was all right. He asked if the plane Cameron had left had been on fire. When Cameron answered in the negative, the farmer asked (scratching his head in befuddlement, to be sure), "Whuffo you jump?" *Whuffo* immediately became the word for non-skydivers, thanks partly to Cameron's powers of dissemination as editor of *Sky Diver,* but also because such a word was sorely needed. Today skydivers still have to deal with the endless refrain from their more landlocked friends: "Why would you want to jump out of a perfectly good airplane?"

Flights of Fancy: Cliff Winters, Jim Poulson, Bob Hannigan

The ground-bound yokels who ask, "Why would you want to jump out of a perfectly good airplane?" would no doubt have asked Cliff Winters, "Why would you want to crash a perfectly good airplane into a house?" for that was his greatest pleasure.

For Winters, who had piloted the plane that crashed while he and Lyle Cameron were filming the plane-to-plane jump for *Ripcord,* batwings were just one small risk in a career packed to the brim with danger—which he ignored completely. Unfortunately, little is known of his winged jumps. How he built them, and when he flew them, is lost to history. We only know that he did. The details of his life, though, may give us some insight on the personality of the kind of a man who takes to human flight. Or possibly he is a freakish exception. If pushing the limits of risk meant giving the sport of skydiving a bad name, then Winters was sinking it in a deep cesspool.

The son of a minister, Winters was soft-spoken and polite,

according to those who knew him. He had learned how to use a parachute while in the 82nd Airborne, and, like many of the pilots of his generation, he learned to fly on the GI Bill. Soon afterward, he was performing winged jumps and other stunts for an air circus. Around the same time he started flying planes in South America, often landing himself in jail for helping revolutionaries. Somewhere along the way he lost a finger to a propeller while crop-dusting. Having recovered the digit, he put it in a jar, pickled it, and, back in the States, enjoyed showing it off at drop zones.

Eventually he "settled" in California, and when he wasn't scrambling out of mangled planes for *Ripcord,* he was performing his own on-the-wing antics (including wing-to-wing transfers) as part of his own air show—often in nothing but swimming trunks. Sometimes he would hang from the wing with one hand, or dangle by a leg from a rope ladder. Winters's show gained popularity in the early sixties, and at times he was performing the entire act nine times a day.

Winters had two stunts that gave him a reputation as a man willing to do anything. The first was his habit of crashing planes into houses. These small, flimsy shacks were built with two telephone poles placed six feet apart on the inside. Winters would take off in a plane with only a gallon of gas in the tank—to prevent an explosion—and half-sawed-off wings. He'd fly the plane straight into the house and cut the engine just before he hit. The poles would rip off the wings, the house would collapse over the fuselage, and Winters would emerge from the wreckage unscathed. On one such crash, Winters switched off the motor too late, and the spinning propeller caught on the crumbling house as it went through, flipping the plane over. Winters lived through that, too, but he learned to place a log across the floor of the shack to tear off the plane's wheels and gears and prevent any further flips.

A friend of Winters and Cameron, Brian Williams, once asked him what kind of cage he had in the cockpit to protect himself.

"No, no, just some pillows in there," answered Winters. "I wrap my legs and elbows with pillows—that's all that's necessary."

"And I thought, 'I'm talking to a madman,' " says Williams.

So it's only fitting that his other famed stunt was jumping in a straitjacket. Originally he had planned to have a secret ripcord somehow in his hand, but he never managed to work out the details. Instead he attached a small, wooden replica of an eight-ball to the ripcord at the shoulder so he could pull it with his teeth. The ball worked like a charm the first time Winters tried the stunt, but the second attempt didn't go so smoothly. Winters left the plane with the ball in his mouth. But the rush of air pulled it—and his dentures, according to one account—out of his mouth immediately. He struggled to reach it, and his harness began to slip off his shoulder. As he spun toward the earth, he snapped at the elusive ball with his teeth (or gums), like a dog after its own tail. There was no reserve, and no way to pull his only parachute. Somehow, though, he worked his harness back onto his shoulder and managed to bite the ball and pull. The next time he tried the stunt, he had an extra strap holding the two shoulder harnesses together.

Winters met his end much the same way Jimmy Goodwin did. At an air show in Chino, California, on Labor Day of 1963, he snap-rolled a biplane too close to the ground. He and the plane were destroyed.

+

We know what happened to Winters, but what happened to his wings? Lyle Cameron's wings now hang in a bar called the Bomb Shelter in Perris, California, Clem Sohn's were once on display in the

Lansing airport, and Tommy Boyd's dangled in the Smithsonian. Doubtless there are many bat-wings stuffed in closets, moth-eaten in attics, and rotting in garbage dumps. But some presumably Californian bat-wing jumper's wings exchanged hands in 1961 in Taft, California, providing more evidence that skydivers of that era would try whatever came their way.

"They had a pair of bat-wings," explains Jim Poulson, another Iowan batman, who bought the wings. "I said 'Bring them over here, I'll jump 'em.' They belonged to some guy—the guy that gave them to me was a crop-duster. He took off and went around the county, got killed in that plane. I jumped those bat-wings quite a few times." In a jump well recalled by parachutists in Taft at the time, Poulson and several wing-free jumpers once went to 18,000, feet, breathing oxygen on the way up. Somehow, someone gave the signal to jump before they were over the drop zone. One skydiver ended up landing as far as five miles away, but Poulson managed to fly back on his wings and made it to within twelve feet of the target.

Encouraged, he enlisted his girlfriend to help him make more. "I jumped a pair of them and they frayed out on me," says Poulson. "One side went out—actually, it was fiberglass, is what it was. I had chains on the outside to give them more weight, a little jack chain to hang a fixture, like you were going to walk a dog with it. It was over twenty pounds . . . it really took off."

Poulson, seventy-six today, still attends Bridge Day, the annual BASE jump in Virginia, every year, and makes a jump with his son.

✦

Poulson may still be jumping, but only one man who flew in the sixties is flying again in the new millennium. This rather large man stood in the BirdMan, Inc., offices in DeLand in January of 2003 on one rather ugly gray day. His body was round and his head was round, and other than some graying facial hair, he was a glistening Kojak bald. When he spoke, as Jari Kuosma measured him for a new Skyflyer suit, Bob Hannigan's voice came out soft, even timid. "I'm five foot ten, 264 pounds," he said, "but I'm going to try to get down to 210."

Eight weeks later, Hannigan was back in Washington State, where he owns a small drop zone, when his package arrived. There was no one there to explain how to use his new wings, so he watched the instructional video, put the suit on, and was soon heading skyward in a plane. "I just dove out the door and brought my wings together, started flying around. I said, 'Hell, this is easy.' " On his second jump he decided to try to bank to one side and spiral down. But he forgot to keep his legs down and went headfirst into an uncontrollable spin. He brought his wings back in, straightened out, and was able to get to the ground without further incident. "That kind of spooked me, but I thought, 'Well, if I'm out of control I can always get back into control. But I better get used to it before I do any tricks.' "

Hannigan had a head start on getting used to it—he'd flown with his own wings forty years earlier. The yearning for more freefall time and better tracking was not limited to the big drop zones in California. Wherever there were planes and parachutes in the sixties, there was a good chance someone was trying wings. "I played a very small part in the development of the wing suit," says Hannigan humbly. But from 1935 to 1995, with minor exceptions, there was no development to speak of, and Hannigan's humility illustrates the point that wings in the sixties were worn in the spirit of experimentation, by those willing to do whatever they could to stay up longer, as well as by those willing to try whatever they could dream up, regardless of risk.

The jumping career that led to bat-wings started with a game of golf. Hannigan was trying to make a putt on a green close to a road when his roommate drove by. "He said 'We're going to Walla Walla to make a skydive.' So I threw my stuff over the fence.

"I jumped off a fire hydrant a few times, put the gear on, and away we went. We jumped from 2,000 feet and there were no static lines, no sleeve, no pilot chute. And the main that we were jumping—the guy had kept it in his basement. Rats had chewed the lines off, and he had just sewed them back on." Surviving such a first jump seems to have made Hannigan eager to see just what else he could survive:

> One good friend of mine, who I used to do demos with, used to always pull low. His name was George Golightly, and he's one of the few black guys that I've seen skydiving, especially in the old days. I said, 'Hey, if you go in, no one is going to give a shit the next day.' He said 'That's all bullshit. You just want all the glory for yourself.' So one thing led to another and we went up and had a low-pull contest. In those days we didn't have altimeters, we had stopwatches so we knew how many seconds we had left.
>
> Well, we jumped out at 7,000 feet, facing each other. So I've got my stopwatch and I keep looking at it, and looking at the ground. But he's not looking at the ground—he's not looking at anything. He's not going to pull until I pull. So I start getting ground effect around 2,000 feet. The earth starts spreading out and it's coming up fast—and I'm way past my time. I look at George and he's just staring at me. So I realized there was only one thing to do. I came in like I was

going to pull. As soon I went in, he pulled. Then, when he pulled, I pulled.

Having triumphed in the low-altitude contest, Hannigan and his friends turned their attention to other challenges, like trying to make contact during free fall.

Up in the northwest corner of the country, jumpers altered parachutes themselves, cutting up their canopies with hot knives, changing the shroud lines, and doing anything they could to slow their fall. "In those days there were no rules," Hannigan says wistfully.

They were desperate to make that hookup in the air, as were skydivers at drop zones all over the country, so in 1965 they turned to wings to try to increase the distance they could track. The main problem they discovered was getting to the ripcord; the wind had a tendency to force the arms to stay outstretched. "We'd go buy different kinds of fabric, then we'd try solid wings, then ones with cuts in them, so you could move your arms. But when you put the cuts in them, then you're just falling straight down." Most of the time the wind would flip Hannigan on his back, where he'd stay for the rest of the free fall, forcing him to use the "belly wart"—his reserve. They did not continue to use their wingsuits after that summer.

They were still after more surface area, though, but decided it would be more natural to have it spread evenly around the body. After giving up on their wings, Hannigan and his friends started making full-body suits, sealed at the wrists and ankles with a snap. Vents let air in, but didn't let it out. They called them "balloon suits": "You really slowed down, you really looked like a balloon, but you really didn't have a lot of control."

Controlled flying finally arrived for Hannigan with his BirdMan wingsuit. On his fourth jump with it, he managed to hook up with another jumper. "I just frogged up into a style tuck—I'm able to fly real tight. What takes time is getting to where you can maximize forward speed, by curving your shoulders and your arms and getting your legs straight without wobbling." He's now able to fall at less than 60 miles per hour. "With all my gear, I'm 280 pounds, so I'm working the suit good."

Clem Sohn, in Hanworth in the spring of 1936, demonstrates how he opens one wing at a time to lessen the "terrific pull" on his body before his wings begin to fly.
Source: British Pathé

A nice day for a white webbing: The founder of BirdMan, Inc., Jari Kuosma, models his Firebird wingsuit.
Courtesy of Bird-Man International OU

A poster of Sohn on a Parisian wall, behind the man himself,
advertises what would be his last jump. Source: Francis Heilmann

Floyd Davis, age 22, before takeoff in
Flint, Michigan, where he fell 6,000 feet
after his parachute fouled in the wings
shown attached to his back.
Courtesy of the Associated Wire Press

Looking sharp: Elmo Bannister in the
pointiest bat-wings of the millennium.
Source: Archives of Tom Sitton

William Picune in his first set of wings. Further innovation would lead to larger wings, closer to those of Sohn.
Source: Pat Picune

Clem Sohn's biggest fan, Roland Kumzak, spreads his square but otherwise Sohn-inspired wings for the camera.
Courtesy of the *Iowa Register & Tribune*

The "Yorkshire Birdman," Harry Ward, testing his bat-wings in a makeshift flight simulator.

Source: *The Yorkshire Birdman* by Harry Ward with Peter Hearn

The members of the Death's Angels Sky Circus (left to right): *George Manus, Elmer Kanta, Jimmy Moll, and the sixteen-year-old Robert X. Leeds standing in his bat-wings.*

Source: Robert X. Leeds

Red Grant, in one of his better moods, tracks over California farmland in the next generation of Tom Sitton–made wings. Source: Tom Sitton

Leo Valentin flies off the newsstand.
Source: Francis Heilmann

The full story of Louis Faure is lost to history, but his wings can still be seen hanging in Pau. Source: Francis Heilmann

André Vassard's wings never tasted air—a roman candle killed him before they had their chance.

Roger Malaussena, inventor of the first inflatable wings (not shown here).

Source: Francis Heilmann

Stuntman Gil Delamare shows off his shards.

Source: Francis Heilmann

Rudolf Richard Boehlen's wingspan was so great that he couldn't stand without a platform . . .
Source: Hans A. Jenny

. . . or land without falling over.
Source: Hans A. Jenny

Walt Peca adjusts Art Lussier's wings in the wilds of Michigan. Source: Charlie Laurin

Impervious, as always, to the windchill factor and all other discomforts, Art Lussier (or possibly Charlie Laurin) spreads his wings moments after exiting the Piper Cub.
Source: Charlie Laurin

AIR SHOW

presented by the MICHIGAN PARACHUTE TEAM
at the SAGINAW MUNICIPAL AIRPORT
3 miles East of Saginaw on Janes rd.

World's only living Batman
Art Lussier

SEE:

✹ A Parachutist falling over a mile before opening his parachute

✹ The Free-Fall contest, the most daring & dangerous contest ever conceived by man

✹ A mass parachute jump

✹ A man jumping an untested experimental parachute

✹ All the stunts ever attempted by parachutists

✹ Sixteen parachute jumps in ninety minutes

World's youngest Parachutist
14 year old - Mike Lussier

FREE Every 100th paid admission wins a free airplane ride
Every 500th paid admission wins a free flying lesson

ADMISSION   Adults 75¢   Children 35¢

Sunday Aug. 17

2:00 P.M.

*The Michigan Parachute
Team advertises "All the
stunts ever attempted by
parachutists."*
Source: Charlie Laurin

*Bird by bird: Lyle Cameron and Tommy Boyd meet for what will be Boyd's last flight
(with Don Molitar in the extensions photographers use to slow their fall.)*
Source: Lyle Cameron Jr.

*Cliff Winters in one of his
rare down to earth moments.*
Source: Smithsonian

Burt Lancaster, if he'd done his own stunts for
The Gypsy Moths. *Instead, it's Jay Benefiel.*
Source: Garth Taggart

*Garth Taggart, about to commit character
Scott Wilson's last jump to film for* The Gypsy
Moths. Source: Jay Gilford/Garth Taggart

Red smoke over Kansas: Taggart, a Gypsy Moth, airborne.
Source: Jay Gilford/Garth Taggart

Not scary enough: Bill Cole in his zip-on wings, which didn't thrill him.
Source: Bill Cole

Tom Sitton prepares to test the world's first ram-air wings, twenty years before Patrick de Gayardon flew his ram-air wingsuit.
Source: Tom Sitton

John Carta invented his Plexiglas feathers to help him fly away from cliff walls. Source: Ken Reed

"You know, I been thinking: nobody has ever ridden a Jet Ski off Niagara Falls, have they?" Carta once wondered aloud. A week later he was killed in a plane crash.
Source: John Carta/Ken Reed

Skysurfing over Chamonix: Patrick de Gayardon at the other sport he practically invented, with Joe Jennings behind the camera.
Source: Joe Jennings.
Photo by Richard Stuart

With steak in hand, Leo Dickinson leaps off a cliff, luring Lucy the peregrine falcon into flying first at him, then with him.
Source: Leo Dickinson, Leo@AdventureArchive.com

Two skier friends watch as Jean-Albert skims down Mount Verbier, just feet above their heads, ten feet above the ground. His shadow keeps up with him on the snow behind him.
Source: Myriam Lang-Willar/ Ride The Planets

*Christoph Aarns and Patrick
Barton shake hands before taking
their carbon fiber wings for a
nearly horizontal test drive.*
Source: Dädalus Service

*Felix Baumgartner, on his way up
to 30,000 feet before his historic
crossing of the English Channel.*
Source: © ulrichgrill.com

The Pyxis, brainchild of Roberto Stickel, will let you soar like a hang glider or fly like a Skyray—and it pops off when you're ready to land. Source: Roberto Stickel

Yep, they're big. Yves Rossy's Jet-Man has a ten-foot wingspan, jet engines, and folds in half. Source: Yves Rossy

Birdman in black: Jeb Corliss about to dock onto Luigi Cani under canopy, a practice stunt toward the eventual goal of touching down without any canopy at all. Source: Luigi Cani

19

Band of Gypsies:
Garth Taggart

*Skydiving had hardly shed its image as a pursuit for half-*suicidal maniacs by 1968, but serious parachutists were jumping with more skill than ever before. Gone were the days of falling through the sky pell-mell, tossed about by the wind like a Ping-Pong ball on bingo night. Though many of the breakthroughs that were achieved by that year seem almost laughable in comparison with what skydivers can do today, at the time they were great strides that demonstrated just how far skydivers had come in their ability to move freely through the air as well as land where they wanted to. The first baton pass in North America had been made in 1958, by Lyle Hoffman and James Pearson. Soon after that, skydivers were passing the baton around in groups and swimming through hula hoops. The first six-way star formation was performed in 1968, and in that same year the Para Commander parachute came out. With its system of vents, it was the most maneuverable parachute yet. A similar parachute called the Crossbow hit the scene then, too. Its major innovation was to move the "belly wart"—the reserve parachute worn on the stomach—off the front and onto the back. By 1967, jumpers in California were making ten-way stars, and international accuracy and style contests had become regular events.

The advances in technique, gear, and free-fall photography, combined with the public's view of the rising sport as something for wild men, meant just one thing: it was time for a Hollywood movie.

James Drought's novel *The Gypsy Moths* had come out in 1964 and made it into the hands of film director John Frankenheimer (Bobby Kennedy, a good friend of Frankenheimer's and a fan of the novel, may have given it to the director to read). The plot is simple, even indispensable: a couple of guys are touring the country as show jumpers, there's antagonism, there's a love affair, there are scenes of nearly fatal disasters, and a scene of fatal disaster. And the bat-wing, so seductive to the daring few, kills, even in fiction.

In one scene toward the end of the book, the character Rettig plans on performing "one of the most dangerous stunts on the program"—a jump in bat-wings. But instead of calling them bat-wings, as they were still known in the parlance of the sport at the time, the suit is called "the cape." And "the cape" is uttered with shuddering fear and awe, as if it were the monster in a poorly funded horror film. But the cause of death in this case would be more psychological than technical. "Rettig had told me about guys he'd heard of or known that had jumped the cape," the narrator explains before the scene where he's to jump with the wings. "A lot of them had never pulled open their chutes and ridden the cape into the ground. And you didn't know whether you were the kind of guy that'd do that until you at least made one cape jump." In the movie version the character goes on to explain that with the freedom and exhilaration a jumper experiences when wearing the cape comes a feeling that the flight can last forever. When Rettig makes his caped jump, he never opens his parachute, never even touches his ripcord, and he slams into the ground not far from the crowd, having flown to the last available inch. Later the narrator takes up the cape, to keep the act alive in their show, and has to resist the urge to try to fly forever, as his friend had.

In order to shoot such tricky scenes, Frankenheimer needed to assemble a team of some of the best skydivers and aerial cinematographers around. The year was 1967, and the television series *Ripcord* was in full swing, inspiring young daredevils to become the next generation of skydivers. When anyone in Hollywood had needed to shoot a skydiving sequence, they had turned to Bob Sinclair, the show's primary stuntman—now the most legendary old-timer skydiver, who is perhaps most famous for taking Johnny Carson on possibly the most famous free fall of all time. But for the second season Lyle Cameron and *his* gang came along, underbid Sinclair, and started shooting for *Ripcord.* The animosity between them remained, and the Hollywood execs for *The Gypsy Moths* wanted to step away from all the poison and find someone new. One had a skydiving relative who knew the filmmaker Carl Boenish, a masterful cinematographer who was up on all the latest technology and techniques. Boenish, as cameraman and skydiver, was to find all the jumpers for the film.

Frankenheimer had only one request: since the stars of the film, Gene Hackman (as Joe Browdy) and Burt Lancaster (as Mike Rettig), were tall men, and would not be making any actual jumps themselves, their parachuting doubles had to be similar in size—nothing under six feet allowed. A jumper in Boenish's circles named Garth Taggart made the cut, as did his pal Russ Benefiel and a handful of other jumping friends. Boenish and Taggart asked one friend and excellent jumper,

Ray Cottingham (who met the height requirement), to join them for the shoot. But Cottingham had been working for Shell Oil for a couple of years and first asked his employers what they thought of letting him resign to make the movie. He came back to Boenish and Taggart and explained that it would be unethical to quit. "That was the last group of people to have loyalty to a company," says Taggart. Cottingham did eventually leave the job for a career in free-fall photography, only to regret that he had waited so long to "break away," as skydivers say.

Taggart, however, had no loyalties, or anything else, holding him back. "The first thing I did when I found out I was going to be one of the guys, I just went to the library and researched it," says Taggart, who with Benefiel would wear the bat-wings for the film. "It turned out that almost everyone from the thirties and forties died. That just made me want to do it more. In those days we didn't think gravity could kill us—I was convinced I could live through bouncing."

When Taggart was a kid, his father—a stoic man, not usually given to fun—had packed the family in the car and taken them to the airport in Richmond, Indiana, to see the flight of a batman. Unfortunately there was too much wind that day, and the jump never happened. But the bird-seed had been planted, and as Taggart grew up and saw bat-wing flights in newsreels, and countless miles of paratrooper footage from World War II, he knew he wanted to be a jumper.

Taggart joined the navy, and right around the time he got out, *Ripcord* had begun to air. A month later he read an article about Bob Sinclair's skydiving school. "That Friday night I was in Elsinore." It was 1962, and the drop zones were filled with tough jumpers who'd made their first jumps during the war. "I remember thinking 'God, I wish I got into this earlier so I could be one of the pioneers.' I was in that second wave. The first was ex-military—no necks, just a bunch of gorillas. I was the first guy on the drop zone with a neck."

His instructor was Denny Manning, son of the legendary Spud Manning, who had inspired Clem Sohn with his stability and controlled movements in the air. Denny was a confident and understanding teacher whose kindly manner soothed his students' fears and gave them confidence that the sport was safe. But when Taggart and his fellow cubs found themselves in a plane with an open door, they were alarmed to discover that the reassuring Manning was not with them. Instead, a burly—and surly—ex-paratrooper was at the edge, shouting at everyone to jump. Taggart survived the experience and went on to become an innovator not only in the technical aspects of jumping—he participated in the first ten-way and the first sixteen-way stars, and filmed some of the first formations—but also in the social aspects of the sport.

These days, skydivers meet frequently at national and international "boogies," which are gatherings neither for competition nor profit, but solely for fun. Taggart started them in the late sixties, largely to give smaller drop zones the opportunity to jump out of the larger planes that would come to participate in the event. Taggart and his pals were leaping together and making formations in ever-greater numbers, and the glee that comes with falling next to fifteen of your friends is not something you achieve with a Cessna. The first boogie took place in Taggart's hometown, Richmond, Indiana, where Taggart and his friends raised money for the boys' and girls' clubs, and arranged to have the boy scouts clean up after them. (The word *boogie* was not Taggart's invention, but was borrowed from New Zealand slang for getting together and having a good time, whatever the activity. The usage was reinforced by Robert Crumb's popular "Keep on Truckin'" character, known as "Boogie Man." By the second boogie, Crumb's long-striding pinhead was appearing on the flyers for the events.) Now boogies are international affairs with jumpers often numbering in the thousands.

Russ Benefiel was more of a loner. He was an inspector for a major aircraft manufacturer, and loved taking part in record-breaking formations, but did not enjoy the drinking and boasting that inevitably followed a day in the air. He seemed closer to his dog, who was always with him when he was on the ground, than he did to any of his fellow jumpers.

But the gathering of actors, filmmakers, and skydivers in Kansas for the filming of *The Gypsy Moths* in 1968 was not a social event. The height restriction that had worked as a convenient way of turning down envious jumpers who wanted to be in the film, but happened to be too short, also worked to turn down local skydivers who hoped to make it into the movie. Coincidentally, everyone in the skydiving camera crew stood taller than six feet, as well. "So when we showed up at the airport in Wichita, they asked us, 'Are all you parachuters so tall?' " says Taggart.

The wings and gear that Taggart and Benefiel were to use needed to satisfy two criteria. "It had to look good for the camera, and let us survive." The cosmetic requirements were easy enough to satisfy; it was the survival part that was the challenge. Skydivers had just started using gear that kept both the main canopy and the reserve on the back. If the main went foul, it could now be cut away so the reserve wouldn't tangle with any already existing mess when it opened. The wings, though, increased the chance that a chute would snag on its way up, and they intensified the vacuum, or "burble," behind the jumper where a pilot chute could get stuck. Add four containers of canned smoke to the person to further complicate matters, and two parachutes were simply not enough. So the caped duo wore a third parachute on the front. "With three open, it might slow us down so we could live if we landed," says Taggart. Instead of cutting away, they planned on just keeping everything they had up in the air, no matter how ill-formed the canopies were. "And another innovation for how not to get killed: we kept an ambulance and paramedics on the ground."

To get the pilot chute to clear the burble, Taggart had to head straight down, picking up speed like a diving falcon. But with all the extra weight, the chutes they were using needed to be large ones, and that meant a hard, hard opening, the kind that makes you see stars. Taggart learned to feel the pilot chute whisking away, and as soon as he did he would sit up, slowing his fall before the main opened, softening the blow. "Yeah, we thought we were pretty hot," he says of his mastery. Taggart and Benefiel made about 150 winged jumps apiece for the movie and managed never to have a malfunction, though Taggart did once land in a sheep pen.

The cameramen's cloth extensions were not enough to slow their fall as much as the wings were slowing Taggart and Benefiel, and at first they only had five to ten seconds to shoot during each jump. The problem was eventually solved by putting cuts in the wings, making them effectively useless for any real flying. "It was strictly for Hollywood. We made no attempts to make it aerodynamic or do anything else."

As preposterous as the cause of death for the character of Rettig might have seemed to actual skydivers of the day, Taggart did understand the "hypnotic effect" free fall could have. He and Jay Gifford, another stuntman on the set, discussed it. "I didn't associate it with the wings at the time, but even without the wings, when you get into a track position, you don't want to break out of that. You're going 180 miles per hour and it feels good. You don't want to stop."

Though he may have been doing well in the air, on the ground

Taggart had a problem—he was pretty much drinking up every cent he was making. On one wing-free jump, his trusty World War II canopy opened inside out and one of the panels exploded. Enough of the chute remained to get him to the ground safely, but because he didn't have enough money for a new canopy, he just sewed the cloth together. For the rest of the filming, he was jumping a 27-foot chute instead of the usual 28.

The most spectacular jump of their lives was for the film but not *in* the film: a night jump into downtown Hollywood on the opening night. The stunt jumpers and film crew descended onto Sunset Boulevard in front of a crowd of moviegoers and 700 skydivers—in their jumpsuits—cheering as they touched down.

But not long after that triumph, Taggart found himself on the East Coast, where his lifestyle was out of sync with the other jumpers. "My drinking was out of control. They didn't start jumping till ten in the morning, and I was too drunk by then. I drank myself right out of that sport." Taggart signed up for Alcoholics Anonymous and hasn't had a drink in thirty years. He also hasn't made more than a few jumps in those thirty years. "You can't not drink and stay in that crowd," he says. He's now the head of a small engineering service company three miles from the ocean in San Clemente.

Benefiel went to school to become a chiropractor and hasn't been heard from since. "If you find him, let us know," says Taggart. "We're all dying to see him."

Thy Words Have Upholden Him
That Was Falling

On the back of Bill Cole's car, tailgaters can read stickers that say, NO FEAR? FEAR GOD! This is both a recommendation for the cocksure and a self-description. No other four words could better sum up Cole, a man of two reigning passions: risking his neck and deciphering the word of the Lord. If there are two distinct types of winged jumpers—the experimenters and the fearless—Cole plummets squarely into the camp of the latter. He seems to have started where Cliff Winters left off.

Cole is now in his seventies, his mobility severely restricted thanks to a mangled foot, ankle, and tailbone, the result of his last jump, in June of 2004. His parachute's steering lines—which are also its brakes—did not descend to reaching distance, and he crashed into the ground hard. "I felt the spinal compression right up my spine to my shoulders," he says. "Now I'm a mass of arthritis from one end to the other." As unpleasant as this must seem, after a lifetime spent just out of reach of death's clutches, Cole's injuries seem like potatoes of the smallest order.

Cole grew up making bombs out of the unexploded ammunition he and his brothers recovered from a pond used by the local rifle range as a dump. Before he'd spent any time under a parachute, he'd been attacked by a bear and had wrestled a Bengal tiger. And his first jump took place without the slightest training. His brother had bragged about making three parachute jumps, and Cole, not to be outdone, went to the airport, watched the jumpers, and said, "I can do this." Less than forty jumps later he was a professional, performing stunts at air shows and appearing in countless television commercials.

Here's a sampling from his log book:

Jump No. 216	Harry had a Christmas sign. It tore out of his hands.
Jump No. 220	Stuck in door, couldn't catch Jerry Brooker.
Jump No. 351	Show jump at football game. I grabbed Bud Spencer's Foot. A-OK.
Jump No. 353	Hooked onto Bud Spencer. Overshot him on first pass. Collided helmets.
Jump No. 354	Just a hop 'n' pop. Snow all over and cooool cool.
Jump No. 358	Helmet fell over my eyes—too big.
Jump No. 436	Left aircraft without any chute. Got 28-foot chute from Larry. Good opening at 3,000 feet. Perfect!

Cole made that 436th jump, his notorious chuteless jump, on August 20, 1969, a year that was filled with oddball jumps for the

Canadian. It started in May, when Cole and three others set a Canadian altitude record while shooting footage for an ad for Carling Red Cap. The commercial was to show a pilot falling through the sky after an ejection, still attached to his seat. For the first take, Cole did the shooting and the crew jumped from 21,500 feet. That same day they broke their own record when they added a thousand feet to the jump, this time with Cole strapped to the seat—possibly the only altitude records ever made sitting down.

A month before the chuteless jump, Cole made some jumps for a television show called *Adventures in Rainbow Island.* For one of them he was to exit the plane embracing a mannequin, and hold on to her for the entire length of the fall and the landing. To tango effectively with her, Cole had to leave his reserve chute behind. He made it out the door and held the mannequin tight through free fall, but when he opened his parachute, one of the lines caught on the doll's neck, removing her head and breaking Cole's wrist. He could no longer hold the remaining body, and the mannequin ended up making her own chuteless jump weeks before Cole would.

A chuteless jump in the United States was an illicit affair. As Rod Pack had proved four years earlier, jumping without a parachute could have consequences for the pilot and others involved. After several practice jumps without a reserve—to make his weight as similar as possible to what it would be when he made the real jump—Cole, his pal Larry Costello, and a cameraman took off in a plane in Ohio and flew it to 13,200 feet over Canada. There they jumped out, and in free fall Cole began trying to make his way over to Costello. But Cole had done something differently this time. To give a better sense for the cameras of a man hurtling helplessly through space, Cole wore his harness inside his jumpsuit, cutting slits for the rings onto which he would attach the pack handed to him in midair. Once out of the plane, Cole found that he could not track the way he was used to, with his jumpsuit looser than usual. After much struggling, the hand-off finally happened at 6,000 feet.

"When I left the aircraft I just acted like there was a chute on my back," Cole explains, "so I didn't worry about it. I had the psychological idea that it was there—it was a psychological jump, that's all."

The jump may have been nothing at all to Cole, but it stirred up a tempest in the world of Canadian skydiving. The Canadian Sport Parachute Association booted him immediately. This had little effect on Cole's jumping career, though, as the CSPA had no legal jurisdiction. The only punishment they could dish out was to expunge him from their membership. This they managed to do twice. In 1973, Cole persuaded the CSPA to let him back in so that he could jump with his son. But soon afterward he mentioned on a talk show the possibility of jumping off the edge of the Grand Canyon. For that they kicked him right out again. Cole explained it in a post on dropzone.com: "Back in 1969, I kinda pissed on some of CSPA's rules . . . kinda like bent them a bit. CSPA, in turn, got pissed off with me and soon I was being pissed *on*. As a result, I pissed on some more of CSPA's rules, bending them more often and a little further than the last time. Again, I was pissed on. I set the Canadian High Alt record, and CSPA decided they would piss on me some more by initiating a set of CSPA "records" from much lower than my jump. This is pissing on me from altitude, so I pissed back on them through the press. They didn't like me pissing on them for pissing on me, so they suspended me for a second life term, and pissed on me again. Well, I was pissed off."

Not content just to hold the Canadian high-altitude record with a jump from 36,916 feet, Cole went on to make the Canadian high-altitude *night* record, from 30,571 feet. He also once tried jumping with a chute that had super-long lines. He landed on a roof and had to be rescued by the fire department. In 1973 he made a *second* chuteless jump, captured in the film *The Endless Fall,* and remains the only person ever to make two such jumps. Perhaps his greatest gaffe occurred while shooting for the Canadian Broadcasting Company, when he let go of a $100,000 camera during free fall. He was sued by the government and went bankrupt.

Somewhere along the line, Cole developed a real taste for getting as close as he could to the face of the earth without hitting it. "How I loved those low openings," he says. "You get to see who's looking up, and you get a real loud thunderclap—when you're that close to the ground, the thunderclap is deafening. That was the idea." At 500 feet, if things go wrong a reserve won't be of much use, so for many jumps he didn't bother wearing one. He also learned how to shake his ass to make sure the pilot chute escaped the burble just behind him. And to get the loudest possible effect, to best shock those below, he used two pilot chutes and packed his main very loosely. "That's not daring, that's just a lot of fun. Now everything is so sophisticated and what makes me laugh is all the bells and whistles they have to tell them different altitude—'Oh, you better pull at 3,000 feet'—all that free time lost."

One of Cole's lowest openings was also his lowest jump. The air show he was working for wanted to have an out-of-control plane fly in from elsewhere—as if it just happened to be flying by the spectacle— and then seem to crash just past a line of trees at the end of the airport. The plan included having a parachutist stay hunched down and hidden in the backseat. As soon as they were past the trees, he would jump out and the actual pilot would dive the plane down and land— the gullible would think they'd just seen a crash and a narrow escape. The problem was finding someone gullible enough to do the stunt.

"Like heck," said one jumper asked to consider the job. "I'll do it for $50,000." Bill Cole, though, did it for $210. When he hopped out of that airplane, he was at 150 feet. The jumper who'd turned down the job later told Cole he was crazy, to which Cole offered his stock response: "Nobody has more fun than me."

Of course, a man willing to leave a plane at 150 feet is not one to be frightened of something like a small set of wings, no matter how many people had died before him trying something similar. Inspired by *The Gypsy Moths,* which hit the theaters in 1969, Cole took the black jumpsuit he was wearing at the time and sewed zippers along the sides of it from ankle to wrist, with a gap on the sides where the harness could slide through. "With that much pressure on the zipper, you'd think it'd tear the teeth out, but it never did," he says (though a note in his logbook states that the "wings came partly off" on one jump). With a friend known as "The Buck-eyed Batman"—not a wing-wearer himself, despite the name—Cole made many winged jumps at air shows. The pair even jumped into a drive-in theater on a night when *The Gypsy Moths* was playing.

But the wings turned out to be too safe to meet Cole's adrenaline needs. "It was an interesting thing to have those wings. There wasn't anyone jumping with them that far back," he says, a bit mistakenly, "but I liked to maximize the risk and then beat it. For me, the wings were no big deal—just like the chuteless jump was no big deal."

Cole never bothered to figure out just how far he was flying, and he continued to jump with his buddies fairly close to the landing spot. "I'd have to turn around, track back, maybe pass the spot, and track back again—and since you can't fly around with those old canopies, I'd end up walking back. I never really liked the wings."

The reckless jumps Cole preferred caused him little fear. "I just knew nothing would happen to me, I knew I wouldn't die. And I don't fear dying because I know where I'm going."

So how does he explain the recent mangled state he's in? "This smashed foot is an answer to a prayer. I was going to meet this woman and I was afraid something was going to happen between her and me, and I was afraid I would give in. I said, 'Lord, do something to prevent something from happening.' "

God seems to have answered those prayers as well as many others Cole has sent heavenward. "I wouldn't change anything—I'd just start sooner. Maybe that would have stopped me from getting married."

Daring Young Man on a
Flying Trapeze: Tom Sitton

"I don't know what a skydiver looks like," says author and veteran jumper Brian Williams, "but Tom Sitton is the last person you'd think would want to jump out of an airplane." Despite the obligatory mustache of the sixties parachutist, Sitton's lankiness, precise language, and careful, problem-solving approach to his activities in the air marked him as a man who was not just a fearless daredevil—he was an engineer. And though he might not have fit the typical skydiver mold, his birdman career has spanned three generations of winged flight. He collaborated with one of the early bat-wing jumpers, went on to produce the world's first ram-air wingsuit, and is even now crafting the first folding semirigid wings.

Sitton was born on September 23, 1938, and within five years he was designing his own airplanes. His love of wings continued through his school years, and as soon as he graduated from high school, he joined the California Air National Guard, where he became a technician. While earning his undergraduate engineering degree at the City College of San Francisco, he joined the flying club, and before he'd had a single solo flight, he was experimenting with the capabilities of the craft he was in. With a more experienced copilot beside him, Sitton started testing the Piper Cub's limits and taking it for loops and spins.

While in school he also took a machine-shop course. The overreaching piloting, combined with the new machining and engineering skills, resulted in a man who could imagine his own aircraft and then bring it into existence. After a stint as a draftsman for Bechtel ("I was pretty good at putting lead on paper"), and a graduate degree from the Northrop Institute of Technology, Sitton took a job with NASA, where he designed the transport for the Lunar Lander.

At the suggestion of a co-worker there, Sitton headed down to the "Chick N Rib," a restaurant in Palmsdale owned by drop-zone owner Wayne Parker, to watch some skydiving films. "I saw these guys flying though hoops—I said, 'I gotta do that,' " says Sitton. And do that he did. He made a few static jumps and then bought a parachute from astronaut and test pilot Bruce Peterson. (When Peterson realized that a mere broken leg could take him off flight status, he decided to sell his gear.) With the prestigious canopy, Sitton made his first free fall, during which he experienced his first struggle for life. When he pulled his ripcord, the pilot chute stuck in the burble behind him as he fell. He understood the problem immediately, and for nineteen seconds he fought to make the air catch the chute and pull open his main canopy. "A hard arch got me out of it," he explains. "I *am* an aeronautical engineer."

When Sitton graduated from Northrop in 1965, he took a job at the Douglas Aircraft Company, soon to be McDonnell Douglas, and there he worked on the Nike antiballistic missile as well as the Delta rocket. But Sitton would not be content to do the theoretical work to send unmanned objects into the sky. In addition to his continued parachute jumping, he had joined the local balloon club, and at one of their meetings he saw stuntman Ralph Wiggins give a talk about his work with smoke balloons. Twenty or so people would hold down a balloon, he had explained, while inside it two men would pour kerosene onto a fire. Eventually the giant bag would fill with smoke, the holders would stop holding, and the balloon would head skyward. Wiggins would run up and jump onto a trapeze hanging below the balloon, get his legs over the bar, and hang from the knees as he floated farther and farther from the earth. After a short time, and a few tricks, the balloon would cool enough to stop flying, and Wiggins would drop from the bar to the gasps of horror from the crowd below. The balloon would upturn, spilling smoke everywhere, and Wiggins would open his parachute. Sitton was drawn to the work on the trapeze as well as to the dropping off of the trapeze. "It seemed like the thing to do," he says.

Sitton asked the organizers of his balloon club if he could jump out of a balloon. "They said, 'No way.' So I said, 'Okay, I can jump out of parachutes.' " And so he began developing a series of unique stunts he would perform once his canopy was open. First he tried the trapeze tricks he had seen Wiggins perform—hanging from the knees and then falling away before opening another parachute—then went on to more-adventurous stuff. He modified his parachute, giving it extra-long lines, then attached a 27-foot-long rope ladder. "I had a remote camera at the top of the ladder," says Sitton. "I'd kick the camera on, pull the releases, and start climbing down. It took me 60 seconds to get down it." In his trademark yellow jumpsuit, he would remove his reserve, attach it to the last rung, and then hang from the trapeze bar at the bottom of the ladder with nothing but a safety cable keeping him attached to the whole rig.

Sitton made one trapeze jump at the inauguration of the reconstructed London Bridge in Arizona in 1971. At 200 feet he was still hanging by the knees, and when he went to pull himself up to make a standing landing, hanging by his hands, he found that his foot was caught in the safety cable. He freed himself by using his free foot to kick out the trapped foot, but thereafter he stopped using the safety cord. "Seems risky, but I'd done all this before—I could hang by my hands for 60 seconds. Of course, if I ran into a thermal . . . I'd thought about it, but not much."

In 1964, on Sitton's twenty-sixth jump, he met the legendary Bob Sinclair on a plane. Sinclair was in the company of a paraplegic in a wetsuit, whom he had agreed to throw out of the plane and into the Pacific. It was to be a static-line jump, and as Sinclair had to follow the paraplegic out to make sure he didn't drown, Sitton agreed to pull the line back into the plane (the paraplegic wrote about the experience in an article titled "Jump, Cripple, Jump," for *Saga* magazine). This was the beginning of a beautiful friendship, and the two remain friends to this day. When Sinclair, who had filmed the first season of *Ripcord,* saw Sitton's trapeze work, he put him in contact with the makers of a television show called *Thrill Seekers,* and many of Sitton's acts appeared there.

Sinclair also introduced Sitton to one man who would have a much bigger influence on Sitton's path through the air. In the early seventies, Red Grant was working at a Budweiser plant near Taft, California—where Sitton was doing his jumping—and not making much money. He'd decided to get back into the bat-wing business to drum up some more funds, but he no longer had his wings and he needed someone who could help him build new ones. Sinclair introduced the two in his loft, which was outfitted with sewing machines and rigging equipment, and before long Sitton was building Grant fresh wings.

Unlike the outfits of the American bat-wing jumpers before him, Grant's last wings had been attached to a yoke or harness that took the pressure off his arms. When he met Sitton, he had the yoke, but no wings. Sitton first made him a new yoke of muffler tubing, which was much lighter than the heavy solid aluminum of the original. For the wings proper, he initially tried to duplicate, from Grant's description, his earlier version.

The new wings were essentially the same spar-and-cloth arrangement that other batmen had used, but they swept forward for better stability. That did not mean spins had been eliminated—it was with these wings that Grant found himself inverted over Niagara Falls. "He had said that those wings had a vicious spin," says Sitton. "I was under canopy at the time, and I went over to him to see if I could do something. But the steel spars were spinning around like a propeller."

The wings were in fact swept too far forward, past something called the "aerodynamic center." Though they were extending Grant's free-fall time by thirty seconds or so, they were catching too much air and were not flying forward very fast. In essence, the wing's pivot point was too far back—imagine stepping on the back end of a surfboard and having the front end pop up. They were certainly stable when flying, but they were so slow that Grant was constantly near the stall point. "Red didn't recognize it because he didn't have his original wings, and he didn't know that much about aerodynamics. And the guy he bought them from probably didn't know much, either."

For a year, Sitton helped Grant fine-tune the wings and built him several sets. He added a fiberglass leading edge to the cloth so that it would cut through the air better. But the bigger problem was the back edge. "I knew about flutter boundaries, I knew about the back of flags, I knew the main problem with small aircraft—that a rudder can go into a flutter mode and destroy itself." On surfaces floppy enough to flap, the air comes off the back edge in vortices, one after the other. These can kick back in a pulse and cause flutter, seriously reducing the efficiency of any wing. So, for the second generation of Grant's wings, Sitton added spars to make the material as stiff as possible.

After a year of watching Grant reap the benefits of his handiwork in the air, often while hanging from a trapeze, Sitton decided it was time to make a flight of his own. He made a few solo jumps with the wings he'd made, then he and Grant tried jumping together. But the winged duo would never work out perfectly. On their first paired jump they did not see each other again till they were on the ground. On a second attempt, a month later, Grant found himself with a Mae West. His reserve fouled, and he suffered a hard landing.

They tried again in Lancaster, California, where they had planned to film what Grant called "the greatest jump of the century." It was to be the first double bat-wing jump ever caught on film. Sitton was rigged up with a camera on the side of his helmet to capture the landmark event, and the filter he had on the lens was rather large. It created a small burble behind it, and the asymmetry was enough to put Sitton in a spin. He had to turn his head to regain control and was unable to film Grant or fly with him.

Grant was known to have something of a temper—he had once punched out someone in a grocery store who had asked where he could find *Mad* magazine—and the faulty jump pushed him over the edge. "He landed, threw his gear down, stomped across the desert, got in his car, and left," says Sitton, who had lent Grant the vehicle as well as $600. "Last I saw of him."

But it was not the last that Sitton saw of bat-wings. In the early 1970s, skydivers were making the switch from round, single-layer parachutes to square ones with two layers and air cells. The semi-rigidity of the canopies meant they no longer just slowed a fall; now they flew and could be steered, as well. To move the concept to wings was a natural leap for Sitton. "I realized that ram-air parachutes were the thing—when you fill a balloon up, you eliminate all that flutter." Before he had even purchased his own square parachute, he was making ram-air wings.

Another major change for the new wings was the degree to which they were swept forward. Sitton made most of his flights with a "yaw string"—a dangling piece of string meant to show the angle of flight and how the air was flowing—and he'd learned that the forward sweep was too great on the other wings.

When Sitton first started jumping with wingsuits himself, Grant had offered him a bit of advice. "Red said, 'I hope you get into trouble once—just to get some respect.' He got his wish." On one of his first jumps with his ram-air wings, Sitton found himself in a very stable position after exiting the plane—but he was flying on his back. No amount of wriggling could change his orientation. Even with the wings folded against his side, they were getting enough air to keep him flying wrong side up, and he ended up having to pull his ripcord while facing the sky. "I was all G-ed out from the opening—the hardest I ever had, little silverfish in front of my eyes. And I lost my gold-plated ripcord."

The scare didn't stop him from experimenting, and he made several more flights with these wings, the last of which was in 1981. Shortly afterward, Bob Sinclair, who had made some jumps for *Ripcord* with "rag and broomstick wings," wrote a letter to the United States Parachute Association asking permission for Sitton and himself to make and use metal wings they were designing. "We promise not to kill ourselves," he wrote. The new wings were to have their own quick release as well as their own parachute, predating the Skyray (see chapter 27) with these details by twenty years. Mike Horan, of the USPA Safety and Training Committee, wrote back that he had no objection at all.

On paper, Sitton had the new wings fully imagined, but they were never to be. Sinclair's attitude toward the whole sport was changing. He closed his loft and his skydiving school and began traveling around the United States in his bus.

Twenty years later, Sitton began to see wingsuits appear at his drop zone, as well as the Skyray and Yves Rossy in the news. Their sophisticated release systems inspired him to begin making wings once again. He wanted something that had the speed of the Skyray but could fit in smaller planes so that any skydiver could use it. The price tag on the Skyray is in the thousands of dollars, and if a skydiver is lucky enough to be able to afford one, it's unlikely he'll find enough partners to make a flock. "Jumping is a group effort. It's quite a thrill, going 200 miles per hour, blasting through clouds, but what do you do for an encore?" Sitton has now built a semirigid wing that is essentially a frame over which a fabric sleeve or a ram-air sleeve can be placed. And the wings are hinged so they can fold back and fit in the smallest of Cessnas.

He has kept the idea of the yoke with a link that will make the two wings operate as one. Handles will allow skydivers to keep the wings tight against the body. "A half-inch shift of the center of gravity puts you anywhere from a stall to 200 miles per hour." For a wind tunnel, he hangs his wings outside the window of his pickup on a set of pulleys. The lines are connected to fish-weighing scales with which he can measure the forces acting on his wings.

Eventually he hopes to make a larger, completely rigid version of the same wings, but apart from fabric rigging, every rivet on the way will come from Sitton. Missives from Sitton read something like this:

> The first shoulder fitting is finished and attached to the center section. Just took a break from the garage where I am machining the left shoulder clevis. Talked to Will at the drop zone today, who was having some trouble sewing the inboard zipper assembly, due, I think, to the tapered nature of the inboard rib around which the zipper assembly wraps. I suggested that instead of a complete sleeve, we put some grommets in the inboard side and attach to the rib with PK screws.

Sitton may be the only personal wing inventor with a degree in aerodynamics, mileage in bat-wings, and the passion to make a wing that trumps everything now in existence. Skyflyers who don't know what PK screws are will someday be glad that Sitton does.

Paying the Toll:
John Carta

Between the winged revivalists of the sixties and the wing-suiters of today, there were few birdmen, largely because the United States Parachute Association (formerly the Parachute Club of America) had banned bat-wings. Early logbooks sold at drop zones contained the following clause: "No wings, cloth extensions, or other forms of control surfaces may be used without written authorization from the main office of the PCA." But for BASE jumpers, flouting rules is second-nature; part of the fun, at least for some, is the sneaking into sites with sheer drops, the scurrying away before authorities arrive, and the feeling of getting away with something.

So it's no surprise that a man like John Carta ended up in wings. Carta had been a Green Beret and was the 118th person to jump from each of the four kinds of places that make up the acronym: Building, Antenna, Span, Earth—making him something of a pioneer in the sport.

Carta was most famous for riding a motorcycle off the 730-foot-high Forset-Hill Bridge in Auburn, California. He also successfully leapt off the Leaning Tower of Pisa as well as the Golden Gate Bridge. Wearing a wetsuit and a parachute, he once did a backflip off New York's George Washington Bridge. A motorboat picked him up out of the water, and he hid his parachute in some hedges along the shore. When he came back to get it the next day, the parachute—and the hedges—were gone. Construction workers were laying the foundation for a new building. On September 10, 1981, Carta jumped from a plane at 10,000 feet, holding a blue flare, and landed on the South Tower of the World Trade Center—exactly twenty years and a day before their destruction. Four days later he tried the stunt again, but missed and complained that he had to take a taxi to get to the towers.

The South Tower landing meant that, unlike tourists who took the more traditional route to the observation deck, Carta didn't have to pay a fee for the view. He did, however, have to pay a fifty-dollar fine for "unlawful parachuting." Perhaps that's why he was more conscientious when, on another jump from an airplane, he landed on the Verrazano Narrows Bridge. He left six quarters for the toll, shed his gear, and used his reserve to BASE-jump into the water.

Though he clearly had a sense of humor about his stunts, he also knew that risking his neck was what gave spectators a thrill—a fact that did not always comfort him. When he set out to make one jump, a small crowd gathered with lawn chairs and coolers of beer. He shouted at them, "This is my life, what are you coming out here with chairs for, what do you think this is?"

However great the risks he assumed, it was his earnest desire to live that eventually brought him to wings. On a jump from Yosemite Falls, he nearly met his end when, after opening his chute, he slammed into the wall of rock. Soon afterward he started thinking about how he could get away from a cliff before opening. His first wings were a single layer of cloth, but these eventually evolved into wings with Plexiglas feathers. Ken Reed, a documentary filmmaker who was working on a piece about Carta, says that when Carta next jumped off Yosemite Falls, now with his wings, he managed to fly at least a third of a mile away from the cliff.

Carta spoke of his wings as the beginning of something that would eventually become a sport, but he would not live to see himself proven right. In August of 1990 he jumped off the twenty-seventh floor of the then-unfinished American Presidents Companies building in Oakland. His parachute did not fully inflate, and he broke his back in three places. He was cited for trespassing by Alameda County, but the charge was later dropped, as the district attorney felt the broken back was punishment enough. Months later, still in casts and on crutches from this last injury, Carta boarded a vintage Lockheed PV2 Harpoon Navy patrol bomber. The pilot flew the plane over an air show in Clear Lake, California, and though it was not part of the planned spectacle, he buzzed the audience several times. The plane crashed, killing the pilot and his seven passengers, including Carta.

Part Four

THE GROWING FLOCK

The Legacy of Patrick de Gayardon

Patrick de Gayardon proudly stretches out in his ram-air wings.
SOURCE: FRANCIS HEILMANN

23

Solo Flight:
Patrick de Gayardon

When you talk to wingsuit jumpers today, some of them pay lip service to "the pioneers who came before" (while others are entirely oblivious of the long history that preceded them). But the word "pioneers" implies a kind of *cumulative* history, of experimenters blazing trails for those that would follow, as if all bat-wing jumpers built on what had been learned by those before them. In almost every case, though, this is not the case. The humans who have tried to fly like birds throughout history are like teenagers in love: they can't learn from anyone else's mistakes, and they generally think they're the only ones.

But if ever there was a man who could be called a pioneer in the world of wingsuits, who truly changed the course of personal flight for all those who would come after him, that man is Patrick de Gayardon, known to skydivers everywhere as Deug. And though his brilliance in the air and his humor, as well as his physical beauty, would inspire those who saw him and those who knew him, he was a man isolated by his monomania.

Gayardon was a French aristocrat, and the son of stuntwoman and skydiver Marie-France de Gayardon, who was killed in a car accident when he was two (see chapter 14). The orphaned Patrick grew up with his grandmother, went to school in Lyon, and learned how to parachute while in the French army. Whether from his mother or from some previous airborne life, Gayardon had flight in his blood. Once he'd served his two years in the military, he became a professional skydiver.

In the early nineties he was on the French eight-way team, and though he was known to be an excellent skydiver, he was not considered a team player. Around the same time, he had begun to experiment with "sky surfing," and when Reebok decided to sponsor him, he quit the team and started his extraordinary solo career. "He had much more fun by himself than staying in the sky with seven other freaks—*people*—and a coach he had to listen to," says Oliver Furrer, a Swiss friend of Gayardon's and a fellow skysurfer who often filmed him.

Though he had not invented the concept, Gayardon developed skysurfing till it was a sport that was much more than just standing on a board and tracking horizontally. With his feet locked on to what was essentially a snowboard, he could perform helicopter twirls, spins, and revolutions, freestyling like no one before him.

He also developed a quick-release system so the board could be immediately jettisoned. He had cause to use it with another invention of his: tandem skysurfing. Gayardon made his first tandem sky-surfing jump with Eric Fradet, a man who today has made more than 25,000 jumps. Fradet was on the back of the board, Gayardon on the front, and they fell in a more or less stable upright position till one of them moved. Gayardon fell forward and Fradet fell backward, but, of course, they could not both cut away from the board at exactly the same time. Gayardon managed it first, and as he fell away, the board whipped with incredible torque before Fradet could free himself. He had to land with two broken ankles.

Once the cutaway system was fixed, by making a release that would free both surfers regardless of who pulled it, Gayardon made the first successful tandem skysurf with Wendy Smith—and this time he was in total control.

Just as Arnold Schwarzenegger elevated, redefined, and popularized the world of bodybuilding while winning its major prize for many consecutive years, Gayardon developed and popularized the sport of skysurfing and went on to win many of its contests. The United States had its first real exposure to the new sport in 1991, when Gayardon made a commercial for Reebok's "Life Is Short/Play Hard" marketing campaign. The sight of Gayardon twirling with his board on television inspired a generation of skydivers to try to do the same, and the commercial is responsible for turning the activity into a sport. Here's how Troy Harman, winner of the of the gold medal for skysurfing in the 1997 X Games, describes seeing the footage shortly after making his first skydive ever:

> What I saw then and there blew me away. It was a Reebok commercial featuring a dude named Patrick de Gayardon skydiving over the French Alps with a snowboard on his feet. He was rippin' out moves left and right to "Suicide Blond" by INXS. It was insane! I got the chills because I knew that I had found the ultimate pursuit.
>
> My life changed at that point.

The sport had become a kind of fandango between the skysurfer and his cameraman. The jumper doing the filming had to be nearly as adept as the man with the board, circling him, flipping upside down, flying past to give the illusion of a more horizontal movement, and knowing every move of the choreography. Gayardon would win the first real international skysurfing tournament in 1993, with Gus Wing circling him behind the camera. A year later, Gayardon and three others would skysurf into the Winter Olympics as part of the opening ceremonies.

Later that year a skysurfer named Rob Harris, who had, needless to say, been inspired by Gayardon, toppled his reign at a competition in Arizona. Harris's moves and timing with his partner, Joe Jennings, were filled with enough grace and beauty to rival any Olympic ice skater, and few have approached his skill since. But Gayardon, even though he had just lost to Harris, immediately took to him. "Patrick had very few close friends," says Andi Duff, who flew camera for Gayardon at the meet. "In half of his mind he was always in the sky, and that made it difficult for people to have a conversation with him—as soon as the conversation went away from skydiving, they lost him. But Harris blew Patrick away, and they became really close friends. When they were talking abut skydiving, that was a totally different sphere. He was known to be the best and then we came in second to Harris, but Patrick didn't give a shit about that. He was just amazed. They got along well on the ground because they both had their heads in the skies." In the locker room after the event, Gayardon invited Harris and Jennings to join him in Florida to shoot some footage for MTV Sports.

At ESPN's first X Games in 1995, Harris and Jennings won the skysurfing event and brought worldwide attention to the sport. But later that year Harris died while making a jump from 5,000 feet for a Mountain Dew commercial—his canopy fouled and he did not have enough time to use his reserve. Gayardon and Joe Jennings scattered Harris's ashes over Rhode Island during the following year's X Games.

By then Gayardon had gained the sponsorship of the Italian watch company Sector to help push their "No Limits" ad campaign and motto. With the new cash flow he could do practically anything he could dream up. Thus began a series of spectacular stunts. A BASE jump from the Eiffel Tower was merely the beginning (when he landed, the gendarmes rushed over to him, ready with the cuffs, but as soon as they recognized his noble countenance, they put them away). For Sector he skysurfed over the North Pole, snowboarded off a cliff in Norway, jumped out of a helicopter and into a cave known as Sótano de las Golondrinas (or the Cave of the Swallows), and BASE-jumped over Angel Falls, the highest waterfall in the world (more than 3,000 feet), deep in the Venezuelan rain forest. In November of 1995 he set a new record for the highest jump without oxygen, when he stepped out of an Ilyushin 76 some 41,910 feet over Moscow. The temperature at that altitude was 67 degrees Fahrenheit below zero.

He also headed to the Arctic Circle with Joe Jennings to jump off a glacier in skis. To get enough footage of him in free fall with his skis on, they first did many jumps onto flat ice. On one of them, Gayardon's ski cracked through the ice. The pair went down on their bellies, removed their packs, and tried not to move too quickly. Moments later the plane landed next to them. The ski had only broken a little ice bubble; they were lying on ice several feet thick.

The BASE jumping, though, was not part of Gayardon's true goals. "He was really afraid of BASE jumping," says Furrer. "He did it sometimes because of the pushing from Sector. If you put $200,000 in front of someone, it's easier to answer the question 'Should I do it, should I not do it?' " For many of the BASE jumps he only made a minimum number of jumps while other jumpers worked, in essence, as stunt doubles for much of the footage.

Gayardon's mind rarely left the sky, and he had long been thinking of a way to stay there longer. His lateral mobility when skysurfing had been something like flying, and it was this more than anything that he wanted to extend. In the late eighties he went to Virginia for Bridge Day, the annual BASE jump off the New River Gorge Bridge (one of the few legal BASE jumps in the United States). There he ran into his friend John LeBlanc, the vice president of Performance Designs, one of the world's largest canopy manufacturers. "I was telling him about my desire to extend free fall," says LeBlanc. "He said, 'Yes, yes, yes—a balloon suit.' But I was thinking of a suit designed for tracking. Something just like a modern parachute, with an upper and lower surface and a mesh-covered inlet. But I was a talker and he was a doer."

Gayardon began studying bird flight, Leo Valentin, and other bat-wing jumpers. "Many of them used rigid parts—from my first jumps on, my instructors would forbid them because they said they were dangerous," Gayardon explained to the French skydiving magazine *ParaMag*. "Most of their wings were mono-surface. The only one who thought of bi-surface wings was Leo Valentin, but they were rigid and it was unfortunately fatal for him." Once he had sponsorship he could take the time to build the ram-air wings he had discussed with LeBlanc, as well as test them in a wind tunnel.

To the untrained eye, Gayardon's wingsuit looked very similar to the canvas wings that Bill Cole, Charlie Laurin, and Bob Hannigan had worn, but with whizzier materials: cloth from wrist to waist and between the legs. The difference was the two layers, made of long cells, that gave the wings thickness, shape, and semirigidity. For the first time, a birdman's wings could fly like the wings of an airplane.

After several trial runs, Gayardon was able to slow his vertical speed to 55 or so miles per hour, increase his horizontal speed to 90 miles per hour, and fly toward the ground at a 35-degree angle.

Having Sector behind him meant he had the time and the money to make his wings a reality, but Sector was not paying him just to tinker and experiment. Gayardon was to come up with two projects a year for the company, and soon after he had learned to fly his suit, he was preparing several extraordinary stunts. With his wings he set a new record for the longest BASE jump: 32 seconds. Then he flew over the peak of Aiguille du Midi in the French Alps, astounding journalists there on a lookout tower when he passed them sixty or so feet away. In the Grand Canyon he performed a similar feat. He made seventy-five jumps there, flying lower and lower each time until he felt comfortable flying from one side to the other often only 150 feet from the rocks. The plan was to keep some part of the canyon just to one side at all times, so if anything went haywire he could try to steer his way into extra altitude (his photographer, Sjarel Boons, following in one of Gayardon's few wingsuits, broke his legs against the lip of the cliff on one jump).

His most famous flight took place in the airspace over Chambéry. There he jumped out of a Pilatus Porter, flew alongside of it and just behind it, and then flew back inside.

Gayardon modified his wings endlessly, and he could rarely be found without his wings and a needle in hand. His conversation, which had always focused on skydiving, began to center on his plans with his wings, though it was often hard to understand him as he spoke with a heavily accented, rapid-fire English. "On the ground he was different," says Duff. "But when he boarded an airplane he just blossomed, like a flower opening up. For me, I felt like he was born in the wrong body."

Though many women made their way to his bed, no one I spoke with had ever known him to have a long-term relationship. "With him you had to accept that in the morning, after breakfast, you had to talk about how he would fly the wingsuit or the surfboard or whatever," Duff says. "At that time I was heavily into skydiving, but even for me it was a little bit overkill."

Gayardon once wound up in the hospital after a motorcycle accident at 60 miles an hour in shorts. Duff visited him, and the contrast between Gayardon's hospital self and his usual self was extreme. "It was funny to see him for once really helpless. You know, if a person is going 180 all day long, it's pretty strange to watch him in slow motion." A week later he was jumping again.

As Gayardon grew more skilled and daring with his wings, he began to open lower and lower, in a kind of real-life demonstration of the seemingly ridiculous phenomenon postulated in *The Gypsy Moths*—that flight in a wingsuit would lure a jumper into thinking he could fly forever. On one jump, Gayardon opened so low that his parachute was still streaming when he hit the ground. Though he landed on snow, it was an accident that would have killed anyone else and must have further fueled Gayardon's notion that he was invincible.

"I think that the problem with wingsuit flying is that you are so close to the dream of flying, you get fooled into it, like Icarus," explains Gayardon's friend Loïc Jean-Albert. "You think you are really flying, but you're not. We're just humans, walking humans. We try to fly the best we can, but we are still far from birds. Patrick got so close, so close to the dream it was hard to tell the difference."

But by the spring of '98, Gayardon had grown somewhat weary. He was as joyous as ever when in the air, but to some it seemed he had grown tired of his life on the ground. "He was a lonely man—sometimes life gets difficult if you don't have people around you who have the same ideas," says Duff. In early May, Gayardon was in DeLand with Oliver Furrer, skysurfing around formations of twenty and thirty skydivers. His friend and cameraman Gus Wing saw Gayardon carelessly packing his parachute between jumps. "That's shit," he said to Gayardon. "You're packing shit."

Several days later, Gayardon was in Hawaii to make a movie with his friend Patrick Passe. He had spent a lot of time on the island and was there to jump with close friends like Wendy Smith and Adrian Nicholas; the latter had flown one of Patrick's wingsuits more than 100 times. For several days they shot footage of Gayardon making tandem skysurfing jumps with Wendy Smith while Nicholas flew around them on his back, as well as of Gayardon and Nicholas flying wingsuits together.

The house they had rented was equipped with two sewing machines, and of course every night Gayardon tinkered with his wingsuit, ever adjusting for a better flight. His canopy container had two deflectors to make the air flow more smoothly over his back. One evening he decided to adjust the deflectors so that he could more easily reach his pilot chute. He used a large upholstery loop needle to sew them back on. The needle went through the container and through several of the lines to his main canopy.

He didn't repack his chute that evening, and he didn't repack it the following morning. He and Nicholas made a jump together, flew around each other, laughing, even joining hands. Adrian pulled at around 3,500 feet. Gayardon flew a bit farther and pulled out his pilot chute at 2,000 feet, but it could not drag out the main canopy, which was sewn into the bag. He tried his reserve, and it fired into the pilot chute and never opened. He let out a last scream and crashed into the banana trees below.

He had made more than 500 jumps with his wingsuit.

+

Weeks later, 250 skydivers from all over the world gathered in France to pay tribute to Gayardon. His ashes were scattered from above. His ashes would also be scattered during the next X Games by Oliver Furrer, just as Gayardon had scattered Rob Harris's ashes. Though he was a demigod to those who mourned him, they may not have guessed that he had truly revolutionized personal flying. Practically every birdman before him had fantasized about a day when everyone could fly. Gayardon had only flown his wings for a year or two, and just a year or two after his death, his imitators would be in the thousands.

"If you ever watch some of his early films," says Adrian Nicholas, "it will make you jealous just to look at his eyes. He looks to be the happiest person you've ever seen. I'm jealous, you know. He looks so wonderfully alive, and you think, 'Oh, I wouldn't mind looking a bit like that myself.' "

"If angels have wings," Nicholas wrote in an obituary for Gayardon, "he's modifying his now."

Over the Volcano:
Chuck Priest

Until 1954, runners had struggled to run a mile under four minutes. Then along came Roger Bannister, cracking the barrier with a good six-tenths of a second to spare. Just a decade before, scientists had thought that it was physically impossible for a human to run a mile in that time. Six weeks after Bannister proved them wrong, John Landy broke the record again. Others soon followed, and now the four-minute mile is considered a basic benchmark for any professional runner.

That Gayardon would have similar imitators was inevitable. His wingsuit flights would do exactly what his skysurfing accomplishments, and what Bannister's breakthrough, had done: show the world what was possible that had never seemed possible before. But in Gayardon's case, it would take six months, rather than six weeks, before his followers would build wingsuits and learn to fly. Gayardon had simply not been flying his wings for very long, and it would take time for the skydiving world to catch up. At the same time, the wingsuit was really considered Gayardon's territory, and many didn't want to seem mere copycats while he was still alive.

While Jari Kuosma and Robert Pecnik were first beginning their BirdMan business, others were building their own Gayardon-inspired wingsuits as well. On his second to last visit to Hawaii, Gayardon met a skydiver there named Chuck Priest, the owner of Da' Kine Rags, a Hawaiian-print jumpsuit producer. Priest had heard of Gayardon's wings just months before the visit, and he'd already been inspired to sketch out a few ideas for his own wingsuit. So, when the two met, Priest was full of questions, and the pair talked for hours about wing-spans, different materials, and what Gayardon had done in the wind tunnel.

The next day, at the drop zone, Gayardon showed Priest his wingsuit—a rarity in and of itself—and then suggested that Priest make a flight on his own. Priest had made only 111 jumps of any kind at that point, but he climbed in and listened to Gayardon's minimal advice: "Open in a track, keep your legs together when you dump." Minutes later, Priest waddled to the plane "like a penguin" and was on his way up.

Because Priest was to jump three miles away from the drop zone and then fly back, he made arrangements to be the last one out of the plane. On the jump run, the other skydivers each shook Priest's hand as they prepared to leave the plane. "Usually we just give each other a slap on the fingers," says Priest, "and these veteran jumpers and tandem guys were looking deep in my eyes as they're going to the door, not saying a word to me. It was just like . . . *pheeeeeeew.*"

In the air, Priest was amazed to hear himself laughing and singing. He flew most of the way back, found that he was still 6,000 feet above the ground, and made a turn. "I zigzagged a little bit, and I thought, 'This is too weird, I've got to open,' so I opened high and landed without incident."

The owner of the drop zone, though, saw the whole flight as an incident, and one he didn't want repeated. He began screaming that no one with under 1,500 jumps could use Gayardon's suit at his establishment.

But the owner had to drive off to pick up some other jumpers who'd landed down the road, so Priest asked Gayardon if he could take another spin. "Well, you're still in the suit," said Gayardon. "And you've got one jump here. I don't."

Priest made his second jump and managed to land safely again. Afterward, the two discussed the idea of making wingsuits to sell in the future. But it was the last time Priest would see Gayardon—he was in California when Gayardon returned to Hawaii for what would be his last flight.

Priest says that after Gayardon's death, "everyone was talking about doing a wingsuit." Oliver Furrer, who had skysurfed with Gayardon and was a friend of Priest's, approached him about a plan he and another friend, Markus Heggli, had drawn up. They were to go to the Swiss Aeronautical Institute, have three wingsuits made, return to Hawaii to learn how to fly them, and then open up the first wingsuit school. Priest agreed, but with his jumpsuit business, he did not have time to go to Switzerland. When the other two returned, they had only two suits. If Priest wanted to fly with them, he would have to quickly make his own. That's just what he did, stitching one together overnight.

When he and Furrer made their first winged flight, Priest took off, leaving Furrer behind. "On the ground he's like, 'What da fuck you have here? What you make?' " Priest's horizontal success had something to do with his larger wingspan and the smooth material he used—stretch vinyl. A third ingredient, Priest would claim, was his good karma.

For their next jump, several months later, Furrer decided that he wanted to make the first wingsuit flight over the volcano Kilauea Caldera on the big island of Hawaii. Priest joined the team at the last minute when another jumper backed out, and would shoot video of the other two flying. This meant that for Priest's fourth flight in a wingsuit, he would be using someone else's parachute, have a camera strapped to his head, and jump into a quasi-legal area at best, since the lava field they would fly over was a national park. Furthermore, they had to convince a helicopter company to remove a door from one of their helicopters, take them up, and let them jump out of it, even though the aircraft—not meant for such purposes—had no handles to hold on to outside the door. Priest also had to track down the owner of a papaya garden at the edge of the lava field, where they hoped to land legally. Having received his blessing, they set out to make their jump. They made two, at $500 each, and landed in front of several busloads of lava-loving tourists who were eager to snap pictures of the unexpected attraction.

After that adventure, Priest decided he needed to make the wings that he thought Gayardon would have wanted him to make. "A few times I sat back in the field where Patrick went in, and I just said, 'I don't even know what I'm asking you, buddy, I'm just wondering how to build this suit, you know.' Got really nothing while I was there except feeling like I connected with him. But then, when I was putting the thing together, ideas came right to me." One of those ideas was to make the wings as thick as the body at the torso. Rather than have them tapered in and sewn to the material on the back of the jumpsuit, the lower surface of the wings (which faces the ground while flying) would attach to the front of the body and the upper surface would attach to the back. He elongated the tail so it would "give more thrust." And inside the cells of each wing he put stiffeners going from front to back to shape them more like a plane's wing—flat on the bottom, rounded on the top—for extra lift.

He also came up with a combination of ingenious solutions for the problem that Gayardon was trying to fix when he fatally sewed up his rig. To reduce the turbulence that was coming off the wings and slamming down on his butt, Priest cut holes in their tops to let the air stream out. He also created an "inflatable pillow" right over the ass. At the waist it stretched the full width of the body, collecting all the air spilling there, but it tapered toward the feet in a teardrop shape, letting out all the air in one controlled stream behind the body.

At around that time, BirdMan started coming out with their first wingsuits, which were basically copies of Gayardon's wings. At one boogie, Priest flew with Jari Kuosma, who, according to Priest, was wide-eyed at the performance of Priest's wings. A year later BirdMan had a very similar wingsuit—butt pillow and all.

Despite his contribution to the shape of wingsuits today, Priest doesn't make wingsuits to sell and uses his only when he's in the mood to "fly up the coast, watch the waves, the breakers, the whales, look around and check things out for a while." He once drew white lines along a road and measured himself flying for nearly four miles. But he says he's "not in it to break any records. I'm in it to go home and love my wife and work on our life together."

Slope Opera:
Loïc Jean-Albert

In the winter of 2003, a young man of twenty-three years took a helicopter to the top of a snow-covered mountain in Switzerland called Verbier. Once above its steep crags, the man calmly hung outside the door in his wingsuit, and when he felt that the right moment had come, he let go and fell away. Within seconds he was gliding down the peak's slope, in a near-perfect parallel to the line of the mountain. For good stretches of this flight he was no more than two body-lengths above the snow, and at one point he passed just over the heads of two people watching from solid ground. When he opened his canopy, his feet hit the snow just seconds later, and he ran to a halt.

Not long after this performance, a short film clip of the flight started appearing on various skydiving websites and circulating among wingsuit enthusiasts. Certainly it is some of the most fantastic footage ever shot in the sport, and people who might otherwise dismiss wingsuits as something for kooks alone were given to saying "Now, *that* is something." The performance won the man, Loïc Jean-Albert, the title of Skydiver of the Year from *Skydiving* magazine. The only other non-American to have been so acknowledged was Patrick de Gayardon.

The torch was passed from Gayardon to Jean-Albert directly. Like Gayardon, Jean-Albert grew up on the drop zone, in his case, quite literally: his parents were skydiving instructors at Réunion island, a French *département* east of Madagascar. French law does not allow children to skydive, no matter how far from the mainland they grow up, so Jean-Albert had to wait until he was sixteen before he made his first jump. A year and a half later, Jean-Albert proved that skydiving ability is at least partially genetic when he was accepted on the French eight-way skydiving team, for which he moved back to France. Gayardon was also on the team, and the two quickly became friends. Jean-Albert began jumping with Gayardon outside team jumps, and helping him pack his rigs and sew his wingsuit. He noticed that Gayardon was always having problems where the wings connected to the torso of the jumpsuit. Jean-Albert began thinking of alternative designs, and he eventually hit upon the idea of a single wing. Rather than have a tight jumpsuit with wings added on, why not just climb into the wing itself? But by the time Jean-Albert was prepared to show Gayardon his new concept, Gayardon was dead.

Jean-Albert went on to make the suit himself, and it was eventually produced and sold as the Crossbow. The difference between Jean-Albert's wingsuit and the BirdMan wingsuits—which are still essentially derivative of Gayardon's wings—is one of maneuverability. When flying straight, both suits have about the same performance, but Jean-Albert's wing is not snug against the body, so he can shift his weight inside it. This lets him do a kind of sideways sliding action, allowing him to turn while remaining flat in the horizontal plane he's moving in, rather than changing the angle of an arm or the body to turn. This move is particularly useful when hooking up with other skyflyers, and ideal for those given more to playing in the air than barreling straight through it.

"I am flying airplanes and trikes [powered hang-gliders] and Paragliders, hang gliders, and other flying machines," says Jean-Albert. "The wingsuit is one of the things that you can fly the best—not in terms of flight angle or glide ratio, but in terms of how you can change the shape of the flying machine. On the plane you just have flaps and ailerons; on the wingsuit you can make it thicker or thinner, shift weight, change the angle of front wings to the tail—you can change so many parameters. It's hard to build an airplane like that."

Though his flight down Verbier, he says, was for him just more play in his wingsuit, he did train for months, gradually working his way up to the now-historic flight. "What's really interesting with the wingsuit is to have a reference to something that is not moving—the cloud or the ground," says Jean-Albert. Having soon had his fill of the former, he turned his attentions to the latter. To keep some form of earth near him without necessarily having to crash into it, he started flying next to cliffs. With each jump he would try to fly closer and closer to the land on one side of him, while keeping the other side open to turn to in case of emergency. As soon as he felt comfortable whizzing alongside cliffs, he began to scope out a mountaintop with a steep ridge so he could bail out on either side if needed. "In Switzerland we found the place. They dropped me at the bottom of the slope—a good angle, a nice cliff to the side." The good angle was about 30 degrees, but Jean-Albert made the judgment by eyeball alone ("It's very instinctive, the way I do things, I don't really measure"). That same day, he made his jump—actually two jumps. The skiers he passed over were meant to be moving along with him, but it turned out that they couldn't keep up with his forward speed. Instead they just stood there and gawked as he passed a few feet overhead. The following day, Jean-Albert made a similar jump at a ski demonstration on a different mountain, and this time the skiers below were stunned to find a birdman swooping down on them.

Whatever skiers and other spectators of the world, startled or otherwise, might think of such stunts, Jean-Albert finds nothing but support in the people who surround him. He's never had any job, let alone a career, outside of skydiving, and practically everyone he knows, including friends and family, is part of the sport. His father has even tried one of his wingsuits. "When they see the video, they think it's dangerous and fast, but they are skydivers, as well, and it's part of the dream."

Birdmen and Birdbirds:
Leo Dickinson

The peregrine falcon is a favorite among falconers because of its famous high-speed earthward dives, which can knock both meal-sized birds and larger trespassers out of the sky. Using gravity combined with its own wing power, it is said to be the fastest bird in the world. Estimates put the peregrine's dives—called stoops—at anywhere from 120 to 200 miles per hour, but the actual speed was not known with any precision, and the dives were not well documented on film until humans caught up with them.

Now that the wingsuit has become a common sight at drop zones everywhere, scientific-minded skydivers don them as casually as they might a lab coat. Leo Dickinson, a veteran skydiver who's been a photographer in the sport for twenty-five years, climbed into a BirdMan wingsuit with the sole purpose of becoming prey—specifically prey for a peregrine.

Dickinson teamed up with bird trainer Lloyd Buck and his bird

Lucy to remedy the situation. The project started with a hot-air balloon tethered 1,600 feet above England. Dickinson, wearing a camera, but not yet a wingsuit, jumped out of it. He was followed by a BBC reporter jumping in tandem with another skydiver and, when Buck, still in the basket, let her go, Lucy.

Lucy followed the falling skydivers but wouldn't come within thirty or so feet of them, most likely because she was scared by the sound of the small drogue parachute used to slow the fall of the pair in tandem. After several attempts, they began jumping without the reporter and continued "throwing breakfast out of balloons," says Dickinson. When he fell on his back and increased his vertical speed to 145 miles per hour, Lucy stayed comfortably by his side.

Then they took things higher. Climbing to altitude in a Cessna, Lucy was as calm as the most seasoned jumper, but when it came time to exit, she didn't like the turbulent wind created by the plane and wouldn't take to the air. So Lloyd started "throwing her out torpedo-style." Once outside the plane, she was perfectly at ease playing around the plane and the jumpers. "She followed the airplane, went to the front of it, did a U-turn, then made a half-mile loop behind it and then caught it up again—without any effort. It was like the airplane was still," says Dickerson. As impressive as this performance was, Lucy was not attacking Dickinson in the desired fashion.

Peregrines don't usually stoop in a perfectly vertical line, as their prey is usually moving across land more or less horizontally. At the speeds a peregrine reaches, the force of a perpendicular collision with some unsuspecting pigeon poking along over a field would probably kill both birds. So, when they come tearing out of the sky, hoping to peg a potential meal, it's usually at something like a 60-degree angle. The obvious way for Dickerson to become more pigeonlike himself was to start flying in a wingsuit. He and Buck made a trip to DeLand and began training in BirdMan wingsuits. (Lucy, though, couldn't come: U.S. law prohibits carrying falcons across international and state lines. "Really ridiculous—they do it of their own accord," says Dickinson.) For a man with nearly 4,000 jumps, the wingsuit was just another technique to learn. "I think it's overdramatized how difficult it is to fly them," he says. "They're not particularly hard to fly. They're quite hard to fly very well—that's a different thing."

Back in England they first trained Lucy to recognize them by running around in fields wearing their wingsuits. Raptors have one of the largest eyeball-to-skull ratios of any animal, and with their binocularly placed eyes and extraordinary ability to focus, they can spot their prey from miles away. "Lloyd was talking on the radio and she was four miles away when she spotted him. She came screaming across the heavens and covered the four miles in not too many seconds."

Once Lucy had internalized the appearance of her wingsuited captors, they decided to make a BASE jump to keep things as natural as possible for the bird. So they set off for a cliff in Italy named Arco—the same 3,700-foot-high cliff where Robert Pecnik and Jari Kuosma had first dreamt up the idea of making BirdMan wingsuits. And in fact Pecnik, who had made a record 59-second delay with his wingsuit from the cliff in 2001, was there to help with filming. Lucy didn't take to him, though, probably because she wasn't fond of his colors—red and white.

Dickinson's purple wingsuit was more to her liking, as was the prime Italian beef he was holding. "That's what gets their attention. They want it and they want it now." Dickinson had only made one BASE jump before he came to Arco with Lucy, but having trained and carefully planned the jump, he was more afraid of what the bird might do to him than of the jump itself. "I didn't get the endorphin buzz people talk about. I think people that do are people that aren't prepared and they're really pushing the boat out." Dickinson planned to give himself a delay of only 20 seconds and to open at 1,000 feet to give himself some extra time if anything should go wrong with the bird. He certainly had no need of performing as well as Pecnik had with his minute-long flight: Lucy hit Dickinson within seconds of his leaving the edge. Sometimes Dickinson would jump when Lucy was a good 250 feet in the air already, and still it was only a matter of seconds before impact. "It's when she wants to hit you," he says.

At first Lucy landed on his leather-protected wrists, often hanging on for a good seven or eight seconds, but then she began to get more aggressive, or, as Dickinson put it, "It started to get a bit personal." The cliff at Arco slopes away at about a 30-degree angle, and with the 45-degree fall that the wingsuit gave him, Dickinson assumed that he would fly away from the cliff and avoid any danger of hitting it. He had not thought that the force of the bird's attack could actually turn him around and send him right back toward the cliff wall. The solution? "Give her the meal instantly—give her the meal instantly, and do your level best to turn back around away from the cliff."

Dickinson made a total of sixteen jumps with Lucy at Arco, and apart from learning how to wrestle raptors in the air, he discovered that she could stoop at 200 miles per hour. Similar studies with free-falling skydivers in DeLand have since clocked another peregrine tearing up the skies at 242 miles per hour.

Most of the world's skyflyers have a ways to go before they can reach such speeds. And though Dickinson's research may have taught them little about how to do so, at least it's given them another important lesson: don't jump out of planes wearing meat.

Part Five

BEYOND

THE

WINGSUIT

Yves Rossy waves off as his inflatable wings inflate.

It's Skyray or the Highway:
Christoph Aarns and Alban Geissler

After two jumps in canvas wings—and a twenty-year history of bat-wing failures before him—Leo Valentin had turned his back on fabric. "Canvas wings would not really allow a man to glide," he wrote. "To glide really, I now realized—and this was the constructive aspect of an experiment which had nearly cost me my life—I had to design a wing with lift. If it were rigid it would support the body." Valentin became the first person to leave a plane wearing rigid wings, and because it was rigid wings that ended up costing him his life, until recently he was the last. Had he survived to continue his experiments, he would have found that their weight would never have let him fly much, despite his initial claims.

Patrick de Gayardon took the lesson to heart and refused to use any kind of stiffener with his wings. "From my first jumps on, my instructors would forbid them because they said they were dangerous.

I kept this in mind," he said. With his success and fame, those who wanted to fly after him kept it in mind, as well.

Now, with the help of strong but light new materials and the interest of a few scientifically oriented minds, rigid wings are proving Gayardon wrong and letting a handful of skilled skydivers take personal flight to extremes Valentin would have marveled at.

This part of the story begins, and continues to evolve, in a place known for the precision of its vehicular manufacturing.

✦

When you get to the Daedalus drop zone, in the heart of Germany's Weserbergland hills, you are already at a high altitude. A half hour's drive from the town of Hamlin, where a famous exterminator and flutist once famously led a pack of children to their deaths, the drop zone sits in the center of a *Naturschutzgebiet,* at the top of small mountain, surrounded by fields of canary-yellow rape. On the way up, a triangular sign depicting a falcon indicates that the area is a sanctuary for birds, and indeed the raptors can easily be seen hovering, circling, and surveying from above without any perceptible movement of their wings. They express little curiosity for the activities of the larger, less graceful creatures that float through their domain.

One of these creatures is a man named Christoph Aarns. With his square jaw, weathered skin, and evenly distributed millimeters of gray hair, Aarns has a stoic, cowboy look to him. And chances are you will find him, after entering the drop zone's gate and passing beneath the Keith Haring winged-man sign above the door of the drop zone's shop, acting as "caller" of a square dance.

That's what it looked like to me, anyway. Sixteen people, in groups of four, were spinning around, holding hands and turning at his command. When he said "Bend at the waist," they bent at the waist, when he said "Raise an arm," they raised an arm. They were, of course, practicing what they would soon repeat while falling through the sky, and Aarns was training them to know their moves perfectly.

Aarns is a unique character in the world of skydiving. As tough and daring as he appears, he is highly attuned to safety issues, and the excitement that comes with the risks of the sport don't interest him at all. "I would love to jump without fear—I don't want to feel all that adrenaline," he says. "I'd love to BASE jump, too, but I'm afraid. I know so many people who've been hurt." These words come from a man with more than 10,000 jumps to his name. So methodical and careful is he in everything he does, from packing his parachute to rehearsing jumps, that he has never once had to use a reserve—a world record of a kind.

That doesn't mean he has steered completely free of disaster. As we talked, his children, an equestrian of seven years and a rabble-rouser of two, played around their mother, who was lounging in a lawn chair. Her foot and lower leg were in a cast holding together the bones of a broken ankle she received while landing in Arizona. And Aarns could not keep his eyes off the sky. Every time the fluttering sound of an emerging parachute came from above, Aarns jumped up to watch and make sure that everyone in the jump load opened their chutes cleanly and got to the ground safely.

Aarns is part owner of the drop zone and naturally wants things to run smoothly, but his concern has been sharpened by an unfortunate occurrence at a boogie there a year earlier. Skydivers had come from all over Germany to attend, and thousands of jumpers were sprawled around the drop zone, watching as twenty-four planes continuously kept the country's best-performing jumpers in the sky while a band rocked out on the mountain. At one point three skydivers came down together, putting on a real show. With smoke trailing behind them from canisters on their ankles, they carved around one another, heading toward the earth, making a giant braid in the sky to the screams and cheers of those below. But they never opened their chutes. When they hit the ground, those cheers turned to silence.

The weavers had been relying on a device called an AAD (automatic activation device), which opens a parachute at a set altitude. Before they had arrived at the Daedalus drop zone, they had visited another at a much lower altitude, and there they had set their AADs, and never reset them. "They just didn't pull," says Aarns. "The main problem was that their priority was to do a nice show. Maybe it was good everyone saw it."

The cautiousness doesn't mean Aarns won't take risks. There just has to be a big enough payoff to make the risk worthwhile. In the mid-eighties, after a long dry spell of birdman activity throughout the world, Aarns developed his own wingsuit. He'd been doing his best to track across the sky and had reached the limits of what one can do with the fairly unaerodynamic human body. Canopies were already getting smaller and smaller, and Aarns had the idea to shrink them down to the extreme and "put myself inside a canopy." The result was a giant trapezoid of double-layered cloth that stretched from limb-end to limb-end—a ram-air wingsuit years before Patrick de Gayardon, let alone Jari Kuosma, started flying theirs. Though it slowed his fall, it did little to help him move across the sky, probably because it was too loose to retain any stiffness. Aarns also developed a kind of kickboard that he strapped to the legs for extra tracking. But he soon became busy as part of the team that made the first 80-way in Germany and later the first 200-way, and he eventually abandoned the wingsuit and tracking board altogether.

It's the mixture of safety consciousness and the urge to fly that makes Aarns the perfect guinea pig for the experiments of Alban Geissler. In a deviation from the traditional pattern in birdman history, Geissler had the dream of human flight without much of the desire to try it himself—certainly a good survival tactic. Unlike the Sohns, Valentins, and Gayardons of the world, Geissler did not come to the idea of using wings while skydiving from skydiving himself. No, he was on the couch, watching TV. While flipping channels he happened upon some footage of a typical skydiver and thought, "I wonder if I could make him fly."

Geissler and Aarns make a striking pair: where Aarns is ruddy, Geissler is pale; where Aarns is of average height, Geissler is tall and lanky; where Aarns is muscular, Geissler is . . . less muscular. And where Aarns has made 10,000-odd jumps, Geissler has made twenty-six (he started jumping after building his first prototype in an effort to try his own invention, but since his girlfriend gets jealous when he flirts with death, chances are he will never fly his own wings). Aarns spends most of his days in the air and in the open air, while Geissler is a tinkerer and vehicle designer in Munich who has engineered earthbound objects from hot rods to heat pumps.

The structure Geissler came up with, called the Skyray, is a sleek carbon-fiber wing that inspires instant lust in the gadget-minded. It's the Lamborghini of personal wings, or at least the Jet Ski of the air, and gives whoever's in it a glide ratio of three to one with a forward speed of 180 miles per hour—faster than most small airplanes. The high-tech textiles, which keep the Skyray at about nine pounds (the lightness is what makes it all possible), earned the wing a place in the Cooper-Hewitt Museum's Extreme Textiles exhibition. But despite its sexy surface and high speeds, the primary design challenge Geissler faced was not one of velocity but one of how-the-hell-do-I-get-this-thing-off-me-in-an-emergency-so-I-don't-kill-myself. "People always told us, 'You will end up like all of them,' " Geissler says. "But those early birdmen missed something—that they should have been thinking first about their security, not about flying. Flying is not so difficult. Security is difficult."

Security for a winged man, as the history of birdmen clearly demonstrates, means keeping him from entanglements and keeping him from the spins. Thanks to inconsistencies and asymmetries in the wing designs of the bat-wing jumpers, they often found themselves in a spin that could send blood rushing to their heads and cause a blackout. If the jumper managed to open his chute before losing consciousness, there was a good chance a rotating wing spar would snag a line or the canopy itself. "That's the biggest problem," Geissler says. "Small areas can develop very big forces, and then you can really fast get into the shit."

The first solution to this problem was to make a set of wings that could pop off if things got hairy. The Skyray has its own harness with a kind of square cutout so that it can fit over the jumper's usual pack. With a single yank of an additional ripcord, the entire apparatus can be jettisoned at any speed. After a short delay the unbound Skyray will deploy its own parachute, pulling it away from the jumper to avoid collision with him or his gear. This parachute will also set the Skyray gently upon the ground, protecting both the Skyray and the unsuspecting pedestrian.

The second solution to the problem is to make the wings so that a spin is impossible in the first place. To achieve this, Geissler fashioned the Skyray with a swept-back delta wing, giving it a triangular shape, much like those found on most fighter jets (including one with the same name). A straight-winged aircraft, like a Cessna, will stall when its angle of attack (which is the angle of the wing's plane against the air hitting it) is greater than 15 degrees. And as one wing begins to create drag, the other creates lift, putting the whole vehicle into rotation. But the Skyray can maintain a 1:1 glide ratio even when the angle of attack is as much as 25 degrees. "It's only when you develop an angle of more than 25 degrees," says Geissler, "that the airstream over the whole wing will detach and create more drag than lift."

The disadvantage of delta wings is that they create more drag in general, but Geissler's smooth design would only be 5 or 6 percent faster if he traded in stability for extra speed by making the wings straighter.

Geissler spent three years designing the Skyray. He first used computer simulations to see how a winged human body behaves in the air. "But airstream detachment is very hard to see with code, and the up-to-date codes all showed different outcomes," he says. "When you have detachment two or three centimeters farther down-stream, it changes everything." To see how the Skyray would per-form in a semi-real-world scenario, he took a scaled-down model to a wind tunnel at the University of Applied Science in Munich. There he tied a dummy, named Ken, to the prototype and discovered that chaotic turbulence at the back of the wing was pushing air back toward the front, just behind the parachute pack. On another air-craft, this might not be such a problem. But a skydiver flying the Skyray needs his parachute to emerge in order to land, and this "backdraft" was so strong that it would likely keep a pilot chute hov-ering just behind the pack, unable to clear the powerful burble to pull out the main canopy. So Geissler resculpted the Skyray and "smoothed the airstream" inward to create two controlled vortices that were away from the pack.

But computers and wind tunnels didn't make the Skyray's first flight much less of a crapshoot. The real world, after all, is notori-ously sticky and imperfect. "Ken is pretty hard, like wood. But a real

human is like jelly with bones," says Geissler. "It's pretty different."
The Skyray-and-human combo is essentially "an aircraft that has a
joint in the middle—your legs." And as legs tend to move freely, it
was not really foreseeable what effect they would have in flight.

What was foreseeable was what might happen to Aarns if he
jumped with the first prototype that Geissler showed him. "Velcro is
not a good idea when you're flying at 200 miles per hour," Aarns says.

When you add endless delays to the mixture of high speed and
uncertainty, you end up with a concoction for producing nausea in
anyone remotely capable of fear. And as the initial test was put off for
many months, when the time finally came to jump with the Skyray,
in Spain, in 1999, some very rapidly beating butterflies had developed
in Aarns's stomach. "It was a very tense situation," says Aarns. "Everyone was scared, even the pilot of the plane. That's what makes us different from animals: we can experience fear with knowledge."

When Aarns finally entered the air for the first time, the turbulence was overwhelming—"like being tied to a washing machine," he
says. When he hit the air at some 200-plus miles per hour he was
unable to stop his forward movement, and the high speed exploded
his pilot parachute. Aarns had to eject the wings, and Geissler watched
from the plane above as the Skyray, under its own canopy, settled into
an olive grove.

Geissler wanted Skyray flyers to be able to use their own gear and
to keep things as simple and as familiar as possible, so he had to re-
design the wings to make them slower so that the pilot chute wouldn't
pop. To tone down the washing-machine effect, he added handles
to the underside of the wings so that Aarns could pull the wings
tight against his body. Over time they found that by letting go of
the handles and going into a typical box shape, the Skyray practically stopped flying, letting Aarns open his parachute from the usual

position and speed. Geissler also added winglets at the ends of the wings and again redirected airflow to avoid turbulence behind the parachute pack.

Since then, Aarns has flown the Skyray nearly 300 times without a hitch. But that doesn't mean making the flight is a breeze. Before he gets on the plane, he goes through a ritual of repeatedly grabbing each ripcord—for the main, reserve, and Skyray ejection. Then he picks up a bucket—"the most important piece of equipment," he says—so that he can sit on it in the plane and not put his weight on the Skyray's wingtips. At altitude, he has to dive straight down after exiting the plane to pick up speed before he straightens out and shoots across the sky. From the ground his trail looks perfectly horizontal (and he has in fact been tracked moving parallel to the earth).

Compared to flying with a wingsuit, which Aarns describes as "floating, slow and smooth," the Skyray is all intensity—"like a bullet, like a dart." As soon as he hits the air, the wings take him far from the plane and any other jumpers. "The moment you jump," Aarns says, "you are a really lonely man."

28

Crossing Over:
Felix Baumgartner

The 21 miles between Dover, England, and Calais, France, have played host to all kinds of record breaking over the years. In 1785, Jean-Pierre Blanchard and John Jeffries were the first to cross the channel in a gas balloon. In 1875, Matthew Webb was the first to swim across it. In 1909, Louis Blériot was the first to make the trip in an airplane. And in 1981, David Kirke was the first to float over in the pouch of an inflatable kangaroo.

In the spirit of historic record breaking that preceded him, an Austrian, Felix Baumgartner, planned to make the first "free fall" from England to France attached to a pair of six-foot carbon-fiber wings that looked very much like the Skyray.

Baumgartner, who has knighted himself "God of the Skies," had talked much about making such an attempt for years, putting the jump off several times. But there was no mounting fear for him in the months before he finally made the leap—at least none on display.

"I don't really have fear—fear slows you down, it blocks you," he said. The air was a second home to him, a place much safer than the surface of the earth. "There are too many people on the ground. On the ground you can be a perfect car driver, but someone else can kill you. In the air most of the time it's just you, so if you do everything perfect, nothing can happen, yeah?"

On July 25, 2003, leaving a hypoxic and unconscious cameraman behind him in the plane, Baumgartner leapt into minus-40-degree air, 30,000 feet above Dover. He was wearing an oxygen tank to survive the thin air, and a transponder to make him visible to other, larger airborne objects. Flying at about 180 miles an hour, he followed another plane over the channel and descended at a rate of 12 yards a second toward the French border. Behind him several additional planes followed, hauling camera crews, while below him rescue boats waited for the possibility of fishing him out of the water.

Once over Calais, he opened his parachute and found his legs tangled in the lines. Still numb from the cold weather, he managed to reach his knife, cut himself free, and touch down safely in front of a crowd of journalists. His first words after the six-and-a-half minute journey: "I made it, which is great."

Images from the flight hit prime-time newscasts and the front page of newspapers all over the world. *The New York Times Magazine* went so far as to list Baumgartner and "Airborne Humans" as the first "idea" in their 2003 "Year in Ideas." The train ride from Heathrow to London now features a looping program showing Baumgartner's flight. His media triumph was solidified when he made it on to Jay Leno.

The Spandexed and helmeted Baumgartner, in the air, framed by a blue sky, and later on the ground, framed by French weeds—slightly dazed and showing a peace sign—had entered the collective unconscious. But that collective's enthusiasm was not unanimous in what it thought of the stunt. A CNN online poll found that 10 percent of those who voted in a survey about the new birdman thought the flight an act of stupidity, 24 percent saw it as "another glorious chapter in the history of flight," 32 percent thought it was all in the name of attention, and 34 percent checked the box with the words "Sounds like fun, sign me up."

To most skydivers and especially BASE jumpers, Baumgartner is reviled at worst and lightly mocked at best. His entire raison d'être is drawing attention, which, though distasteful to some, is not in itself cause for wrath. But the publicity has caused authorities to begin to monitor the lofty sites he'd used as launching pads, spoiling the opportunity for BASE jumpers thereafter. As a soloist who doesn't do his stunts for the sport itself or the skydiving community, he has made news of his jump from the world's tallest bridge in Millau, as well as a hop off the giant Jesus statue that looks out over Rio de Janeiro. The latter is a jump he calls the lowest BASE jump ever, and the number that Baumgartner uses, 95 feet, is the height of the statue from head to toe. But the statue stands on a hill, and Baumgartner did not land at its feet but farther down the slope. Furthermore, before Baumgartner had ever visited the site, other BASE jumpers had climbed the statue, usually at sunrise, made the jump, and scurried away before drawing attention, media or otherwise.

Baumgartner extends the media campaign to his own skin. As he was the 502nd person to jump from a building, an antenna, a span, and earth, he had a logo designed of that number, which he had tattooed on his back and "copyrighted all over the world."

However little respect he has for and receives from his peers, Baumgartner has a kind of backhanded respect for the winged flyers who came before him. "These days we have perfect skydiving stuff— wingsuits are already perfectly developed—and it's not really dangerous," he says. "But those guys. They are the real guys, because at that time they had no knowledge, they were just trying. If you look at those old movies they all look kind of stupid. Franz Reichelt? It looks like 'What the fuck?' It looks so stupid. They had no idea, they tried to copy a bird. But they had vision and they had balls and they tried."

He does not have the same things to say about his more immediate predecessors. The contours and swept-back delta wings of Baumgartner's gear made it look like a larger version of the Skyray, and many of the articles that reported on the flight mistakenly identified the wings as such. This is because Baumgartner and his sponsor, Red Bull, started out with a Skyray, purchasing one of the first models that Geissler made. Geissler and Aarns were initially pleased to have a corporate sponsor and a media-savvy daredevil parading their product around the globe. Baumgartner had been doing BASE jumps and other stunts for the company for several years, and to have that kind of marketing and money behind them seemed at first like a great break.

But it soon turned out that Baumgartner was too reckless for Geissler and Aarns. He pulled his chute while flying his Skyray at full speed, without first going into box position. While on an island-hopping tour with other wingsuiters, he took off on his own, as if the gathering were a race. Once he let a B-25 bomber tow him across the sky by a wire attached to the fuselage. The resistance tore a piece out of the plane and very nearly took it down. When the Red Bull contract ran out, Geissler and Aarns, not wanting a dead Skyray flyer as early publicity, chose not to renew it.

As did Baumgartner. He had been thinking of trying to take the Skyray across the Channel almost from the start, and Geissler had simply told him that the math said it wouldn't work (and he has hinted that with Baumgartner's bigger wings, the math still says it doesn't work). "No" was not the kind of answer Baumgartner wanted to hear. "I put too much force on these guys, and they couldn't stand the pressure," Baumgartner explained. "But they are boys." Baumgartner took the project to a company called Carbotech, just a few miles from where he lived, and began experimenting with larger wings.

The media explosion after the crossing moved Geissler to comment. "Felix Baumgartner seems (but I'm not sure) to have crossed the channel with a wing he built as a copy from two prototype wings we sold to Red Bull two years ago," he wrote on dropzone.com. "Congratulations for realizing this media-event to him! But he is not and will never be the best SKYRAY flyer! He proved this himself! He needed to build a much bigger wing to get the same glide ratio Christoph Aarns or Patrick Barton got with the SKYRAY prototypes!"

Whether or not Baumgartner's abilities as a skydiver and skyflyer are world-class may be up for debate, but his abilities at working the media are world-class without question. His next stunt, if rumors are to be believed, will undoubtedly draw the eyes of the world: he is reported to be conducting secret experiments in an effort to land without a parachute. He is not, however, the only one. As he himself says, "You have to be the first one. The second one is the first loser."

The Shape of Things to Come:
Roberto Stickel

Aviation firsts come naturally to Roberto Stickel, whose uncle's uncle, as he puts it, was Alberto Santos-Dumont, the Brazilian aviation pioneer who flew the first powered aircraft in Europe (and who Brazilians claim actually beat the Wright brothers altogether). In 1974 a friend of Stickel's, Pedro Paulo "Pepe" Lopes, brought the first hang glider to Brazil after a trip to the United States. With it, Stickel and Lopes started Brazil's first hang-gliding club, and soon they were designing their own kites.

For a man with a lineage such as Stickel's, tooling around in the air at slow speeds on wings conceived in foreign lands was simply not an achievement of sufficient grandeur. Though he first entered the air under a hang glider, his ultimate goal was a personal flight of unlimited freedom. He wanted to experience the open-air soaring of a wingsuit, the speed of the Skyray, and the extended flight of a glider, all with one set of wings.

Having grown weary of cloth-and-pole wings, Stickel bought the only rigid-winged hang glider then in existence in Brazil. He fell in love with its speed, mastered it, and eventually flew it in the world championships in Japan. But the glider was difficult to assemble and, more important, required great speed—for human legs—to leave the ground. "It was always a kind of nightmare to take off with this wing," says Stickel. "To take off running, you would die to reach the speed. Very dangerous." So he set out to make a "variable wing" hang glider.

To take off easily at low speeds, a wing needs to be thick and long, but to be capable of aerobatics and greater speeds, it should be short and thin. Aeronautical engineers in the military, at NASA, and at many universities and labs have long struggled to have it both ways for planes and spacecraft. But Stickel was at it long before even he really knew what he was doing.

Despite a degree in civil engineering, Stickel knew nothing about aerodynamics, and what he came up with was pure improvisation. His wing was full of hinges, and a web of cables and pulleys inside it made it possible for him to alter its shape midflight. "It was something that would never work to sell to someone," he says. "A very naive concept. Oh, I made something very special . . . but too complicated to sell." His friends begged him to stop, insisting that he would die.

And he very nearly did.

"At that time I had physical problems—ulcers—because it was scaring my life. Every weekend I was changing something, always making some kind of mistake, and again and again going out of control, spinning very fast, crying in the middle of the air, 'I will die'— but always landing safely, never breaking even a leg."

One of the main challenges Stickel faced was making his wings light enough. The kind of featherweight aluminum that was being used in the United States for rigid hang gliders was (and still is) un-available in Brazil. Stickel approached an American company in Oak-land, California, Manta Products, with the idea of developing the wings and selling them commercially. But in 1982 the world's greatest rigid-wing flyer, Eric Raymond, lost his first competition in Death Valley. The loss put a sudden end to worldwide interest in rigid wings for the small hang-gliding community (who generally didn't want to invest in something that was expensive and heavy), and hang-gliding technology did not progress for the next twenty years. Manta Prod-ucts withdrew from the plan, and if this weren't enough to put the ki-bosh on any hopes of developing Stickel's variable wing, the single existing prototype was stolen.

Stickel abandoned hang gliding, but did not give up on making a wing that could fly as fast and as long as he wanted. He threw out the idea of taking off from the ground, but was unwilling to make the compromises in wing size that Yves Rossy (see chapter 30) and Alban Geissler would make for their wings to fit in and out of a plane door. And coming at the aeronautics as a hang glider pilot rather than a skydiver, he could not be satisfied with a flight that lasted no more than a few minutes.

Stickel named the wings he developed to meet his multiple needs the Pyxis, after the constellation, with a nod to the Pixies. (The fact that in botanical circles it also means "a capsule whose upper part falls off when the seeds are released" is pure coincidence). The Pyxis is a small, carbon-fiber pod with ultra-long, thin wings. Its aesthetic is fifties futuristic, and it has the personality of one of the cuter Pokémon characters. The flyer lies prone in a kind of pod with a clear bubble around the head through which he can take in the view. The rounded curves—and the pod—give the impression that it has recently punctured the atmosphere after a long trip from the planet Krypton. Plowing into the earth at great speed, however, is not part of the itinerary. With its wingspan of more than 31 feet, anyone flying the Pyxis can stay in the air, with a good thermal, all day. Speed freaks looking to perform aerobatics or just increase their velocity can easily change the wings to get what they're after.

Stickel's dream is that complete beginners will be able to fly the Pyxis without a problem. That means skipping the dangerous parts of flying any aircraft: taking off and landing. The Pyxis goes up coupled to the belly of any airplane, be it a Twin Otter or an ultralight. Since it weighs less than 50 pounds and is, of course, designed to fly itself, it will have little effect on the flight of whatever aircraft it's piggybacked to. The arrangement also obviates the issue of how to safely squeeze out of a plane door.

To avoid having to land, the flyer uses a parachute. And to keep the pilot from getting caught in the parachute, Stickel has come up with a clever opening mechanism. The pilot simply pulls a trigger, and the top of the Pyxis comes off and becomes a large, kitelike drogue, pulling the parachute far away from the human and into clean, turbulence-free air. A hinge on the bottom front of the pod opens as the parachute yanks the skydiver into an upright position, and the rest of the journey is a typical descent under a canopy. Should anything go wrong before then, a separate trigger releases the Pyxis, which, like the Skyray, then coasts to the ground under its own reserve. The pilot's gear is the same parachute he uses while skydiving. "The same equipment," says Stickel. "You are a skydiver, you are just joking with something else."

To figure out just how the business with the parachute should work, Stickel took up skydiving himself. Skydiving, however, did not take to him. "I liked it very much," he says. "Twenty years ago the people from skydiving were so square about flying by yourself. They liked to do those figures in the air. Why? They couldn't accept someone doing what they wanted in the air. 'No, you have to do the figures with us, you have to go up with a team.' So I had to stop." But after a mere twenty jumps, Stickel knew how to use a parachute, which was all he really needed.

The only problem with the Pyxis, so far, is that it does not yet exist—not in a size big enough for a human pilot, anyway. Rather than risk his own neck flying the Pyxis for the first time, Stickel built a version one-third the size of the planned final product and outfitted it with the tiny servos used in model airplane flying these days. He quickly discovered that the wings needed a tail for stability. He also discovered that flying the model by remote control was very easy. So he decided that the full-size model should also have an onboard computer.

But the primary reason that skydivers and hang gliders—the more daring of whom are always eager to try the newest and coolest—are not now floating through the sky for hours in their Pyxises is that the engineers who have helped Stickel thus far are now busy building Chinese satellites. The model made its last flight in 2003, and since then work on the project has stalled. "It's very near, maybe fifteen days of work," says Stickel, "but they have no room to make it, their place is filled with satellite stuff."

Turn On the Warm Jets: Yves Rossy

The length, lightness, and shape of most of the wings mentioned in this book so far have increased the glide ratios, air time, and distances flown for many. But without using a thermal—rising warm air that can push lighter aircraft upward—as hang gliders and engine-free sailplanes do, no birdman will ever fly truly horizontally for a significant amount of time without attaching some sort of additional power. Every winged skydiver has had the thought of using an engine with his assemblage, just as the inventors of the Wright brothers' era did. But only one man so far has taken this step, the Swiss Yves Rossy.

With his lean and angular body and close-cropped, thinning hair, Rossy looks like a happy-go-lucky Vladimir Putin. Rossy's happiness and luck have something to do with his accomplishing—and surviving—a rattle bag of stunts to rival any daredevil alive today.

Rossy was trained as a pilot in the Swiss army, and by the age of twenty-nine he was flying for Swissair, a job he still maintains. Having learned the ropes of skydiving in the army, Rossy took it up for sport and soon afterward began his career of elaborate and oddball stunts.

In 1991 he made a trip around *a* world (Switzerland) in one day: After flying a DC-9 from Geneva to Zurich, he took the controls of a Venom airplane and performed some aerobatics before switching to a motorbike, then a mountain bike for the leg to Zermatt. A lift then brought him to the top of a mountain that he skied and then snow-boarded down before hiking to the top of the Breithorn. He para-chuted down the other side of that peak, grabbed a train to a bridge, and bungee-jumped off it. A helicopter picked him up and let him out at 6,000 feet so that he could skydive to the next segment: rafting and kayaking to Château-d'Oex. Afterward he drove another motor-cycle to another jump, followed it with a truck ride, a horse ride, water skis, and a boat that brought him back to where he'd started.

After he had made 150 jumps, he began surfing the skies instead of just diving through them. This branch of air travel had been pop-ularized by Patrick de Gayardon, of course, but Rossy would take it to quirkier extremes. In 1994 he dropped into a friend's wedding party wearing a bowler, suspenders, and a red bow tie. In one hand he carried a bunch of roses, and strapped to his feet was a heart not much bigger than a welcome mat, which he surfed down to the newlyweds. He also made a miniature version of the French fighter plane Mirage III and skysurfed by standing on its wings, outfitted in a fighter pilot's helmet and oxygen mask.*

Until 1995, the peak of Geneva's "Jet d'Eau"—a fountain of water that shoots up 450 feet—remained untouched by human hand or surfboard. Rossy put an end to that when, after opening his canopy

---

*However much Rossy went in for surfing of the goofy kind, his skills were top-notch. In 1993, Rossy came in second at the Skysurfing World Championships.

during one jump, he steered himself right through the powerful jet's zenith, risking death in the turbulence created by the ever-varying height of the tip.

A man like Rossy cannot just take a ride in a hot-air balloon. Nor would he be content merely to jump out of its basket. If Yves Rossy must be seen dallying with a vehicle of such torpor, he would have to be surfing off the top of it. Rossy earned a place in the *Guinness Book of Records* when he did just that. This required building a platform on the top of the blue balloon to keep him from sinking down as he stood on its top while it floated to altitude. Without it, his weight would create an indentation so large he would not be able to surf, or climb, his way out. He also had a little strip attached to the side of the balloon to smooth his journey off its side.

Rossy earned a second entry in that great book of records in June 1996, when he pulled off a trick more suited to the original barnstormers. He went up in a yellow Boeing Stearman—a biplane first produced in the thirties—climbed out of the cockpit, and walked to the end of the wing. Grasping a handle on the far edge of the wing, Rossy waited while a second plane inched its way alongside the first. Once it was in striking distance, Rossy took hold of a handle on the second plane and flew for thirty seconds suspended between them before letting go and parachuting to the ground.

The audacity of such stunts, as well as his skysurfing skills, eventually led to a friendship with Patrick de Gayardon, and in the early nineties they often found themselves in competition with each other. They both seemed to realize at the same time that they couldn't take skysurfing much further than they had. "I was making wings to surf—skysurfing with the shape of a wing," Rossy says of his Mirage III model. "It's not logical. Birds are not flying on their feet." While Gayardon was flying with the first version of his wingsuit, Rossy was getting a similar glide ratio—1:1—with his wing-surfing. But when Gayardon died in 1998, Rossy joined the community of avant-garde adventurers who wanted to continue where Gayardon had left off.

For Gayardon, and many of those who modeled their wingsuits after his, it was crucial to keep the wings free of solid parts. "He didn't want anything rigid on him," says Rossy. "It was for him something forbidden. Only fabric. He told me—and everybody—'Once you have something rigid around you, sooner or later you will be dead.'" But Rossy thought that the length of the human arm, on even the tallest, most chimp-proportioned of individuals, was too much of a limiting factor. And though he wanted to carry on what Gayardon had started, he also wanted to be known for doing something new.

> You cannot profile the body to make it a perfect aerodynamic body—it's impossible. You need the head where she is, the arms cannot be placed elsewhere, you need the shoulders free. So the best thing is like a bird: the body is under the wings with perfect aerodynamic parts. With just fabric, you will never have a really good upside of the wing, where the under-pressure is forming—the upper wing must be clean such that you have lift. But with the wingsuit, you don't have enough span and you never will get aerodynamic enough to permit a long stabilized flight. You have some very good performance in the beginning, but you cannot hold a perfect position. The muscles can't hold it, it's a big effort and you perspire. And they can't be motorized—where do you put two 100-pound engines and the fuel and so on?

Rossy teamed up with two companies: Act Composites, which develops new materials for unique projects, and Prospective Concepts, a company steeped in the art of building oddball vehicles (like an upside-down hot air balloon; a light plane that can take off without a runway by catapulting itself off the ground; and an inflatable aircraft). Rossy would become their second inflatable aircraft. Named "Flying Man," these wings folded up so that Rossy could fit in an airplane as well as stabilize his fall before flying after exiting. Once in the air, he simply pulled a cord to open a valve that unfolded the wings and made them rigid, like some kind of high-speed inflating air mattress. When the wings were fully extended, Rossy had a wingspan of more than eight feet, and with them he was able to fly across Lake Geneva, a distance of seven and a half miles.

The Flying Man wings let Rossy steer his way across the lake with muscle movements largely the same as those used to control free fall. He could go in any direction he liked but one: up. So after a few flights he put Flying Man aside to devote himself to "Jet Man."

Rossy knew of a company called Jet-Cat, which built small jet engines for model airplanes. He wanted to use a wing design similar to that of the Flying Man and attach two of these engines, but the inflatable structure, though rigid, would not be strong enough to support the additional weight. Act Composites took full control of the project, building Rossy's wings of solid carbon—tough and light—that folded and unfolded with a hinge instead of an air valve. The wingspan now reached ten feet.

With fuel, batteries, wires, and heat, Rossy ran the risk of turning into more of a fireball than a firebird. The wings would need a mechanism so that they could be quickly jettisoned, adding an extra layer of complexity (and cost) to an already complex design. Early on, Rossy ran into several problems. He wanted to open the wings as soon as he was in the air, but it was almost impossible to have them open together at exactly the same time. With asymmetrical wings on his back and not enough speed to make them fly on his first test flights, he found himself in a spin after and had to ditch the prototype—many times. Another major hurdle was just trying to get the engines to start. They were designed to fly at altitudes typical for any aircraft, but as they were meant for models, the designers had no reason to make them so they could start anywhere but on the ground. Eventually, with the help of injectors and compressors—and a lot of additional cash, all Rossy's—his team found a way to start the jets at 14,000 feet.

"It's the opposite of the way I think as a pilot," says Rossy. "The project was not economical—a huge amount of energy for a little pleasure. When you go to an investor and say you need $80,000 to fly with a wing on your back with two jets on, the guy looks at you and takes you as a crazy guy, and says, 'Yeah, come back when you're ready.' That's why I did it a little bit alone."

If any of today's skyflyers embody the experimental glee combined with the personal neck-risking that permeated the golden age of flight, Rossy does. Leonard Opdycke, the editor of *WWI Aero,* looks back at the history of flight and bemoans today's lack of inventiveness and personal investment. "The whole early period, just before World War I, was the most exciting time for flight," he told me. "They really weren't sure how to do it—the whole thing was up for grabs. Historians look back and see their bizarre machinery, and they treat them with scorn. In fact, those guys were risking their lives and put a lot of money in those things. We don't have that anymore." Rossy, perhaps more than anyone in a similar line of work, meets the criteria of draining his own pocketbook and putting his bodily person on the line.

Rossy approached every jump with ever-mounting fear. Six times he was thrown into a wicked spin and had to cut away from the whole system. "Every time, I couldn't say what was field, forest, or sea." But even as he approached unconsciousness, he was reluctant to separate himself from his wings. "I did know that it's my only prototype—if I throw it away it will break a bit more or totally one time." Again and again he had to test the wings with dummy weights in place of the motors to figure out where best to attach them.

On July 24, 2004, Rossy made his first jump with the real jets. After stabilizing himself and gliding for a few seconds to pick up speed, he turned the engines on. Immediately he was flying at 115 miles per hour and perfectly horizontal. For four minutes Rossy was flying "like a child playing airplane," he says. "You want to go left, turn your head left. This phase was a dream. I do paraglider, I do hang glider—it's not the same. Now I fly with my body, not through steering something." Partway through the flight he turned on the smoke, and a gray trail came fuming out behind him. But the dream ended when he hit a pocket of turbulence and had to turn off the engines and open his parachute. He still had ten minutes' worth of fuel.

It was yet another record for Yves Rossy. He could now claim, as the Aero-News Network put it, to be the "first man to fly horizontally with wings attached to a flight suit of his own design and two small jet engines."

> I would like to be a part of that birdman lineage. I have such respect for those guys, they had no technology, no aerodynamic. So many people died from these tests but they were so convinced that it would work—so magnificent in spirit. The guy that is so absolutely sure his vector will be horizontal when he goes off the cliff—unfortunately it didn't work, but at the moment he jumped, he was sure. I hope when they see me from paradise, I hope they are enjoying what I do.

CHAPTER

31

The Final Frontier:
Earth

If you ever find yourself trying to explain to a whuffo or
an otherwise uninformed individual what a batwing, a wingsuit, or a
Skyray is, you will most likely first be confronted with looks of aston-
ishment, amazement, and wonder. But before you have gone far into
your explanation, you are sure to be asked how these birdmen land,
and when you answer that "they open a parachute, of course," you will
see a hint of mild disappointment muddy the otherwise fascinated face.
The idea that a skydiver trying to fly with wings still needs additional
equipment to land makes the whole pursuit seem slightly impure.

However unlikely it is that people will ever regularly "soar from
the housetops" in any future, far or near, as Clem Sohn and others
claimed, it is even more unlikely that they will be able to land without
a parachute. No matter how much drag is reduced with smooth or pit-
ted materials, no matter how many vortices get redirected, no matter
how strong the shoulder that shapes the airfoil, no wing that could fit

through an airplane door could achieve a glide ratio high enough to set anyone down whole, on flat ground. But what will never become commonplace for the common skydiver, or anyone else, will certainly be accomplished by one, or a small handful, of the most daring and most talented in the sport in a matter of years. Provided, of course, that the "flat ground" becomes something less than flat.

Whoever it is in the coming years who jumps from an airplane of his own volition, lands without a parachute, and lives will not be able to claim he was the first. The possibility of surviving a fall from an airplane has already been proven by a lucky—extremely lucky—few.

The glory goes to the Russian lieutenant I. M. Chisov. In 1942, after his plane had been hit by German fire, he abandoned it at nearly 22,000 feet. He went unconscious during the fall, and when he awoke he found himself on a steep slope in three feet of snow, with a broken hip and a banged-up head, but very much alive.

A year later a U.S. ball-turret gunner named Alan Magee found himself in a disintegrating B-17 over St.-Nazaire, France, and leapt from a hole that had opened up in the plane. He, too, was at 22,000 feet and passed out during the descent, but there was no snowy slope to greet him. Instead he smashed through the skylight of the city's train station, broke a leg and an ankle, mucked up his nose and his eye, and nearly lost an arm. The German soldiers who quickly greeted him were so amazed by his survival that they took special care of him. He led a healthy and active life till his death in 2004.

A year after Magee's drop, tail gunner Nicholas Alkemade left his damaged bomber at 18,000 feet over Berlin. Trees, shrubs, and snow cushioned his fall, and other than some scrapes and minor injuries to his leg, he was unharmed.

The lesson, for those hoping to make their own chuteless landing, is to be sure to land on a snow-covered slope or snow-covered vegetation, or fall through glass. As the last of these seems inherently more risky, those now planning an entirely voluntary version of such a jump have tended to focus on the snowy slope.

The concept of trying to land on a slope with skis began with Patrick de Gayardon, who spoke of such a plan to many of his friends. He didn't live to make an attempt, but the idea has been taken up by his followers.

New Zealander Chuck Berry, for instance, has made practice jumps from a helicopter wearing his wingsuit and a pair of skis. "It's not like I'm inventing new technologies from scratch," Berry says. "Ski jumpers have already perfected how to fly through the air and land at high speeds. Putting the wingsuit into the equation brings the airspeed down to what they're doing." When Berry says "equation," he means it literally: he spent eighteen years as an aircraft engineer and comes to the problem of landing chuteless with more than just cojones. (That's not to say he hasn't done his share of cojones-driven stunts: he's exited a helicopter while riding a BMX bike and has flown in his wingsuit from one coast to the other at the northern tip of New Zealand. He's also a downhill skier and high-speed hang glider pilot, well accustomed to zipping down mountainsides.)

"The key to the whole thing, the way I see it, is you've got to arrive parallel to the planet," says Berry. "That's why I'm choosing to land on a slope. I'm convinced that if you can touch down, it doesn't really matter what speed you're going." Berry is supposedly still tinkering with his wingsuit and skis, trying to get that extra dollop of lift for the moment his skis scrape snow.

Other wingsuiters remain skeptical. "Talk is so cheap," says Adrian Nicholas, who was flying with Patrick de Gayardon when he died.

"Patrick's style was always to wait until he'd done something and then say, 'Hey, look what I did.' Let's hope Chuck is very, very careful."

Jari Kuosma is more unimpressed than skeptical. "There are stories from the war of people falling from airplanes without a parachute and landing on a snowy hill," he says. "So to me that's not really a professional landing. When you land on a runway like an airplane, then you can call it a landing." The BirdMan manual that comes with every suit states clearly that "the user of this equipment MUST NOT attempt to land a wing suit without a fully open parachute."

Berry, though, has heard it all before:

> Most people are nonbelievers, but that's because they don't have the knowledge and the skill that we've developed through, like, eighteen years of skydiving. You're sort of dealing with different concept levels and different skill levels. And if I didn't do anything because everyone was frightened, then I'd never achieve anything, so you've got to be quite careful about taking on other people's fears.

Much of his plan makes perfect sense: he's practicing getting closer and closer to the slope, gradually lining things up, and he's trying find a mountain with a cliff on one side so he can ditch the whole plan and open his parachute if things go wrong.

And Berry may be more comfortable than the rest of us with things going wrong. "I've talked to a lot of people with different theories about landing wingsuits," he says. "Part of my theory is . . . I've had motorbike accidents at 90 miles an hour, which is actually faster than I'll be going when I land the wingsuit. And, um, yeah, I walked away. I was like, 'Oh wow, that didn't kill me.' " Whether Berry will be able to say something similar after his attempted landing remains to be seen.

Another jumper named Rod Driver visited New Zealand with the sole purpose of making a parachute-free mountain landing on a surfboard. Friends and other skydivers persuaded him not to at the last minute. Since then he has reportedly been scoping out ideal slopes in Alaska.

"You've got to get rid of the snow slope," says BASE jumper Jeb Corliss. "Too many variables, too many things can go wrong." In Corliss's vision of a canopy-free touchdown, a spill of any kind cannot be a possibility. "In all honesty, if you break a fingernail it's not successful. You have to land it and be willing to do it again."

Corliss, who wears only black, including his wingsuit and canopy, has been arrested in four countries and is one of the world's few professional BASE jumpers. He started flying BirdMan wingsuits when they were first introduced—he claims to have the fourth or fifth one ever made—but his intention was never to soar and play in the clouds. "Skydiving seemed boring and pointless to me. And with a wingsuit it seemed more boring—now you're in the air longer!—*ugggh*. The purpose was to learn to take them off a cliff."

Corliss's distaste for broken nails and other injuries may spring from the fact that he's seen his share of disaster and has a fairly precise sense of what it means for things to go wrong.

In November 2003, he and his friend Dwaine Weston, both wearing wingsuits, jumped out of a plane and started flying toward the Royal Gorge Bridge over the Arkansas River in Colorado. Corliss was to pass below the bridge while Weston zipped over it, but as he approached, Weston must have decided to buzz the spectators below as close as possible. As Corliss flew out from beneath the bridge, he dodged a falling object—part of Weston's leg. Weston had hit the bridge's railing. He died on the rocks below.

When jumping at a waterfall in South Africa, Corliss could not steer away from the falling water after opening his parachute. The torrent collapsed the canopy, and when he crashed into the water below, he broke his back and several ribs.

"My goal is to not break myself into little bits," he says. "I've been laying in bed with my back broken in three places, staring at a ceiling. That sucks. I don't want to repeat the process." Fingernails, back, and ribs are all too much at risk for something like a mountain slope landing.

> Anyone can land with skis. Yeah, then what do you do? One hundred twenty miles per hour but you're going down on your face. How do your transition that energy? You have a chance of surviving it, maybe, without injuries—sometimes—but that's not acceptable. If you're going to survive it nine out of ten times totally shattered and broken . . . if that's how a canopy worked—one out of ten times—it's pointless. The jumper's got to land, then wipe himself off, say, "Is that all you got?" and then do it again. The only acceptable way is if it's repeatable, over and over and over again.

Corliss is keeping the details of his solution, which will involve four different types of new technology, tightly under wraps. The concept is simple and obvious, he says, and the only thing holding him back—or anyone else who knew of the idea—from an actual attempt is the usual problem of money. Engineers he has approached with the concept have all agreed that it's entirely feasible, but would cost between four and six million dollars. And it would take a year to build.

Corliss is sponsored by GoFast, a sports drink after the same kind of media attention that Red Bull manages to attract, but they are not willing to put up that kind of cash.

Corliss *has* offered little clues to what he has in mind. The technology has nothing to do with the wingsuit itself, he says, and wing-free skydivers capable of achieving a 1:1 glide ratio with their bodies alone may be able to use it to land, as well. "From touching down to stopping, there's 100 percent control—no rag-dolling, no slipping." Most likely it's some kind of a special sloped and curved runway, something like the Summit Plummet water slide at Disney World's Blizzard Beach, where daring visitors start their descent in a near free fall. After a few seconds the drop is slowly broken by a long gentle curve. The difficult part for a wingsuit flyer would be lining up with the runway, however perfectly it matched the angle of their fall. "Even with my method, which I believe is the safest way of doing it, if you fuck up you will die—it's not 'Oh, I twisted my ankle.' "

Just as Chuck Berry shrugs off naysayers as the kind of people who hold up human progress, Corliss has complete faith that human ingenuity will eventually find a way for a parachute-free landing.

> If a flying squirrel or sugar glider can do it, why can't we? A sugar glider's bones are hollow—until your bones are hollow, it won't be *that* way. That's what's cool about humans. We can't breathe underwater, but we figured out how to do it. It's kind of a similar thing. That's what makes human beings so special, our ability to evolve quickly. How many millions of years did it take for a squirrel to fly? For us it took a hundred.

It might seem that the obvious person to make a landing on a slope, be it natural or man-made, would be Loïc Jean-Albert, who practically skimmed down the surface of Mount Verbier's dome. "What we are all aiming at is flying," he says. "Natural flying. And you need to be able to take off and land, to be a little bird. It's the dream of everyone since the beginning of humans." A year after his near-surface flight, he was telling reporters that he did in fact plan to land without a parachute. "My main goal is to develop an air brake so that at the last moment I can flare out the suit and touch down," he said. "There are two possibilities: either braking so that I can land on a well-prepared snow slope, or slowing down enough so I can run to a stop."

But what led him to make his famous jump and land standing was the cautiousness and patience he brings to the sport. Perhaps the same people who had a word with Rod Driver spoke to Jean-Albert, as well.

> With today's technique and today's wingsuits, for me it's too dangerous. I will do it when I think it's safe enough, when there's a 98-percent chance of having no injuries. I could do it the same way at Verbier, and touch the ground at 80 miles per hour—skiers are wiping out at these speeds—but most of them have broken legs and broken whatever. So it's not in my plans for the near future, it's something I'm thinking of.

For wingsuiters still gung-ho on trying to land like a little bird, Robert Pecnik, co-founder of BirdMan wingsuits, suggests this experiment:

> If you are still thinking of landing the wingsuit, do one normal parachute jump, but when you open the canopy, try to position your body horizontally (can be done by

hooking your feet around rear risers) and try to land a small elliptical canopy in that position. After that painful experience, multiply pain and injuries by nine (three times the speed = nine times the force of impact = nine times the consequences), and decide if you are willing to give it a try.

Trowbridge's poem of 1910 was a real hit when first published, and remained sufficiently popular into the 1930s that reporters would use its title offhandedly in stories about batmen. Its message continued the long tradition of poetic mockery of those who try to fly too high.

DARIUS GREEN AND HIS FLYING MACHINE

John T. Trowbridge

If ever there lived a Yankee lad,
Wise or otherwise, good or bad,
Who, seeing the birds fly, didn't jump
With flapping arms from stake or
 stump,
Or, spreading the tail
Of his coat for a sail,
Take a soaring leap from post or rail,
And wonder why
He couldn't fly,
And flap and flutter and wish and try—
If ever you knew a country dunce
Who didn't try that as often as once,
All I can say is, that's a sign
He never would do for a hero of mine.

An aspiring genius was D. Green:
The son of a farmer—age fourteen;
His body was long and lank and lean,
Just right for flying, as will be seen;
He had two eyes, each bright as a bean,
And a freckled nose that grew between,
A little awry—for I must mention

That he had riveted his attention
Upon his wonderful invention,
Twisting his tongue as he twisted the
 strings,
Working his face as he worked the
 wings,
And with every turn of gimlet and
 screw
Turning and screwing his mouth
 round, too,
Till his nose seemed bent
To catch the scent,
Around some corner, of new-baked
 pies,
And his wrinkled cheeks and his
 squinting eyes
Grew puckered into a queer grimace,
That made him look very droll in the
 face,
And also very wise.

And wise he must have been, to do
 more

Than ever a genius did before,
Excepting Daedalus of yore
And his son Icarus, who wore
Upon their backs
Those wings of wax
He had read of in the old almanacs,
Darius was clearly of the opinion
That the air is also man's dominion,
And that, with paddle or fin or pinion,
We soon or late
Shall navigate
The azure as now we sail the sea.
The thing looks simple enough to me
And if you doubt it, Hear how Darius
    reasoned about it.

"Birds can fly,
An' why can't I?
Must we give in,"
Says he with a grin,
"'T the bluebird an' phoebe
Are smarter'n we be?
Jest fold our hands an' see the swaller,
An' blackbird an' catbird beat us holler?
Does the leetle, chatterin', sassy wren,
No bigger'n my thumb, know more
    than men?
Jest show me that!
Er prove 't the bat
Has got more brains than's in my hat
An' I'll back down, an' not till then!"

He argued further: "Ner I can't see
What's th' use o' wings to a bumblebee
For to git a livin' with, more'n to me—
Ain't my business
Important's his'n is?
That Icarus
Was a silly cuss,
Him an' his daddy Daedalus.

They might 'a' knowed wings made
    o' wax
Wouldn't stan' sun-heat an' hard
    whacks.
I'll make mine o' luther,
Er suthin' er other."

And he said to himself, as he tinkered
    and planned:
"But I ain't goin' to show my hand
To mummies that never can
    understand
The fust idee that's big an' grand.
They'd 'a' laft an' made fun
O' Creation itself afore 'twas done."
So he kept his secret from all the rest
Safely buttoned within his vest;
And in the loft above the shed
Himself he locks, with thimble and
    thread
And wax and hammer and buckles and
    screws,
And all such things as geniuses use;
Two bats for patterns, curious fellows!
A charcoal-pot and a pair of bellows;
An old hoop-skirt or two, as well as
Some wire and several old umbrellas;
A carriage-cover, for tail and wings;
A piece of harness; and straps and
    strings;
And a big strong box,
In which he locks
These and a hundred other things.

His grinning brothers, Reuben and
    Burke
And Nathan and Jotham and
    Salomon, lurk
Around the corner to see him work,
Sitting cross-legged, like a Turk,

Drawing the waxed end through with
    a jerk,
And boring the holes with a comical
    quirk
Of his wise old head, and a knowing
    smirk.
But vainly they mounted each other's
    backs,
And poked through knot-holes and
    pried through cracks;
With wood from the pile and straw
    from the stacks
He plugged the knot-holes and calked
    the cracks;
And a bucket of water, which one
    would think
He had brought up into the loft to
    drink
When he chanced to dry.
Stood always nigh,
For Darius was sly!
And whenever at work he happened
    to spy
At chink or crevice a blinking eye,
He let a dipper of water fly.
"Take that ! an' ef ever ye get a peep,
Guess ye'll ketch a weasel asleep!"
And he sings as he locks
His big strong box:

"The weasel's head is small an' trim,
An' he is leetle an' long an' slim,
An' quick of motion an' nimble of limb,
An' ef you'll be
Advised by me
Keep wide awake when ye're ketchin'
    him!"
So day after day
He stitched and tinkered and
    hammered away,

Till at last 'twas done,
The greatest invention under the sun!
"An' now," says Darius, "hooray fer
    some fun!"

'Twas the Fourth of July,
And the weather was dry,
And not a cloud was on all the sky,
Save a few tight fleeces, which here
    and there,
Half mist, half air,
Like foam on the ocean went floating
    by:
Just as lovely a morning as ever was
    seen
For a nice little trip in a flying-machine.

Thought cunning Darius, "Now I
    sha'n't go
Along 'ith the fellers to see the show.
I'll say I've got sich a terrible cough!
An' then, when the folks 'ave all
    gone off
I'll hev full swing
For to try the thing,
An' practyse a leetle on the wing."
"Aint goin' to see the celebration?"
Says Brother Nate. "No; botheration!
I've got sich a cold—a toothache-I—
My gracious!-feel's though I shou'd fly !"

Said Jotham "Sho!
Guess ye better go."
But Darius said, "No !
Shouldn't wonder 'f yeou might see
    me, though,
'Long 'bout noon, ef I git red
O' this Jumpin', thumpin' pain 'n my
    head."
For all the while to himself he said:

"I'll tell ye what!
I'll fly a few times around the lot,
To see how 't seems, then soon's I've got
The hang o' the thing, ez likely's not,
I'll astonish the nation,
And all creation,
By flyin' over the celebration!
Over their heads I'll sail like an eagle;
I'll balance myself on my wings like a
    sea-gull;
I'll dance on the chimbleys; I'll stand
    on the steeple;
I'll flop up to winders an' scare the
    people!
I'll light on the libbe'ty-pole, an' crow;
An' I'll say to the gawpin' fools below,
'What world's this 'ere
That I've come near?'
Fer I'll make 'em believe I'm a chap
    f'm the moon!
An' I'll try a race 'ith their ol' bulloon."
He crept from his bed;
And, seeing the others were gone, he
    said,
"I'm a-gittin' over the cold 'n my head."
And away he sped,
To open the wonderful box in the
    shed.

His brothers had walked but a little way
When Jotham to Nathan chanced to
    say,
"What on airth is he up to, hey?"
"Don'o, the' 's suthin' er other to pay,
Er he wouldn't a stayed to hum to-day."
Says Burke, "His toothache's all 'n his
    eye!
He never'd miss a Fo'th-o'-July,
Ef he hedn't some machine to try.
Le's hurry back and hide in the barn,

An' pay him fer tellin' us that yarn!"
"Agreed!" Through the orchard they
    creep back,
Along by the fences, behind the stack,
And one by one, through a hole in the
    wall,
In under the dusty barn they crawl,
Dressed in their Sunday garments all;
And a very astonishing sight was that,
When each in his cobwebbed coat
    and hat
Came up through the floor like an
    ancient rat.
And there they hid;
And Reuben slid
The fastenings back, and the door
    undid.
"Keep dark!" said he,
"While I squint an' see what the' is to
    see."

As knights of old put on their mail,
From head to foot
An iron suit,
Iron jacket and iron boot,
Iron breeches, and on the head
No hat, but an iron pot instead,
And under the chin the bail,
I believe they called the thing a helm;
And the lid they carried they called a
    shield;
And, thus accoutred, they took the
    field,
Sallying forth to overwhelm
The dragons and pagans that plagued
    the realm:
So this modern knight
Prepared for flight,
Put on his wings and strapped them
    tight;

Jointed and jaunty, strong and light;
Buckled them fast to shoulder and
    hip,—
Ten feet they measured from tip to tip!
And a helm had he, but that he wore,
Not on his head like those of yore,
But more like the helm of a ship.

"Hush!" Reuben said,
"He's up in the shed!
He's opened the winder—I see his
    head!
He stretches it out,
An' pokes it about,
Lookin' to see 'f the coast is clear,
An' nobody near;
Guess he don'o' who's hid in here!
He's riggin' a spring-board over the sill!
Stop laffin', Solomon! Burke, keep still!
He's a climbin' out now—of all the
    things!
What's he got on? I van, it's wings!
An' that t'other thing? I vum, it's a tail!
An' there he sets like a hawk on a rail!
Steppin' careful, he travels the length
Of his spring-board, and teeters to try
    its strength.
Now he stretches his wings, like a
    monstrous bat;
Peeks over his shoulder, this way an'
    that,
Fer to see 'f the' 's anyone passin' by;
But the' 's on'y a ca'f an' a goslin' nigh.
They turn up at him a wonderin' eye,
To see—The dragon! he's goin' to fly!
Away he goes! Jimmy! what a jump!
Flop-flop—an' plump
To the ground with a thump!
Flutt'rin an' flound'rin', all in a lump!"

As a demon is hurled by an angel's
    spear,
Heels over head, to his proper
    sphere—
Heels over head, and head over heels,
Dizzily down the abyss he wheels—
So fell Darius. Upon his crown,
In the midst of the barnyard, he came
    down,
In a wonderful whirl of tangled strings,
Broken braces and broken springs,
Broken tail and broken wings,
Shooting-stars, and various things!
Away with a bellow fled the calf,
And what was that? Did the gosling
    laugh?
'Tis a merry roar
Front the old barn-door,
And he hears the voice of Jotham
    cryin',
"Say, D'rius! how de you like flying?"
Slowly, ruefully, where he lay,
Darius just turned and looked that way,
As he stanched his sorrowful nose with
    his cuff.
"Wall, I like flyin' well enough,"
He said; "but the' ain't sich a
    thunderin' sight
O' fun in 't when ye come to light."

Moral I just have room for the moral
    here:
And this is the moral—Stick to your
    sphere.
Or if you insist, as you have the right,
On spreading your wings for a loftier
    flight,
The moral is—Take care how you
    light.

The following poem is about John Damian's flight. For detailed notes and explanations, please visit www.lib.rochester.edu/camelot/teams/dunfrm2.htm

A Ballad of the Friar of Tungland

William Dunbar (1460–1530)

As yung Aurora with cristall haile
In orient schew hir visage paile,
A swevyng swyth did me assaile
 Of sonis of Sathanis seid.
Me thocht a Turk of Tartary
Come throw the boundis of Barbary
And lay forloppin in Lumbardy
 Full lang in waithman weid.

Fra baptasing for to eschew,
Thair a religious man he slew
And cled him in his abeit new,
 For he couth wryte and reid.
Quhen kend was his dissimulance
And all his cursit govirnance,
For feir he fled and come in France,
 With littill of Lumbard leid.
To be a leiche he fenyt him thair,
Quhilk mony a man micht rew
 evirmair,
For he left nowthir seik nor sair
 Unslane or he hyne yeid.
Vane organis he full clenely carvit.
Quhen of his straik so mony starvit,
Dreid he had gottin that he desarvit,
 He fled away gud speid.

In Scotland than the narrest way
He come his cunnyng till assay.
To sum man thair it was no play,
 The preving of his sciens.

In pottingry he wrocht grit pyne,
He murdreist mony in medecyne.
The Jow was of a grit engyne,
 And generit was of gyans.

In leichecraft he was homecyd.
He wald haif, for a nycht to byd,
A haiknay and the hurt manis hyd,
 So meikle he was of myance.
His yrnis was rude as ony rawchtir.
Quhair he leit blude it was no lawchtir.
Full mony instrument for slawchtir
 Was in his gardevyance.

He cowth gif cure for laxatyve
To gar a wicht hors want his lyve.
Quhaevir assay wald, man or wyve,
 Thair hippis yeid hiddy giddy.
His practikis nevir war put to preif
Bot suddane deid or grit mischeif.
He had purgatioun to mak a theif
 To dee withowt a widdy.

Unto no Mes pressit this prelat
For sound of sacring bell nor skellat.
As blaksmyth bruikit was his pallatt
 For battering at the study.
Thocht he come hame a new maid
 channoun,
He had dispensit with matynnis
 channoun.

On him come nowther stole nor
    fannoun
    For smowking of the smydy.

Me thocht seir fassonis he assailyeit
To mak the quintessance, and failyeit.
And quhen he saw that nocht availyeit,
    A fedrem on he tuke,
And schupe in Turky for to fle.
And quhen that he did mont on he,
All fowill ferleit quhat he sowld be,
    That evir did on him luke.

Sum held he had bene Dedalus,
Sum the Menatair marvelus,
Sum Martis blaksmyth, Vulcanus,
    And sum Saturnus kuke.
And evir the tuschettis at him tuggit,
The rukis him rent, the ravynis him
    druggit,
The hudit crawis his hair furth ruggit,
    The hevin he micht not bruke.

The myttane and Sanct Martynis fowle
Wend he had bene the hornit howle,
Thay set aupone him with a yowle
    And gaif him dynt for dynt.
The golk, the gormaw, and the gled
Beft him with buffettis quhill he bled,
The sparhalk to the spring him sped
    Als fers as fyre of flynt.

The tarsall gaif him tug for tug,
A stanchell hang in ilka lug,
The pyot furth his pennis did rug,
    The stork straik ay but stynt,
The bissart, bissy but rebuik,
Scho was so cleverus of hir cluik
His bawis he micht not langer bruik,
    Scho held thame at ane hint.

Thik was the clud of kayis and crawis,
Of marleyonis, mittanis, and of mawis,
That bikkrit at his berd with blawis,
    In battell him abowt.
Thay nybbillit him with noyis and
    cry,
The rerd of thame rais to the sky,
And evir he cryit on Fortoun, "Fy!"
    His lyfe was into dowt.

The ja him skrippit with a skryke
And skornit him, as it was lyk.
The egill strong at him did stryke
    And rawcht him mony a rowt.
For feir uncunnandly he cawkit,
Quhill all his pennis war drownd and
    drawkit.
He maid a hundreth nolt all hawkit
    Beneth him with a spout.

He schewre his feddreme that was
    schene,
And slippit out of it full clene,
And in a myre up to the ene
    Amang the glar did glyd.
The fowlis all at the fedrem dang
As at a monster thame amang,
Quhill all the pennis of it owtsprang
    In till the air full wyde.

And he lay at the plunge evirmair,
Sa lang as any ravin did rair.
The crawis him socht with cryis of
    cair
    In every schaw besyde.
Had he reveild bene to the ruikis,
Thay had him revin all with thair
    cluikis.
Thre dayis in dub amang the dukis
    He did with dirt him hyde.

The air was dirkit with the fowlis
That come with yawmeris and yowlis,
With skryking, skrymming, and with
    scowlis,
      To tak him in the tyde.

I walknit with the noyis and schowte,
So hiddowis beir was me abowte.
Sensyne I curs that cankerit rowte,
      Quhairevir I go or ryde.

The following is the beginning of an elegiac poem prepared for a French ceremony after Clem Sohn's death (translated by Burkhard Bilger):

And now, Prince of the clouds, where the archangels of the Lord, which you embody, move in unfathomable translucence, Clem Sohn, my beloved son of glory, roll the cold boulder from your tomb and take flight to the harmonious vibrations of my lute! Conquer the bardic hearts of antique bronze, thou apotheosis of the triumphant future of the sky, until the end of time! Be thou the Phoenix reborn from its own ashes, Prometheus loosed of his deathly chains—superior and infinite predestination!—thou incomparable and superhuman destiny!

Phoebe, virgin of serene nights, encompasses me in the prodigious nimbus of her prodigious phosphorescence— and universal peace envelops me like a miracle. My sublime Heroes appear before me. Ah! Clem Sohn, you cross over to me, your immaculate wings unfurled across the cosmic dust—the immensity of tumultuous oceans. O celestial dramaturge, with vertiginous grace you descend upon your Poet, O beauty. . . .

Introduction   DeLand of the Free: Wingsuits for Whuffos

I met with Jari Kuosma and interviewed him many times from 2002 to 2005. The bulk of the material in the introduction comes from those meetings, and much of it appeared in "The Birdman of DeLand," *Forbes FYI,* Summer 2003.

For an excellent retelling of how the Wright brothers succeeded, and what kind of competition they faced, see James Tobin's *To Conquer the Air: The Wright Brothers and the Great Race for Flight* (Free Press, 2003).

If you are a wingsuit flyer or preparing to become one, be sure to read the first wingsuit how-to book—Scott Campos's *Skyflying: Wingsuits in Motion* (SkyMonkey Publishing, 2005).

Chapter 1   One Small Step for Man = One Giant Step for Man, *and*
Chapter 2   The Plummet Continues

For the full details of the Icarus myth, see Robert Graves, *The Greek Myths* (Penguin, 1960). To understand how flight permeates human history and myth, see Bayla Singer, *Like Sex with Gods: An Unorthodox History of Flying* (Texas A&M University Press, 2003). One of the most helpful resources for anyone interested in early flight is the appendix to Clive Hart's *The Prehistory of Flight* (University of California Press, 1985). The quote from Grace Wiggins comes from an interview I conducted with her.

Other sources include the following:

Octave Chanute, *Progress in Flying Machines,* first published in the *The Railroad and Engineering Journal,* 1891–1893.

Charles Harvard Gibbs-Smith, *Flight Through the Ages: A Complete, Illustrated Chronology from the Dreams of Early History to the Age of Space Exploration* (Crowell, 1974).

Peter Haining, *The Compleat Birdman: An Illustrated History of Man-Powered Flight* (Robert Hale Ltd., 1976).

Richard P. Hallion, *Taking Flight: Inventing the Aerial Age from Antiquity Through the First War* (Oxford University Press, 2003).

Hank Harrison, *A Hole in the Wind: Hang Gliding and the Quest for Flight* (Bobbs-Merrill, 1979).

Clive Hart, *The Dream of Flight: Aeronautics from Classical Times to the Renaissance* (Faber, 1972).

Berthold Laufer, *The Prehistory of Aviation* (Kraus Reprint Co., 1973).

William of Malmesbury, *William of Malmesbury's Chronicle of the Kings of England: From the Earliest Period to the Reign of King Stephen* (Bell and Sons, 1883).

Valerie Moolman, *The Road to Kitty Hawk* (Time-Life Books, 1980).

Roger Shattuck, "Tumult in the Clouds," *The New York Review of Books,* November 6, 2003.

Suetonius, *The Twelve Caesars* (Penguin, 1957).

Ernest Edward Walker, *Aviation: Or, Human Flight Through the Ages, with Drawings, Illustrations and Photographs* (Aeronautics Education Foundation, 1939).

Lynn White Jr., *Eilmer of Malmesbury: An 11th-Century Aviator* from Kranzberg, Melvin, *Technology and Culture: An Anthology* (Schocken Books, 1972).

Chapter 3   The Sohn Also Falls: Clem Sohn

Information about Sohn came from interviews with Elaine Thelen and Roy Kramer, cousins of Sohn's, and from papers they provided, as well as the following sources:

"Jumper, 12,000 Ft. Up, Trusts Self to 'Bat Wings,' " *New York Times,* February 28, 1935.

"Steps From Plane to Test 'Bat Wings'; They Work; He's Safe," *Chicago Daily Tribune,* February 28, 1935.

" 'Winged Man' Guides Drop: We'll All Do It Some Day, He Predicts," *New York Herald Tribune,* February 28, 1935.

"Transport: Wing Man," *Time,* March 11, 1935.

"Parachute Jumper Glides on Canvas Wings," *Popular Mechanics* 64 (July 1935).

"Moline Airman in Race Crash; Then Wins Cup," *Chicago Daily Tribune,* September 1, 1935.

Paul Gallico, "Sohn's Bat—Like Parachute, Interesting, If Not Perfect," *Washington Post,* September 3, 1935.

"Flyers Risk Gale in Meet," *Los Angeles Times,* December 14, 1935.

"A Birdman Shows How He Flies: With Heavy Canvas Wings and Tail Strapped to His Shoulders and Legs, Mr. Clem Sohn Steps Off an Airplane 10,000 Feet Up," *American Weekly,* 1936.

"A Human Glider: From 10,000 Ft. by Wings and Parachute," *The Times,* May 4, 1936.

J. Maynard Hill, "Lansing Stunt Flyers Enjoy Flirting with Death in the Clouds," *Lansing* [Michigan] *State Journal,* October 25, 1936.

" 'BatMan' Dies in 1,000-Ft. Plunge at Paris as Two Parachutes Fail," *New York Herald Tribune,* 1937.

Norris Ingells, "The Human Bat's Daring Last Flight," *Lansing* [Michigan] *State Journal,* April 21, 1987.

Homer Shannon, "The Man Who Nearly Flew Like a Bird," *True Flying Saucers and UFO Quarterly,* Spring 1980.

Manuel Castro, "From the Past . . . Lansing's 'Batman' Earned World Fame," *Metropolitan Quarterly,* Winter 1989–90.

Footage of Sohn in the air can be seen at www.britishpathe.com.

Chapter 4 Mocking Birds Don't Sing: Floyd Davis and Others

FLOYD DAVIS

" 'Human Bat' Dive Kills Sky Leaper: Youth Falls 6000 Feet to Death as 'Chute Fouls on Wing Fastened to Back," *Los Angeles Times,* April 1, 1935.

"Two Die in Collision," *Chicago Daily Tribune,* April 1, 1935.

EARL STEIN

"The Reading Aero Club—After 40," article from the booklet, "The Reading Aero Club 1932–1972." http://www.berkshistory.org/airport/reading_aero_club.html.

"The Fair Today," *New York Times,* September 30, 1939.

SOVIET IN ALUMINUM

"News in Bulletins," *Washington Post,* April 21, 1935.

JIMMY CARAWAY

"Sky Leaper Dies as Chute Fails," *Los Angeles Times,* August 31, 1938.

DONNIE MARSHALL

Ashlee Griggs, "A Look at the 20th Century: 1938," *Augusta* [Georgia] *Chronicle,* Web posted May 22, 1999.

ELMO BANNISTER

"Air Maneuvers Big Event of Week," *New York Times,* January 1, 1939.

GEORGE COOK

"L.A. 'Human Bat' Breaks Back in Fall: Daredevil Plunges to Earth Before 6000," *Los Angeles Times,* June 4, 1939.

WALTER "CHIEF" THATCHER

"Circus 'Bat Man' Is Killed in Accident," Associated Press, July 20, 1939.

JIMMIE GOODWIN

Don Dwiggins, *The Air Devils* (J. B. Lippincott, 1966).

———, *Flying Daredevils of the Roaring Twenties* (Tab Books, 1981).

"Bat Man Will Try Wings at Blythe Today," *Los Angeles Times,* January 22, 1939.

"Death Dodgers Will Perform at Airport," *Ashland* [Ohio] *Times-Gazette,* July 21, 1939.

"Spin Result of Acrobatics," press release from Civil Aeronautics Board, November 24, 1941.

CLIFF ROSE

Don Dwiggins, *The Barnstormers: Flying Daredevils of the Roaring Twenties* (Tab Books, 1981).

Chapter 5   Garden State Bird: William Picune

Much of this chapter comes from interviews with Adelaide and Pat Picune, who also sent me many personal papers. Additional sources include the following:

"Parachute Saves Jersey's 'Darius Green' as Wind Frays 'Wings' in 9,800-Foot Drop," *New York Times,* May 13, 1935.
"Parachute Saves Youth When His Wings Fail," *New York Herald Tribune,* May 13, 1935.
"Jersey 'Bat-Wing' Flier Lands Safely in a Tree," *New York Times,* May 20, 1935.
"He Flies Through the Air with the Greatest of Ease: 'Chute Leaper Turns to 'Bat Wing' Stunts," *Washington Post,* June 16, 1935.
"Air Meet to Be Held Sept. 5–7," *Concord* [New Hampshire] *Union Leader,* September 3, 1936.
"Picune Thrills Spectators in Delayed Parachute Jump," *Concord* [New Hampshire] *Union Leader,* September 7, 1936.
Alan Wayne, "JFK-Based Captain Recalls Lindbergh's Final Flight," *Friendly Times,* September 13, 1974.
"Four Teterboro Pioneers to Be Inducted," *Propwash,* Winter 1979.

Chapter 6   High Planes Drifter: Roland Kumzak

"Air 'Bat' Sohn to Jump Here," *Des Moines Register,* May 4, 1935.
George Shane, "20,000 Strain Eyes In Vain As Batman Drops: He Arrives This Time But Dull Sky Hides Stunt From Crowd," *Des Moines Register,* May 6, 1935.
Jane Risdon, "The Iowa Bat-Man—Roland Kumzak," *Annals of Iowa,* Summer 1966.

Chapter 7   New Falls from Sioux Falls: Manus "Mickey" Morgan

"A Man Who 'Flies' Like a Bat," *Parachute Times,* December 12, 1937.
"Stunt Man Plans Plane Jump from Four-Mile Height," *Los Angeles Times,* March 5, 1938.
"Bat-Flyer to Perform at Oakland Air Races," *Chicago Daily Tribune,* May 20, 1938.
"Man Spirals 3,000 Feet on Bat Wings," *PIC,* February 7, 1939.
"Human Glider," *Popular Mechanics,* September 1939.

"The Little Woman Finally Says Okay, So I'm Out for the Human Bat Record Again," *CCCC,* October 14, 1940.

Chapter 8 Mamas, If You Don't Want Your Babies to Grow to Be Bird-Boys: Tommy Boyd

I spoke with Tom DeLashmutt, who owns Oak Hill Farm, which Boyd ended up working on. Most of the information comes from the following:

"Youth is Snatched into Air by Plane," *New York Times,* January 10, 1948.
Jim Pope, "The Shock Was Bad, But It Was Welcome," *Loudoun* [Virginia] *Times-Mirror.*
Louise Lague, "A Batman Kicks Off Air Expo," *Washington* [D.C.] *Star-News,* March 29, 1974.
Phil Casey, "A 'Batman' Who Survived," *Washington Post,* March 30, 1974.

Chapter 9 When Erks Turn Loony: Harry Ward

The bulk of the material in this chapter comes from Harry Ward with Peter Hearn, *The Yorkshire Birdman: Memoirs of a Pioneer Parachutist* (Robert Hale Limited, 1990).
Other sources:

Peter Hearn, *The Sky People: A History of Parachuting* (Airlife, 1997).
Francis Heilmann, "Harry Ward, The Yorkshire Birdman," *ParaMag,* July 2004.
"Squadron Leader Harry Ward, AFC, Parachutist, Dies at Age 97," Dropzone.com, September 17, 2000 (http://www.dropzone.com/news/SquadronLeaderHarryWardA.shtml).

Chapter 10 They Fell for It: Robert X. Leeds

All quotes in this chapter come from interviews I conducted with Leeds. Some biographical background information comes from his book *How to Almost Make a Million Dollars* (Epic, 2004).

Chapter 11 International Playbird: Roy W. Grant

Much of this material comes from interviews with Tom Sitton, and also from Martin Caidin, *Barnstorming* (Bantam Books, 1965).

Chapter 12 When a Finn Is a Wing: Viktor Andro

Eero Pakarinen, *Lentosirkus Pilvien Huimapäät* (Finland: Karisto, 1977).

Chapter 13 *L'homme-oiseau:* Leo Valentin

Quotes and most information come from Valentin's *Bird Man* (Hutchinson, 1955).

Other sources:

"Bird Man's Wings Flop; 250,000 Boo His Attempt to Flap," *Chicago Daily Tribune,* May 1, 1950.

"End of a Winged Man," *Life,* June 4, 1956.

" 'Birdman' Falls to Death: Wings Splintered at 8,000 Ft.," *The Times,* May 22, 1956.

"Wooden Wings Fail; 100,000 See Him Die," *Daily News,* May 22, 1956.

"Bird Man . . . Leo Valentin," *Sky Diver,* July 1963.

Michael Horan, *Parachuting Folklore: The Evolution of Freefall* (Parachuting Resources, 1980).

Craig Ryan, *The Pre-Astronauts: Manned Ballooning on the Threshold of Space* (Naval Institute Press, 1995).

Clive Barker, *The Essential Clive Barker: Selected Fictions* (HarperCollins, 1999).

Footage of Valentin going up on the outside of a plane can be seen at www.britishpathe.com.

Chapter 14   Mocking Birds Still Don't Sing: Louis Faure and Others.

Francis Heilmann, "Sur les Ailes du Destin," *ParaMag,* September 2004.

René Roy, "De Mon Temps . . . C'était Quand Même Autre Chose!" *ParaMag,* November 1992.

———, "De Mon Temps . . . C'était Quand Même Autre Chose!: Les Hommes-Oiseaux: Seconde Epoque," *ParaMag,* December 1992.

———, "De Mon Temps . . . C'était Quand Même Autre Chose!: Les Derniers Hommes-Oiseaux," *ParaMag,* April 1993.

———, "De Mon Temps . . . C'était Quand Même Autre Chose!: Les Derniers Hommes-Oiseaux (Suite et Fin)," *ParaMag,* May 1993.

Chapter 15   Shiver of Death: Rudolf R. Boelheln

Francis Heilmann, "Rudolf Boehlen, le Maître de la Mort," *ParaMag,* August, 2004. Footage of Boehlen in the air can be seen at www.britishpathe.com.

Chapter 16   Michigan Shenanigans: Charlie Laurin and Art Lussier

Sources for this chapter include Laurin's unpublished memoirs, *The Last Barnstormers,* as well as extensive interviews with Charlie Laurin, Art Lussier, Walt Peca, Jim McCusker, and Willard Stahl.

Chapter 17   Spy vs. Sky: Lyle Cameron

Interviewees for this chapter include Lyle Cameron Jr., Brian Williams, and Walt Peca. Other sources include the following:

Lyle Cameron, "Ramblings . . . of L.C.," *Sky Diver* magazine, March 1965.

Howard Gregory, *Parachutes Unforgettable Jumps III,* third edition (Howard Gregory Associates, 1986).

Chapter 18   Flights of Fancy: Cliff Winters, Jim Poulson, Bob Hannigan

All information about Poulson and Hannigan came straight from them. For Cliff Winters, I talked to Brian Williams and Walt Peca.

Lyle Cameron, "Cliff Winters: Veteran Hollywood Stunt Man," *Sky Diver,* November 1961.
Howard Gregory, *Parachutes Unforgettable Jumps III,* third edition (Howard Gregory Associates, 1986).

Chapter 19   Band of Gypsies: Garth Taggart

Other than interviews with Garth Taggart, information for this chapter came from correspondence with James Drought's sons Hank and Alex, as well as the following:

James Drought, *The Gypsy Moths* (Skylight Press, 1964). Read it online at http://drought.com/works.htm.
Jerry Rouillard, "Will the REAL 'Gypsy Moths' Please Chute Up," *Parachutist,* November 1969.
There's also an excellent documentary on the stunt jumping done for the film on *The Gypsy Moths* DVD.

Chapter 20   Thy Words Have Upholden Him That Was Falling: Bill Cole

Interviews, correspondence, and papers sent to me by Cole make up the majority of the information in this chapter. For the full story of his second chuteless jump, be sure to read Mike Swain's book *The Endless Fall* (CeShore, 2000).

Chapter 21   Daring Young Man on a Flying Trapeze: Tom Sitton

Everything in this chapter comes from interviews with Sitton and Brian Williams.

Chapter 22   Paying the Toll: John Carta

In addition to interviews with Ken Reed, information for this chapter came from the following sources:

"Chutist Lands Unhurt Atop the Trade Center," *New York Times,* September 11, 1981.
"Parachutist Is Arrested," *New York Times,* February 18, 1987.
"Boat Rescues Chutist After His Bridge Leap," *New York Times,* March 16, 1987.
"National Digest: Only a Third of Americans Happy with Their Looks, Poll Discloses," *St. Petersburg* [Florida] *Times,* August 19, 1990.

"Parachutist Not Charged," *Washington Post,* August 19, 1990.

Stephen Schwartz, "Parachutist Among 8 Crash Victims: Officials Release Identities of 5 on Plane that Hit Clear Lake," *San Francisco Chronicle,* August 19, 1990.

Chapter 23 Solo Flight: Patrick de Gayardon
Interviews with Oliver Furrer, Andi Duff, Loïc Jean-Albert, Adrian Nicholas, and Gus Wing make up the larger portion of what's presented here.

"Can Reebok Find Happiness with a New Ad Campaign? Firm Still Searching for a Lasting Theme," *Boston Globe,* August 2, 1991.

Richard Sandomir, "Taking Sport to the Extreme: When Error Can Cost a Life," *New York Times,* June 25, 1996.

Andrea Kannapell, "Taking Sports to the Limit," *New York Times,* October 11, 1998.

Bruno Passe, "Wing Flight," *ParaMag,* February 1998; also ParaMag Online, para-mag.com.

Patrick Passe, "The Longest Flight," ParaMag Online.

Adrian Nicholas, "People in the Sport: Patrick de Gayardon," June 1998, bpa.org.uk.

Bruno Passe, "Deug, Many Folks Came to Honor Your Memory," ParaMag Online.

Daniel Michaels, "It's a Bird . . . It's a Plane . . . No, It Isn't—It's a Man, and the 'Wingsuit' That Allows Him to Fly Sparks Words of Caution," *Wall Street Journal,* September 30, 1999.

"Il Sogno di Icaro," http://www.faciaruli.it/paracadutismo.html.

Joe Jennings, http://www.skydive.tv/patrick.htm.

Troy Hartman, http://www.troyhartman.com/skysurfing.htm.

Watch Gayardon fly at http://www.poxon.org/Craig/Skydive/PatrickDeGayardon/photos.html.

Chapter 24 Over the Volcano: Chuck Priest
In addition to personal communications with Priest and Oliver Furrer, I gathered some facts from the following article:

Stephanie Kendrick, "Look! Up in the Sky . . . No, It's Not a Bird, a Plane or Superman. But the Man of Steel Might Want to Buy One of Chuck Priest's Suits," *Honolulu Star-Bulletin,* May 4, 1999.

Chapter 25 Slope Opera: Loïc Jean-Albert
In addition to interviews with Jean-Albert, this chapter came from the following sources:

Bruno Passe, "L'Aile-Combinaison," *ParaMag,* June 1999.

Bruno Passe, "La Science Du Vol," *ParaMag,* May 2004.
To watch Jean-Albert fly, see http://www.flyyourbody.com.

Chapter 26 Birdmen and Birdbirds: Leo Dickinson
Information comes from interviews with Leo Dickinson, as well as the following articles:

"Lucy Stoops to Conquer," *InCamera,* January 2004.
Tom Harpole, "Falling with the Falcon," *Air & Space,* February/March 2005.

Chapter 27 It's Skyray or the Highway: Christoph Aarns and Alban Geissler
I spoke with Geissler many times, and met him and Aarns at the Daedalus drop zone. You can watch Aarns fly at http://freesky.de/movpics.html.

Chapter 28 Crossing Over: Felix Baumgartner
Interviews and countless news reports make up the bulk of this chapter. More can be found at http://www.felixbaumgartner.com.

Chapter 29 The Shape of Things to Come: Roberto Stickel
All the information in this chapter is taken from interviews with Stickel. To further explore his design, see http://www.necostickel.com.br/.

Chapter 30 Turn on the Warm Jets: Yves Rossy
In addition to interviews with Rossy, much of the material comes from his website, http://www.yves-rossy.com/. Also see "French Rocketeer Flies!" on Aero-News.net, September 4, 2004.

Chapter 31 The Final Frontier: Earth
In addition to interviews with Jeb Corlis, Chuck Berry, Loïc Jean-Albert, Jari Kuosma, and Adrian Nicholas, some of this chapter comes from the following:

The Free-Fall Research Page: http://www.greenharbor.com/fffolder/ffallers.html.
Paul Logan, "Man Survived 22,000-Foot Fall Out of Bomber," *Albuquerque Journal,* February 3, 2004.
Charles Duhigg, "The Void Calls," *Los Angeles Times,* June 29, 2004.
Huw Williams, "Winging It: You'd Have to Be Crazy to Jump Out of an Aeroplane Without a Parachute, But One Man Believes That He Can Do it and Survive," *Mail on Sunday* [London], July 11, 2004.

For more spectacular footage of Jeb Corlis, Jari Kuosma, and many other wingsuiters in action, be sure to visit www.skydivingmovies.com.

This book could not have sprouted its wings without the generosity and help of countless people, winged and otherwise. Most important are all the living birdmen who offered me as much of their time as I needed to understand what they did in air. In particular Jari Kuosma, Charlie Laurin, Tom Sitton, and Roberto Stickel have given me hour upon hour of their time to explain much more than just themselves.

Many skydivers who are not subjects of this book are also owed thanks: Stacey Carl, Kevin Orkin, Andi Duff, Oliver Furrer, Vladi Pesa, and Brian Williams are all sharp thinkers who know how to spin a yarn. In particular, Francis Heilmann heaped assistance as well as photos upon me. Heilmann is a great storyteller, a photographer with a keen eye, a very clever wingsuit innovator, and a birdman historian of the first order.

Gus Wing, who died this year doing what he loved, was one of the kindest and most generous people I've met. He went out of his way to help me and the photographer I was with, and, like anyone who spent even ten minutes with him, we were inspired by his enthusiasm and his warmth. His passing is a great loss for the sport of skydiving and for anyone who knew him on any level.

Adrian Nicholas died in a non-wingsuit related skydiving accident just as I was finishing this book, and his death came as a shock to me as well as to the skydiving community. There was hardly a moment when he wasn't jumping, in a plane about to jump, or in a plane heading to another country. His stunts—jumping a Leonardo-designed parachute and setting the record for the longest wingsuit flight—as well as his infectious energy inspired everyone who talked to him, including myself. He will be missed by thousands.

Elaine Thelen, Roy Kramer, and Pat Picune have a passion for their winged relatives, and it's thanks to their assistance as well as their excellent archival instincts that I've been able to tell the story of the first bat-wing jumpers.

Melissa Keiser, an archives specialist at the National Air and Space Museum, is an amazing resource for anyone looking into any aspect of the history of flight. She went well out of her way to help me when I had little idea where to begin, and spent hours digging up every mention of birdmen in the museum's archives.

Kevin Gibson, who kindly gave me the run of the USPA's library, turns out to be not only a great skydiver but also a great fingerpicking guitar player who told me where the road is. And he can cook, too.

I, and many European birdmen featured herein, need to thank Serena Winters, who superbly translated (as far as I can tell) a foot-high stack of French articles for little more than a vague promise of future babysitting. No one else worked harder to help me. Similarly, Vesa Toropainen was good enough to translate from the Finnish—without any promises from me, vague or otherwise. And Burkhard Bilger did a wonderful job of rendering flowery French into English (though not without some badgering).

The whole project started thanks to the encouragement and support of the ever-wry Thomas Jackson, was furthered by the incomparable Dan Mandel, and was polished by the only other person I know who is never wrong, Julia Pastore.

My mother and father did everything they could to make me a person who would not jump out of planes. But they were certainly eager to hear free-fall stories after I'd touched the ground, and, thanks to their support, I was able to complete this book.

I owe much to my dear cousin Amanda (and her roommates), who gave me a couch to sleep on while I rooted through various archives in Washington.

And I must give a special thanks to the long-suffering Shenglan, who didn't want me to die and unquestionably put up with much.